Traveling Solo

"A comprehensive guide for anyone contemplating a solo vacation. Berman, a firm believer that 'alone' need not mean lonely, outlines a range of rewarding group vacations for all ages."
—*New York* magazine

"Earns our respect for a job well done . . . If you're about to plan a vacation on your own, read this first."
—*Modern Maturity*

"For a complete resource guide, nothing will equal the revised *Traveling Solo.*"
—*New Choices* magazine

"The best researched guide currently available, *Traveling Solo* delineates many travel options available to single travelers of all tastes and interests. The book includes a wide range of sections for the various types of vacations, specifications as to the common range of participants, and candid comments from former trip participants."
—Amazon.com

"Anyone considering traveling by themselves would be wise to consult this well-organized and innovative travel guide."
—*Iowa City Press-Citizen*

"Berman has done the single traveler a tremendous service with this guide. . . . tells single travelers what they really want and need to know."
—*Library Journal*

"To explore all the ways to travel alone or to find travel mates, invest in a book, *Traveling Solo,* by Eleanor Berman."
—*Sun-Sentinel*

Help Us Keep This Guide Up to Date

Every effort has been made by the author and editors to make this guide as accurate and useful as possible. However, many things can change after a guide is published—establishments close, phone numbers change, facilities come under new management, etc.

We would love to hear from you concerning your experiences with this guide and how you feel it could be improved and be kept up to date. Though we may not be able to respond to all comments and suggestions, we'll take them to heart, and we'll also make certain to share them with the author. Please send your comments and suggestions to the following address:

The Globe Pequot Press
Reader Response/Editorial Department
P.O. Box 833
Old Saybrook, CT 06475

Or you may e-mail us at:
editorial@globe-pequot.com

Thanks for your input, and happy travels!

Traveling Solo

{ Advice and Ideas for More Than 250 Great Vacations }

Second Edition

Eleanor BERMAN

The Globe Pequot Press

Guilford, Connecticut

Text design by Bill Brown Design
Cover illustration by Pam Meier

Library of Congress Cataloging-in-Publication Data
　Berman, Eleanor, 1934–
　　Traveling solo: advice and ideas for more than 250 great vacations /
Eleanor Berman. —2nd ed.
　　p. cm.
　　Rev. ed. of: Traveling on your own. 1st ed. c1990
　　Includes bibliographical references and index.
　　ISBN 0–7627–0418–7
　　1. Travel.　I. Berman, Eleanor, 1934–　Traveling on your own.
II. Title.
　G151.B483　1999
　910'.2'02—dc21　　　　　　　　　　　　　　　　　　　98–54364
　　　　　　　　　　　　　　　　　　　　　　　　　　　　CIP

Manufactured in the United States of America
Second Globe Pequot Edition/Second Printing

Contents

Section I:
Great Group Vacations
for Solo Travelers

Section II:
Solo Travel Know-How

Introduction

The first time I traveled by myself, I was newly divorced and scared to death. I never dreamed at that point that travel writing was to become my profession, almost forcing me to become adept at getting around on my own. I was just a travel lover determined that lack of a companion was not going to keep me at home. Happily, I discovered that the excitement of my first visit to San Francisco overcame my qualms. I did meet people along the way—not every day or for every meal, but often enough to keep me from feeling totally alone. I discovered to my surprise that there were unique pleasures to being completely on my own. And I had a wonderful time.

That was a long time ago, but I still remember my initial fear, and I have special empathy when someone asks me plaintively, "But where can I go alone?"

Having now traveled extensively for both business and pleasure, I've learned that there are many happy answers to that question; that, in fact, solo travel can have special advantages simply because you can tailor it exactly to your own tastes.

The purpose of this book is to point out some of the myriad possibilities for rewarding solo vacations, as well as offer some of the know-how that makes for more confident travel on your own. My aim is to help you discover that you don't always need a traveling companion to have a wonderful time—that alone need not mean lonely.

No one asked or paid to be included in this book. I chose programs and tours strictly because they represented a wide range of activities that seemed to offer an opportunity for comfortable and exciting singular vacations. I tried to stay with those that have been around long enough to have a proven record. The basic information was provided by the operator of each program, as were the names of most of the references quoted. The comments were requested because the trips I could experience personally were necessarily limited (you will find my remarks under E.B.). Wherever possible, I wanted to hear from travelers who could give firsthand reports.

The best way to ensure that any vacation is successful is to gather as much information as possible before you make a choice. That is doubly true when you are planning a trip alone, without a companion to help cushion disappointments. Use the listings in this book as a guide and a starting point only, to be followed up by research with travel agents, friends, and specialized magazines. If you're considering a particular group trip or activity, ask for current information and *references,* and phone directly to clear up unanswered questions before you sign on. You might follow my example and ask for names of past solo participants who can tell you whether they felt comfortable as part of such a group.

I've tried to give the cons as well as the pros for some of these trips in the hopes that they will be of value to you in making a choice. Inevitably, these are personal assessments, and my tastes may not always match your own.

The pages that follow present only a sampling of trips, and I may have omitted some equally rewarding possibilities for solo travel. If you know of any, please write to me care of The Globe Pequot Press and share them for a future edition.

If this book gives you new ideas, encourages you to overcome your fears of traveling by yourself, and helps you to make the right choices for *you,* my mission will have been accomplished.

FLORIDA

The
PALM BEACH
GIRL"

PEP AND SPEED
BRIGHT AND BREEZY !
HAPPY FUN

On Your Own: The Rewards

NOT VERY LONG AGO IN NEW YORK CITY, A LECTURE WAS HELD that packed the auditorium. The topic: vacations for singles.

The turnout was not surprising. We are living in a world where the number of single people is increasing dramatically. According to the U.S. Census Bureau, the number of never-married adults over age 18 more than doubled from 1970 to 1994, rising from 21 to 44 million, and the 30- to 34-age range tripled in size. Adding those who are divorced or widowed, unmarried adults now comprise 39 percent of the over-18 population.

And solo travelers comprise a growing number of vacationers. In their quarterly forecast for a recent summer, the United States Travel Data Center, the research arm of the Travel Industry Association of America, reported that 9 million people were planning summer vacation trips on their own in this one season alone. And this does not count the large number of solo business travelers who will extend their stays for a few days of vacation pleasure.

Yet information for those who want to plan a vacation alone has been hard to come by. Most people know about Club Med and some of the tours designed for single travelers. But there is also a world of exciting travel to be enjoyed on your own that is not labeled "For singles only."

Many people are at a loss when it comes to finding these vacations because information is scattered. The occasional lecture or article may not be available when you really need it. Few guidebooks look at travel issues from the point of view of a single traveler. Travel agents also are limited by this lack of reference material.

The aim of *Traveling Solo* is to fill that gap, to bring together in one sourcebook the wide range of rewarding vacations that can be enjoyed without a traveling companion.

Today no one, young or old, needs to stay at home for lack of company. The exciting possibilities for travel are as varied as the ages, budgets, and interests of those millions of singles. And while that old stickler, the single supplement, still makes it more expensive to travel alone, for those who need to economize there are ways to match up with compatible roommates to share the costs.

One chapter ahead will include the range of programs exclusively for singles, but most of the options in this book are not limited by marital status. They are choices based on personal interests, places, and programs where you can feel equally comfortable with or without a partner. Many of them include family-style meals, eliminating the need to eat alone, a prospect that is daunting to many travelers.

The first chapters are divided into various categories of vacation experiences, from shaping up your body to stretching your mind, from active adventure to relaxing in the sun. There is something here for everyone, from travelers in their 20s to adventure-seekers over age 50.

Many of these ideas can be found in other guides. The difference here is that the information was compiled with the single traveler in mind—single in this case meaning simply traveling alone.

The data supplied by the organizer of each trip is supplemented wherever possible by firsthand accounts from past solo travelers—including myself. If there are no reports, it is because no references were made available. Big tour companies and cruise lines in particular were generally unwilling to give out names of past clients.

Exact prices change rapidly, so the trips here are designated by general price categories as follows:

I = $150 a day or less including meals
M = $150–$200 daily
E = $200–$250 daily
EE = More than $250 per day

Transportation is not included in these estimates except for tours or unless it is specifically mentioned.

For your information, "single supplement" refers to the common practice of adding a surcharge for solo travelers. Though it is a source of expense and annoyance to everyone who travels alone, the supplement has a practical reason; it is an attempt to make up for the lost revenue of a second person in the room. Some wise hoteliers and tour operators have realized that single travelers are valuable customers and have minimized or eliminated the supplement. Many offer guaranteed "shares," which means that they will provide you with another single person of your sex as a roommate or they will waive the supplement if they cannot find someone to share the room.

The term "homestay" means an arrangement of accommodations in another person's home.

The last section of the book is for those who want to travel completely on their own, with ideas and guidance for doing so safely and comfortably.

One issue should be stressed from the start. This is not a book about how to find Mr. or Ms. Right on your vacation. Cupid is notoriously unreliable about where and when he aims his arrows, and there is no surer way to doom your trip than to base its success on whether or not you find romance on your travels.

The trips here encourage you to look at solo travel not as a way to find someone else, but as a time to find yourself. That is the secret of a truly successful solo vacation.

Certainly there are challenges in traveling by yourself. Dining alone is a big one, and successful solo travel requires more advance research, more careful planning, and more resourcefulness than a trip for two. All these topics will be covered in the pages ahead.

But what stops most people from traveling alone is less logistics than attitude. If you've never traveled by yourself, it may seem frightening. It's easy to feel nervous, shy, self-conscious, and even self-pitying when you seem to be one in a world of twos. The tendency is to imagine that people will look at you and say, "Poor thing—all alone."

In truth, traveling alone says nothing about you whatever except that you have a spirit of independence and adventure. Who's to say you don't have a wonderful friend at home who can't get away for this particular trip?

Furthermore, rather than feeling sorry for you, many of the couples you are envying may be jealous of your spirit and your freedom. Travel shared can be wonderful—but it can sometimes pose its own problems. Neither friends nor lovers are always in harmony in their enthusiasm or energy levels. If she loves Gothic cathedrals but he'd rather scuba dive, tensions can loom. Nothing is more frustrating than a companion who wants to use up all of your free time shopping—unless it is a travel mate who taps a foot impatiently every time *you* want to browse in a store. Travel partners sometimes lack your stamina, or, even worse, may keep up a pace that wears you out.

So, travel with a partner means compromises. Solo travel, on the other hand, can be the ultimate self-indulgence, the chance to tailor a vacation strictly to your own tastes, energies, and timetable—to go where you please, do exactly what you want when you want, and meet interesting new people of all ages and both sexes, married and single, in the process.

Without the insulation of a partner, you may find that you are more open to experiencing a new environment. You notice more, impressions are more vivid, you can take time to linger—and reactions are completely your own, uncolored by someone else's opinions.

By yourself you can feel freer to broaden your horizons and try out new roles, to live out a few fantasies perhaps, like riding a horse or rafting a river or painting a sunset—activities you might hesitate to attempt in front of the folks back home.

Because there is far more incentive to meet other people when you are by yourself, you tend to become more outgoing, to seek out new friends—and to find them.

What's more, many travelers who set out a bit shaky about traveling solo return feeling very good about themselves, with a stronger sense of competence, self-assurance, and independence for having proved that they can make it on their own.

Traveling alone has its challenges, but it can also be a wonderful opportunity. In the pages ahead you'll find a world of ideas for rewarding adventures. Make the most of them by selecting those that are uniquely right for you.

Making Choices

In planning a successful solo vacation, the first and most important tip to keep in mind is a simple one: Know yourself.

You may consider literally thousands of possibilities or vacations, from tennis camps and museum tours to cruising the Nile or trekking in

Nepal. Or you may choose to explore a great city on your own. One of the pitfalls of planning a trip alone is the temptation to choose what you think other single people are doing rather than doing the research to find something suited to your own tastes.

Yes, lots of people go on rafting trips by themselves, but if you hate camping and would be terrified by swirling rapids, it makes little sense to head for a river. Remember that the greatest advantage to traveling by yourself is the freedom to do exactly what you like best.

And while trips for "singles" may seem more comfortable than being a single among couples, it is a mistake to limit yourself only to this category. Consider these trips, certainly, but if you sign up for a trip solely for single company and discover that all you have in common with your fellow travelers is your marital status, the trip will be a washout.

The first question to ask yourself, then, is what you want from your vacation. Here are some points to consider:

- Do you need to relax and wind down or do you want a pick-me-up, a totally new adventure to spice up your life?
- What kind of physical shape are you in—and how much physical challenge do you want on your trip?
- Do you want to expand your present hobbies or interests or develop a new one?
- Is there some particular area you want to visit? If so, do you prefer seeing a little bit of a lot of places or spending time getting to know one destination in depth?
- Are you seeking a warm climate?
- How important is the quality of the food and lodging?
- Will you be happier making arrangements on your own and moving at your own pace, or would you be more secure as part of a group with all the planning done for you?

The more carefully you analyze what you are hoping for, the more likely you are to find it. Suppose, for example, that you want to visit the south of France. Your goals are to see the countryside, get some exercise, meet other people ages 30 to 40, and sample gourmet food. Many luxury tours could supply the gourmet part of the formula, but they would provide little exercise and probably attract an older clientele. An upscale biking or hiking trip might fill all of the requirements. What remains then is to research who offers such trips in this area and contact each with the right questions.

If you have the same destination in mind, but want a less strenuous trip, you might look into a learning vacation—one that stresses cooking, learning a foreign language, architecture, photography, or art. For a younger scene, consider tours geared to those under 35.

When your sights are set on sunshine, beware. A Caribbean island or the Mexican Riviera can hold perils for single travelers. Romantic resorts naturally attract loving couples, and there is nothing more depressing than feeling like odd man out in a lovers' hideaway. Look for other possibilities instead. Depending on your tastes, a trip to the Yucatan ruins in Mexico, a tennis camp in Florida, or painting lessons in the Caribbean are warm-weather options that should offer companions whose enthusiasms match your own. Windjammer sailing cruises attract lots of active, sociable people in the Caribbean, or you could check into a sunny spa resort that tends to draw many solo participants, married and single alike.

Should you join a tour or take off on your own? A lot depends on your travel experience and disposition. Do you dislike regimentation and prefer setting your own pace? Are you content to amuse yourself at home on occasion with solo walks, shopping expeditions, or museum visits? Are you able to talk to strangers? Are you willing to spend time and effort researching and planning your trip? Most of all, are you an optimist, ready to make the most of what you have rather than pining about what is missing? If the answers are yes, don't hesitate to try a trip by yourself; often going solo is the most rewarding way to go.

A good way to test the waters is to join a group or a tour, then afterward spend extra time in a city on your own. Or you might break up a solo city visit with short group tours to nearby attractions, providing a chance for a day or two of companionship.

Browse through all of the categories of vacations included in this book, including suggestions for travel on your own. You should find enough ideas to get you happily to almost any part of the world that intrigues you, and inspiration to try some new travel experiences as well. The key to traveling happily on your own is simply to do it in the way that will be most comfortable and enjoyable for *you*.

Section One

Great Group Vacations for Solo Travelers

Learn a Sport

SPORTS ARE THE PERFECT VACATION ICEBREAKER WHEN YOU are alone. It is easy to get to know others when you are learning new techniques together. Whether you improve your old game or pick up a new one, you'll also be adding a valuable dimension to your life when you get home. On a sports vacation, everyone is a winner.

Which sports are offered? Almost any you can name. From tennis and golf to scuba diving or mountain climbing, if you want to learn it, you can find someone to teach you on your vacation. You can learn to cross-country ski, canoe, ride a horse—or even live out your fantasy of being a major leaguer at a spring training baseball camp.

Tips for Enjoying Sports Camps
- Try to avoid blisters. If you buy new shoes for the trip, leave plenty of time to break them in at home before you go.
- Be prepared for hours out-of-doors with proper protection—sunscreen, sunglasses or a visor, and a protective hat.
- Start an exercise routine at home, stressing aerobics, for about a month before you go. Beginner or expert, you'll get more out of sports instruction if you build up your stamina in advance.

Here's a survey of the sporting vacation world.

Tennis

Tennis camp is one of the most popular sports vacations. Since there is a wide variation in facilities and rates, your first decision in choosing a tennis camp should be based on its ambience—resort versus campus dormitory-style living. This is often a matter of budget as well as preference, since resorts are obviously more expensive. Locations with group dining are often more sociable for single participants, but tennis instruction at resorts can provide a way to meet people on a resort vacation that might otherwise be lonely.

Your next decision depends on how intensive an instructional program you prefer. Finally, the season will make a difference. Decide whether you want to head for the mountains or the sunshine—or maybe let tennis camp solve the problem of planning a Caribbean vacation on your own.

While the lodgings and atmosphere may vary, the essential teaching programs all are much like the program I experienced at the Topnotch resort in Stowe, Vermont.

The instruction began with an orientation session and a few minutes of individual play with instructors who graded and divided us by ability into groups of four. Then we spent about an hour learning the right way to volley at the net.

During the next few days, we moved on to forehand, backhand, serve, overhead, and short strokes, with special drills devised to work on each stroke. Each day began with about fifteen minutes of warm-up exercises. One morning we were videotaped and got to see firsthand what we were doing right and wrong. Another day we got a private half-hour lesson to work on individual problems. On the last day we received an honest but upbeat evaluation sheet, with tips as to what to watch out for at home. The pros were excellent—outgoing, encouraging, and fun as well as fine teachers.

Will tennis camp work miracles on a mediocre tennis game? Unfortunately, you can't radically change your game in a few days, and most camps don't try. Instead they work on improving your existing strokes. With such concentrated practice, you do see encouraging improvement—and at the same time meet many people who share your interest in the sport.

Following is a listing of a variety of tennis camps.

The most spartan—those on school campuses—attract the most singles because everyone dines together.

Tennis Tips

Before you sign up for any tennis program, you should know the answers to the following questions:
- What is the instructor/student ratio? It should be no higher than one instructor per four students.
- How long has the program been running?
- What are the qualifications of the pros—are they certified by the U.S. Tennis Association and /or the U.S. Professional Tennis Association?
- Are there ample indoor courts so your vacation won't be washed out if it rains?

TOTAL TENNIS

Box 28, Saugerties, NY 12477;
(800) 221-6496 or (914) 247-9177;
WWW.TOTALTENNIS.COM (I)

YEARS IN BUSINESS:	19
AGE RANGE:	20–60
MOST COMMON AGE:	30–45
PERCENT ALONE:	50
NUMBER OF PARTICIPANTS:	60
MALE/FEMALE RATIO:	50/50

WILL TRY TO ARRANGE SHARES, BUT THE SINGLE SUPPLEMENT, WHEN ROOMS ARE AVAILABLE, IS MODEST.

This program has moved from summer quarters on a school campus to a permanent, year-round facility on the sixty-seven-acre grounds of a former resort overlooking the northern Catskill Mountains.

Facilities include thirteen red clay courts, seven all-weather courts, and five indoor courts. Participants are divided by ability into groups of four for five hours of daily instruction. Juice and fruit are served during breaks. Programs last from two to seven days; all include at least one private lesson.

Forty-three guest rooms in newly renovated buildings have air conditioning and private bathrooms. Most rooms have terraces; ten rooms in the Main Lodge have unobstructed mountain views.

The congenial Main Lodge features fireplaces in the reception area, living room and library, dining, TV/movie and card rooms, and fabulous views. The Barn houses massage therapy rooms and is used for dancing two nights weekly. Other evening activities include tennis talks, films, and current movies.

A swimming pool cools guests in summer, and in winter, a golf club ¼ mile down the road provides change-of-pace cross-country skiing and ice skating on a natural pond. For those who still have energy when the clinics end at 4:00 P.M., Saugerties is an antiquing center, and 10 miles away a host of shops beckon in charming Woodstock.

COMMENTS *Male, 30s: You have to work to get the most from this, but being serious about a game is an escape. Though hours of instruction seems like hard work, the atmosphere is friendly, and everyone has fun. Evenings can be social but are usually laid-back and quiet. There is a wide range of ages, with most people in their 20s and 30s and others up to their 60s. There are always many singles, a good mix of men and women, and no one has to worry about finding people at compatible levels of play.*
Female, 30s: Low-key, friendly, and open. Good instruction. I felt perfectly comfortable alone.

TENNIS CAMPS LTD. AT SWARTHMORE COLLEGE

444 EAST 82ND STREET,
NEW YORK, NY 10028;
(212) 879-0225 OR (800) 223-2442.
(I–M)

YEARS IN BUSINESS:	17
AGE RANGE:	30–65
MOST COMMON AGE:	35–45
PERCENT ALONE:	80
NUMBER OF PARTICIPANTS:	24 PER WEEK
MALE/FEMALE RATIO:	50/50
LATE JUNE TO MID-AUGUST; NO SINGLE SUPPLEMENT IN DORM LODGING; SINGLES WEEKS OFFERED	

Held on the manicured acres of Swarthmore College, 12 miles from Philadelphia, this summer program attracts many singles. Five-day clinics include five hours of instruction (with a 4:1 student-to-instructor ratio) and three half-hour private lessons. There is a choice of accommodations. Dorms, where everyone dines together, are recommended for meeting people. Strathaven, with modern hotel accommodations, and Ashton House, a Victorian mansion on campus, are more comfortable alternatives with a modest supplement. Both of the latter serve breakfast and lunch only; you are on your own for dinner. Campers have use of the school's indoor swimming pool, the outdoor pool at Strathaven, and Nautilus equipment. Three-day weekend clinics are also available.

COMMENTS *Female, 50s: I've gone for four successive summers and plan to go back. I choose the singles weeks since more people come alone. It is very relaxed, and there's a variety of people, from early 20s to 70s, about evenly divided between male and female, and backgrounds vary from a housewife to an ex-marine. You can be alone if you want, but someone is always looking for company for dinner or a movie. The staff really goes out of its way to make everyone comfortable, and they are good about getting people together. They suggest places to eat and often go along.*

Male, 30s: The instruction is terrific, and you get a lot of tennis—six hours a day. I don't play regularly, and I liked this because there was enough playing time to reinforce what we were learning. My game improved a lot. I chose the dorm accommodations, spartan and simple, with a shower down the hall. There was a wide mix in ages, 20s to 60s, a good mix of men and women. Most of the other people were either couples or friends who came together, but it was very easy being alone because every day had a focus. The instructors were enthusiastic and helpful and very sociable. On Saturday night a whole group, including the instructors, went into Philadelphia for dinner. It was a very good experience.

TOPNOTCH AT STOWE RESORT AND SPA

4000 MOUNTAIN ROAD, P.O. BOX 1458,
STOWE, VT 05672;
(802) 253-8585 OR (800) 451-8686;
TWO-HOUR PROGRAM, M
FOUR-HOUR PROGRAM, E (NO MEALS)

YEARS IN BUSINESS:	26
AGE RANGE:	35–65
MOST COMMON AGE FOR TENNIS:	35–65
PERCENT ALONE:	VARIES
NUMBER OF PARTICIPANTS:	VARIES
MALE/FEMALE RATIO:	VARIES
YEAR-ROUND	

Topnotch is exactly that: a beautiful setting in the Green Mountains and a first-class resort offering horseback riding, mountain biking, and a lovely spa as well as tennis. A tennis–spa package is available. The tennis program has been rated number one in the Northeast by *Tennis* magazine. Singles weeks are held in mid-June and early September. Ten outdoor courts are supplemented with four indoor courts in case of rain.

Topnotch no longer holds an organized tennis week like the one I attended. Though there is a minimum stay of three days, you can begin on any day, and the participants will vary from day to day, even during singles weeks. There is a choice of two- or four-hour programs, and everyone gets a half-hour private lesson for every three-day stay.

COMMENTS   *E.B.: Topnotch has been doing this for a long time, and they do it very well. Be prepared for a lot of tennis, even if you choose just two hours of instruction. What with playing with fellow campers in the afternoon, practicing my serve, working on strokes with the ball machine, and taking part in friendly tournaments, four hours of tennis was the average every day.*

But our group was on its own after the day's lessons ended, and many couples chose to eat at area restaurants rather than in the dining room. It was harder getting to know people well than if one were in a group that shares meals. A singles week might be a better choice. During those weeks, everyone gathers for cocktails late in the day and almost naturally stays together for dinner. There is no predicting male/female ratio. Some groups have even had the unusual problem of too many men!

Female, 20s: The singles week was very social, with an equal number of men and women. Ages were from early 20s to late 40s. We all went out to dinner and the bars together. The program was very well run. The people were interesting, from all over the U.S. and Canada. The accommodations were wonderful.

Male, 30s: The tennis program is staffed by pros of exceptional ability in tennis and also in dealing with people. To a man, they are polite, supportive, and lots of fun to be with. Their acute observations of my strokes and personalized attention were much appreciated. What is so nice is that after a very short time at Topnotch, you feel you really know the pros and other players.

JOHN NEWCOMBE TENNIS RANCH

P.O. Box 310469, New Braunfels, TX 78131; (830) 625-9105 or (800) 444-6204; WWW.LONE-STAR.NET/MALL/NEWKS/INDEX (E)

Australian John Newcombe, former U.S. Open and Wimbledon champion, believes that tennis should be fun. When "Newk" and his partners converted this former dude ranch, the program they created reflected his philosophy of good tennis and good times.

YEARS IN BUSINESS:	30
AGE RANGE:	30–60s
MOST COMMON AGE:	VARIES EACH WEEK
PERCENT ALONE:	20
NUMBER OF PARTICIPANTS:	MAXIMUM OF 80
MALE/FEMALE RATIO:	30/70
YEAR-ROUND WEEKLY AND WEEKEND PROGRAMS	

The program begins with tips from the various pros. Then come two and a half hours of drill work on the courts, developing shot techniques, reflexes, concentration, and conditioning. Video replays and a roving coach reinforce the teaching. Each group of four moves from court to court and from pro to pro.

If you choose the intensive program, afternoon brings more drills, strategy sessions, and supervised match play. Otherwise you can relax at the pool or in the Jacuzzi.

Good food and lots of it is one of the big attractions here. Accommodations are in courtside condominiums; unfortunately, there is no matching program, so there is no way around a single supplement—possibly the reason why singles are in the minority. Given the Texas climate, the best times to come are spring and fall. Avoid school vacation weeks, when the resort fills up with families.

NICK BOLLETTIERI SPORTS ACADEMY

5500 34TH STREET WEST, BRADENTON, FL 34210; (941) 755-1000 OR (800) USA-NICK; WWW.BOLLETTIERI.COM (I–M)

YEARS IN BUSINESS:	20+
AGE RANGE:	19–80
MOST COMMON AGE:	27–40
PERCENT ALONE:	40
NUMBER OF PARTICIPANTS:	VARIES
MALE/FEMALE RATIO:	3/1
YEAR-ROUND; WILL TRY TO ARRANGE SHARES	
ADDITIONAL LOCATIONS AT SOME RESORTS AND ON SEVERAL SCHOOL CAMPUSES IN SUMMER.	

Bollettieri, whose school has produced the likes of André Agassi, Monica Seles, and Jim Courier, runs one of the largest tennis-training operations in the world. The Bradenton headquarters boasts more than seventy-nine courts, eight of them indoors. Tennis programs are available for all levels. Instruction includes drills on strokes and videotaping as well as physical training and mental strategies. Tennis is just one of the options at the Sports Academy, a fifty-acre complex at which instruction is also offered in golf, soccer, and baseball.

Guests are housed in recently upgraded on-site apartments, and served buffet-style meals. A large swimming pool and a Jacuzzi are available along with a recreation center, computer learning center, and a sports therapy center. Longboat Key beaches and Sarasota shopping are minutes away. Free transportation is offered to and from the Sarasota/Bradenton airport.

RAMEY TENNIS SCHOOL

5931 HIGHWAY 56, OWENSBORO, KY 42301;
(501) 771-4723; WWW.MINDSPRING.COM/~JRAMEY (I)
TWO-, THREE-, AND FIVE-DAY PROGRAMS.

YEARS IN BUSINESS:	30+
AGE RANGE:	19–70
MOST COMMON AGE:	35–55
PERCENT ALONE:	75
NUMBER OF PARTICIPANTS:	21
MALE/FEMALE RATIO:	VARIES
YEAR-ROUND, WEEK-LONG, AND WEEKEND PROGRAMS; WILL TRY TO ARRANGE SHARES	

This "total immersion" program, located in a pleasant country setting among farms and orchards, is geared to high achievers, with the day planned from 8:00 A.M. to 9:00 P.M. Tennis takes up to five hours daily or can be extended for diehards. Strategy sessions, stroke presentations, tennis videos, and a tennis psychology program are on the full agenda. Four campers work with one pro and also get to work individually with director Joan Ramey, a U.S. Professional Tennis Association Master Professional. Campers are housed in cottages with cooking facilities or in nearby motels. Facilities include three indoor and three outdoor tennis courts, an outdoor pool, a Nautilus fitness room, sauna, racquetball courts, and a lighted sand volleyball court. A masseuse can be arranged to ease tired muscles. Food is home cooked and farm fresh. Horseback instruction is available at the riding stables, and campers have the option of combining tennis and riding programs.

COMMENTS *Male, 40s: The ages varied from teens to 50s; people were mainly from the Midwest. You naturally get to know people, especially those in your tennis group, but we all ate meals as a group, making it even easier. Food was excellent, the accommodations fine, the program well run. It was a great experience.*

Male, 40s: There were some singles, but mostly couples or two friends who came together. But I was alone, and I didn't feel lonely. It was easy to meet people, even though I stayed at a motel in town, because we all ate together. The food was the high point of the trip. I was very impressed also by the structure of the lessons. We worked for eight hours a day, but it was spaced so that you didn't get worn out.

NEW ENGLAND TENNIS HOLIDAYS

P.O. Box 1648
North Conway, NH 03850;
(800) 869-0949 (M)

YEARS IN BUSINESS: SINCE 1987
AGE RANGES: LATE 30s TO EARLY 60s
MOST COMMON AGE: 40
PERCENT ALONE: OVER 50
NUMBER OF PARTICIPANTS: UP TO 24, 10-15 ON AVERAGE
MALE/FEMALE RATIO: ROUGHLY 50/50
MAY THROUGH SEPTEMBER

Two ski areas, Cranmore in North Conway, New Hampshire, and Sugarbush in Warren, Vermont, are headquarters for this program. Participants are housed in inns or condos near the mountain. Breakfast is at the lodging, lunch at the courts; the group goes out together for meals in area restaurants.

Players are evaluated, divided by ability into groups of four for instruction on all types of strokes, and taught singles and doubles strategies. Videos of each individual on the court help reinforce instruction. Indoor courts ensure play, rain or shine. *Tennis Magazine* rates this program highly.

JOHN GARDINER'S TENNIS RANCH

P.O. Box 228, Carmel Valley, CA 93924;
(408) 659-2207; www.jgtr.com (EE)

JOHN GARDINER'S RESORT ON CAMELBACK

5700 East McDonald Drive, Scottsdale, AZ 85253;
(602) 948-2100 or (800) 245-2051;
www.arizonaguide.com/gardinertennis (M-EE)

The number of single participants is very small, but these two facilities deserve mention as the ultimate luxury in tennis camps. The intimate California ranch, a pioneer in tennis instruction now past its thirtieth year in business, provides court space for twenty-eight players. Guests are requested to wear tennis whites; for dinner, men wear jackets and ties and women dress up. Dinner is served buffet style and there are no tables for two, so guests do get to know each other. They may range from Texas ranchers to feminist lawyers, but all tend to be interesting and well-heeled people. The program includes five hours of instruction daily and all meals. The camp operates March to November.

The Scottsdale facility, bigger and more luxurious, is set in the beautiful Arizona desert and offers lodging in spacious casitas on the grounds. It upholds the high instructional standards of the original ranch, but the program is less intense, with three and a half hours of instruction daily. The fee for the seven-day program includes two half-hour massages; three-day packages offer one massage. Meals are served both indoors and out to take advantage of the scenery. Both tennis clinics are kicked off with a champagne reception on the night of arrival.

There are many more tennis camp options on campuses around the country in summer. Here are a few possibilities:

- OBERLIN COLLEGE, C/O DR. BOB PIRON, RICE HALL, OBERLIN COLLEGE, OBERLIN, OHIO 44074; (216) 775-8763 OR (800) 433-6060.
- UNIVERSITY OF CALIFORNIA, IRVINE AND UNIVERSITY OF CALIFORNIA, SANTA CRUZ, BOTH C/O U.S. SPORTS, 919 SIR FRANCIS DRAKE BOULEVARD, KENTFIELD, CA 94904; (800) 645-3226.
- DUKE UNIVERSITY, P.O. BOX 2553, DURHAM, NC 27715; (919) 479-0854.

Resorts with large tennis instructional programs include:

ARTHUR ASHE TENNIS CENTER

DORAL RESORT, 4400 NW 87TH AVENUE, MIAMI, FL 33178; (305) 591-6454.

NAPLES BATH AND TENNIS CLUB, 4995 AIRPORT ROAD NORTH,

NAPLES, FL 33942; (813) 261-5777 OR (800) 225-9692.

HARRY HOPMAN TENNIS ACADEMY, SADDLEBROOK RESORT,

5700 SADDLEBROOK WAY, WESLEY CHAPEL, FL 33543 (NEAR TAMPA); (813) 973-1111 OR (800) 729-8383.

COLONY BEACH AND TENNIS RESORT

1620 GULF OF MEXICO DRIVE, LONGBOAT KEY, FL 34228; (941) 383-6464 OR (800) 282-1138.

BOCA RATON TENNIS CENTER, BOCA RATON RESORT AND CLUB,

P.O. BOX 5025, BOCA RATON, FL 33431; (407) 395-3000 OR (800) 327-0101.

THE POINTE ON SOUTH MOUNTAIN TENNIS CLUB

THE POINTE-HILTON RESORT, 777 SOUTH POINTE PARKWAY, PHOENIX, AZ 85044; (602) 432-6453 OR (800) 876-4683.

LITCHFIELD BEACH RESORT, P.O. Box 320, Pawleys Island, SC 29585; (803) 237-3070 or (800) 344-5590.

WINTERGREEN RESORT, P.O. Box 706, Wintergreen, VA; (804) 325-2200 or (800) 325-2200.

For further listings of tennis schools, consult the following resources:

PETERSON'S TENNIS CAMPS & CLINICS, 1995, Peterson's Publishing, Princeton, NJ; (609) 243-9111.

FODOR'S GREAT AMERICAN SPORTS AND ADVENTURE VACATIONS, 1996, Fodors Publishing, New York; (212) 751-2600.

TENNIS MAGAZINE, 5520 Park Avenue, Box 395, Trumbull, CT 06611; (203) 373-7000. Prints an annual listing of tennis camps and clinics in its February issue.

....

Golf

Golf schools based at top resorts give single vacationers a focus to the day and a way to meet people, as well as the chance to improve their game. With locations from coast to coast, they provide opportunities for a comfortable resort vacation year-round.

THE GOLF SCHOOL

Mount Snow Resort, Mount Snow, VT 05356; (802) 464-3333 or (800) 240-2555; WWW.THEGOLFSCHOOL.COM (E)

Years in business:	Since 1978
Age range:	12–75
Most common age:	50s
Percent alone:	25–30
Number of participants:	50–80
Male/female ratio:	More males
Offered year-round; suitable for beginners	

This popular school has winter headquarters in Crystal River, Florida, and warm-weather bases at Ocean City, Maryland, and four scenic New England ski resorts—Mt. Snow, Killington, and Sugarbush in Vermont and Sugarloaf/USA in Maine. Schools are

also held at courses in Amherst, NH, Binghamton, NY, and Fredericksburg, VA, with accommodations at nearby hotels or motels. All offer a
low teaching ratio—four students per instructor—and instruction that
ranges from fundamentals for beginners to fine nuances for the experts.
Videotape plus other training aids and classroom instruction are part of
the two-, three-, four-, and five-day programs offered. Special offerings
include clinics for women and juniors and a parent–child program. Balls
and clubs are provided, so beginners don't have to worry about equipment.

COMMENTS *Female, 40s: A special effort is made to make single
people feel comfortable. There is a get-together party and buffet dinner the first night, a banquet the last night, and a "captain's table" so
that you can always find company for dinner. There were many more
single males than females! The small teaching groups mean you get to
know people well. A good learning experience, a lot of golf, and a lot
of fun.*

GOLF DIGEST SCHOOLS

5520 Park Avenue, Box 395, Trumbull, CT
06611; (203) 373-7130 or
(800) 243-6121;
www.golf.com/golfdigest/schools (EE)

YEARS IN BUSINESS:	26
AGE RANGE:	25–65
MOST COMMON AGE:	OVER 35
PERCENT ALONE:	HIGH
NUMBER OF PARTICIPANTS:	4–28
MALE/FEMALE RATIO:	VARIES, BUT MORE MEN
OFFERED YEAR-ROUND. SUITABLE FOR BEGINNERS; SINGLE SUPPLEMENT CHARGED	

Schools at nearly twenty resorts around the country operate under
the auspices of this golfing magazine. Many top pros are teachers, and instruction is geared to every level from beginner to advanced. Classes are
held at the practice tee, the practice bunker, and the putting green, as
well as on the golf course. Videotapes are also used. The welcoming cocktail reception and dinner with instructors is a good chance to meet other
participants; programs close with another reception and special dinner.
Among the resorts and golf clubs participating are Innisbrook Resort and
Golf Club, Tarpon Springs, Florida; Carmel Valley Golf and Country
Club, California; Sea Island Golf Club, St. Simons Island, Georgia; Sun
Valley Golf Club, Sun Valley, Idaho; Pine Meadow Golf Club,

Mundelein, Illinois; the Golf Club at Chateau Elan, Brazelton, Georgia; and the Williamsburg Inn in Virginia.

COMMENTS *Female, 40s: I've attended two schools, with very different lodgings—villas at one, a lodge at another, but both were quite comfortable. Generally there are couples and men alone; women are in the minority. You all start as strangers, then quickly become friendly. Many people get together for dinner. I never ate alone. Ages were from 20s to 70s; the larger group is divided into smaller sections, and you get to know your own group very well.*

CRAFT-ZAVICHAS GOLF SCHOOL

600 DITTMER, PUEBLO, CO 81005;
(719) 564–4449 OR (800) 858–9633. (E)

YEARS IN BUSINESS:	30
AGE RANGE:	30 AND UP
MOST COMMON AGE:	55
PERCENT ALONE:	30
NUMBER OF PARTICIPANTS:	24–30
MALE/FEMALE RATIO:	30/70
YEAR-ROUND. SUITABLE FOR BEGINNERS; WILL TRY TO ARRANGE SHARES	

The second-oldest golf school in the country (and the only one operated by a woman) holds clinics that range from two and a half to five days at a variety of resort locations. Groups are divided into classes of four or less, with male instructors for the men and female instructors for the women. In addition to the personal instruction, split-screen, slow-motion video analysis is given to each student to take home. The atmosphere is friendly, with many meals planned with students and instructors in attendance.

COMMENTS *Male, 60s: I went alone, and it was fine, though there were hardly any other singles. There are many couples where only one plays golf, so it works out. The people were from all over the U.S. and about evenly divided between males and females. The program was well organized, with good instruction. Classes are small: five students to one instructor. The days are full, and I was too tired to worry about doing anything at night. They do a great job.*
Female, 40s: I've been there twice, first alone and I came back with my sister. About one-third of the people come by themselves. The food was only so-so, but the staff was excellent—I dropped my handicap by seven strokes after my first time there. You get lots of individual atten-

tion. The staff really concentrates on you and your game. It's pretty easy to meet people. You all wear name tags, and you meet lots of people at meals. Many people return—over half the people there had been before. I highly recommend the women-only classes—especially to women going alone—since there is no distraction so you concentrate on your golf, which is what you're there to do.

JOHN JACOBS' GOLF SCHOOLS

7825 EAST REDFIELD ROAD, SCOTTSDALE, AZ 85260; (602) 991-8587 OR (800) 822-1255; WWW. JACOBSGOLF.COM (M–EE: COST VARIES WITH THE RESORT CHOSEN)

YEARS IN BUSINESS:	28
AGE RANGE:	20–70
MOST COMMON AGE:	40–55
PERCENT ALONE:	20
NUMBER OF PARTICIPANTS:	VARIES
MALE/FEMALE RATIO:	60/40
OFFERED YEAR-ROUND	
GUARANTEED SHARES IF REQUESTED THIRTY-ONE DAYS IN ADVANCE	

A long-established program that graduates more than 12,000 students annually, the John Jacobs' Golf Schools are found in more than 30 locations from Point Clear, Alabama, to Palm Desert, California. Three-, four-, and five-day sessions include a comprehensive teaching program and opening and closing dinner parties with instructors and classmates.

For additional golf school possibilities, see the following:
Golf Digest, 5520 PARK AVENUE, BOX 395, TRUMBULL, CT 06611; (203) 373-7000.
Golf Magazine, 380 MADISON AVENUE, NEW YORK, NY 10017; (212) 687-3000.

....

Horseback Riding

Horseback Riding, Western Style

Why don't more single people go to ranches? It's hard to imagine a more informal, relaxing vacation. Everybody is in jeans; nobody puts on airs; "dudes" come from all over the country and are all ages.

This is a favorite family vacation, but while solo guests are few, ranches are the best examples I know of why an easy ambience, family-style meals, and a common pursuit are more important for a good vacation than the presence of lots of "singles." I've not met anyone who went to a ranch alone who did not report a wonderful time.

Besides riding, many ranches offer activities such as river-rafting, short pack trips, and hiking. They are the perfect introduction to the panoramas and pleasures of the American West.

Ranches vary in ambience, but the routines at most of them are similar. Guests mount up the first day so that the wranglers can judge their ability. Beginners get instructions in starting, stopping, turning, and getting to know a horse. Your horse is assigned according to your ability to ride. Each day adult rides are offered morning and afternoon for both beginners and advanced riders.

Since many people arrive with little or no riding experience, lessons also are offered every day to help you sit tall in the saddle. Some wind up the week galloping across the meadows; others are content to stay with the "slow ride" each day, a trek into the wilderness that is no less beautiful when the horses move at a reassuring, steady walk.

Evenings bring informal group activities from nature talks and slides to square dancing. Sometimes there is a trip to a nearby rodeo.

If you want to avoid the family scene, come in spring or fall, when school is in session.

I've visited two very different kinds of ranches, both places that I would recommend to anyone who loves the outdoors and wants to learn to ride.

TANQUE VERDE RANCH

14301 EAST SPEEDWAY, TUCSON, AZ 85748;
(520) 296–6275 OR (800) 234–DUDE. (E–EE)

In a sublime setting 2,800 feet high in the foothills of three mountain ranges, Tanque Verde Ranch sits amidst millions of acres of national forest and adjoins the Saguaro National Monument, a veritable forest of giant cactus. Guests ride over silent, open desert, up rocky canyons, and into towering mountains. The food is plentiful and delicious, especially cookouts over a mesquite fire; almost every belt was out at least a notch by the end of the week. A tradition here is the early morning ride where a chuck-wagon breakfast of eggs and pancakes awaits in the desert, served up against a backdrop of cactus haloed by the glow of the morning sun.

The main building of the ranch is historic, dating to the 1880s, but the fifty-nine air-conditioned rooms in modern casitas are downright luxurious. The ranch has Arizona's largest riding stable, with more than 100 mounts. Five tennis courts, indoor and outdoor pools, and a workout room are available when you are not in the saddle. Nature programs and walks are an added feature for those who are interested.

Despite the comparatively large number of guests here, singles need not feel left out. As the brochure says, "It's easy to be alone, but hard to feel lonely." I met a friendly couple in the van from the airport who invited me to their table at dinner that night, and I never lacked for company the rest of the week. Meals are family style, so each day was an opportunity to meet more people. The other two singles in residence during my stay were a male visitor from Japan, about age 35, and a woman in her 60s.

COMMENTS *Female, 30s: I've been there ten times, three or four times alone, and I'd tell anyone to come alone. It's very comfortable, the kind of place where you can feel really safe, relax, and have fun. No one is looking at you because you're there by yourself. I made friends quickly each time, and I got to know the staff, too—they were always good for conversation and companionship. There's always something going on, so you can be alone or with people whenever you want. It is evenly split among men and women, but not many men by themselves. The food is great and plentiful. They have a new chef, and the menu is lighter now, more health oriented.*
Female, 40s: I first went here with my husband and kids, then was divorced, and I've gone alone for the past four years. There are very few singles, but it's very easy to meet people, starting at meals, which are served family style at tables for ten. A separate kids' program for much of the day means you aren't surrounded by children even though many families do come. I love the fact that it is so quiet, that you can be alone or with people as you choose. I'm planning to go back next year!

VISTA VERDE RANCH

P.O. Box 465, Steamboat Springs, CO 80477;
(970) 879-3858 or (800) 526-7433; www.vistaverde.com (E–EE)

This is an equally stupendous setting in the high meadows north of Steamboat Springs. At 7,800 feet, surrounded by national forest and wilderness areas and the 12,000-foot peaks of the Rockies, the air was crystal clear and the views glorious. Though food and accommodations are upscale and amenities include private hot tubs, a sauna, and fitness equipment, this is a working ranch, with cattle, plenty of farm animals, and its own stable of more than sixty horses. With a maximum of thirty-five guests and a friendly staff, making friends was a snap. Besides enjoying riding, eating, and evening entertainment together, guests share adventures such as white-water rafting trips, hot-air balloon rides, hiking, kayaking, mountain biking, and rock climbing. If you don't feel at home and don't know everyone well by the time the week is over, it's your own fault. Special weeks featuring cattle drives, pack trips, and fly-fishing are especially recommended for single guests, and the hiking is superb in early June, when wildflowers and waterfalls abound.

At both ranches, the guests were well educated, interesting, and went out of their way to include someone who was alone.

COMMENTS *Female, 30s: I've been there six times total, with someone and on the cattle drive alone. There aren't many singles—on all my trips I've encountered only two other singles—one male in his 40s and one woman on the cattle drive with me. But it was nice to go alone because it seems like they pay more attention to you to make sure you're having a good time. The staff treated me like family— they were very welcoming and took care of me. It's a great experience that I'd recommend to anyone.*

CASTLE ROCK GUEST RANCH AND ADVENTURE RESORT

412 County Road, 6NS, Cody, WY 82414;
(307) 587-2076. (E)

Castle Rock rates a mention for its varied program, which supplements riding instruction and ranch life with a chance to try out easy adventures such as llama treks, mountain biking, kayaking, rafting, sailing, windsurfing, and rock climbing. Trips to see the sights of Cody and Yellowstone National Park are included in the rates.

COMMENTS *Male, late 30s: I went with my daughter. There were mostly families, just a few singles with kids and a few couples. Most adults were in their 30s and 40s. The days were structured, but the atmosphere was very relaxed. They had set riding times each day and many planned activities, such as kayaking, climbing, fishing, and llama packing. They also have a pool, so there is always something to do. They play games the first day that introduce everyone, and it is very friendly. The food was wonderful, the accommodations okay— sort of suburban rustic. The instruction was great, and I had a wonderful time.*

Female, 40s: It was a totally positive experience. Guests were mostly couples, a few families, and one other single parent with his son, from all over the U.S. and from Europe. Everyone was easy to get along with and compatible. You could do as much or as little as you wanted, with the group or on your own. The food was served buffet style and was outstanding. The staff was top-notch. I would recommend it to any single traveler but especially to those with kids.

LAZY HILLS GUEST RANCH
BOX G, INGRAM, TX 78025;
(830) 367–5600 OR (800) 880–0632; WWW.LAZYHILLS.COM (I).
WILL TRY TO ARRANGE SHARES

In business for more than thirty-five years, this is a family-owned, working ranch in beautiful country, a good choice for those who want to sample Texas-style ranching. Besides riding, the ranch offers swimming, tennis, basketball, volleyball, hiking, fishing, hayrides, and cookouts. Owners say that it is a good choice for singles, even though they are few in number, because they are included when they want to be, yet are not pressured to participate in activities.

COMMENTS *Female, 30s: I've gone a number of times, alone and with my son. It is a working ranch with trail rides, tennis, a pool, a lovely environment. Meals are served family style, so you get to know*

How to Choose a Ranch

There are enough ranches out West to fill a separate book, and because none attract a large number of single guests, the best bet is to get a comprehensive listing, narrow the choices by location, and write for brochures. The first determining factor will be price, since ranches can range from $600 to $2,000 a week and from five-star to pure rustic. When you have a few possibilities in mind, call them directly. You'll get a good idea of the flavor of the place just from the way you are received on the telephone. Here are a few considerations you should learn from the brochure or the owner:

- Emphasis: Are single adults welcome? How many came last year? Do more come at certain times of year?
- Rates: Many ranches give a break to single adults with only a modest added supplement.
- Location: To experience the true beauty of the West, pick a ranch with mountain views and access to rides in the wilderness. If you are traveling alone, you may prefer a ranch that provides transportation services or that is easy for you to reach from a major airport.
- Size: Outgoing people will do fine almost anywhere, but on the whole, it is easier to meet people at a smaller ranch.
- Ambience: Is this an authentic working ranch or a resort? Are accommodations modern or rustic?
- Amenities: If you are a new rider, chances are you will soon be a "tenderseat." You may welcome facilities such as whirlpools or the ministrations of a masseuse on the premises—services that can be found even on working ranches these days.
- Facilities: Do you care about a pool or tennis courts in addition to riding? If so, check whether they are available.
- Activities: Are there options beyond the ranch itself—trips to the rodeo, rafting expeditions, fishing, et cetera? Is there an evening program?
- Staff: What is the ratio of staff to guests? Who gives the riding instruction? How much teaching experience do they have?
- Horses: Are there more horses than guests? Will you be assigned the same horse each day?
- References: Every ranch should be able to provide you with the names of guests who have visited recently. Call them before you decide where to go.

everyone. Guests come from all over the world and range in age from 20s to 90s. There have been a number of single people on my visits, more women than men.

Female, 40s: There were few other singles, but I had a wonderful time. It was easy to be there solo because the owners made sure I was never by myself if I didn't want to be. The area is very beautiful and peaceful. The hayrides were absolutely wonderful. I would recommend this place to anyone.

Here are sources that can supply ranch listings; some can also offer advice on selection:

COLORADO DUDE AND GUEST RANCH ASSOCIATION

P.O. Box 300, Tabernash, CO 80478; (970) 887–3128; www.stout.entertain.com. Publishes annual state directory and offers guidance.

THE DUDE RANCHERS ASSOCIATION

P.O. Box 471, Laporte, CO 80535; (970) 223–8440; www.duderanch.org. Publishes annual directory including ranches in Arizona, Arkansas, California, Colorado, Montana, Nevada, New Mexico, Oregon, South Dakota, Texas, and Wyoming. The association will give advice on choosing a ranch.

OLD WEST DUDE RANCH VACATIONS, AMERICAN WILDERNESS EXPERIENCES, INC.

P.O. Box 1486, Boulder, CO 80306; (800) 444–DUDE, (303) 444–2622; www.gorp.com/oldwest

Handles sixty-seven ranches in Arizona, Colorado, Idaho, Montana, New Mexico, Wyoming, and British Columbia and offers a central reservation service with guidance in selecting the best place for your needs. Their catalog indicates ranches with special rates for single guests.

ARIZONA DIVISION OF TOURISM

1702 North Third Street, Phoenix, AZ 85004; (602) 230–7733 or (800) 842–8257; www.arizonaguide.com

TRAVEL MONTANA

1424 Ninth Avenue, Helena, MT 59620; (800) 541–1447; www.visitmt.com

WYOMING TRAVEL COMMISSION

I-25 at College Drive, Cheyenne, WY 82002-0660;
(800) 225-5996; in state, (307) 777-7777. Publishes state listing. www.commerce.state.wy.us/west

For more information on individual Western ranches, consult Gene Kilgore's Ranch Vacations, John Muir Press, (800) 888-7504.

Horseback Riding, Eastern Style

For easterners who can't make the trip out West, here are a few places that teach riding in rustic, informal, and scenic surroundings:

JORDAN HOLLOW FARM

Route 2, Box 375, Stanley, VA 22851; (888) 418-7000 or (540) 778-2285.

WEST RIVER LODGE

RR 1, Box 693, Newfane, VT 05345; (802) 365-7745.

KEDRON VALLEY INN

Route 106, South Woodstock, VT 05071; (802) 457-1473 or (800) 836-1193.

ROCKING HORSE RANCH

Highland, NY 12528; (800) 43-RANCH or (914) 681-2927.

PINE GROVE RANCH

Cherrytown Road, Kerhonkson, NY 12448; (914) 626-7365 or (800) 346-4626.

ROARING BROOK RANCH & TENNIS RESORT

Lake George, NY 12845; (518) 668-5767.

Baseball

Every guy—or gal—who has ever fantasized about being a major leaguer can make the dream come true at one-week spring training camps where guests become the rookies and former greats of the sport turn coach. Said one participant, "You walk into the clubhouse, grab a cup of coffee, head for your locker, and get your freshly laundered uniform, with your name stitched on the shirt above your number. You look around and you see baseball stars, telling stories about the old days, and you're one of them . . . for one week, you're on the team." This participant, one of three women in the camp, not only got to play but actually got a hit in the final game, a thrill she will never forget.

Baseball camps, aptly named "Dream Weeks" by one promoter, attract as many nonathletes as aces. Nobody under age 30 is allowed. Campers are coached in every phase of the game by former greats. They get drafted for teams, play each other, and sometimes play the pros. Talk is centered on baseball—past, present, and future. Most participants haven't played ball for years—but they have a ball! Who comes to baseball camp? One recent roster included surgeons, lawyers, a dentist, a comic-book distributor, a real estate broker, a bartender, two mailmen, a plumber, and a congressional analyst.

The programs are basically alike, and most will try to arrange shares. All are in the EE category, but participants find them a once-in-a-lifetime fantasy come true.

COMMENTS *Male, 40s: I've attended the Randy Hundley Cubs camp twice. I went alone and was placed with a roommate. You can't help meeting people. Most of the men were over 40, married but traveling on their own, and Cub fans from the Midwest. It is well run.*
Male, 30s: I've been to baseball camp three times and I am going again. It is so easy to meet people—there is instant "team spirit." The men are mostly married, from 30 to 50; there were very few women. I had a great time each time and am looking forward to returning.

Baseball camps for adults include:

DREAM WEEK, INC.
P.O. Box 115, Huntingdon Valley, PA 19006;
(215) 938–1200 or (800) 888–4376.
Weeks and weekends offered feature the Phillies,
the St. Louis Cardinals, and Atlanta Braves.

RANDY HUNDLEY'S FANTASY BASEBALL CAMPS, INC.

130 South Northwest Highway, Palatine, IL 60067;
(847) 991–9595.
Nirvana for Chicago Cubs fans.

LOS ANGELES DODGERS ADULT BASEBALL CAMP

Box 2887, Vero Beach, FL 32961;
(561) 569–4900 or (800) 334–7529.
Former stars from both Brooklyn and L.A. Dodgers take part.

NEW YORK YANKEES FANTASY CAMP

3102 North Himes Avenue, Tampa, FL 33207;
(800) 368–2267.
A chance to mingle with Yankee greats.

Sailing

Attending sailing school is a wonderful combination of learning a skill and experiencing the exhilaration of being at sea. In a week you learn the ropes from port to starboard. You start on land, learning what to expect, then head on board with instructors. Pretty soon the crew mates are working as a team, beginning to speak the language of sailing, and getting to know their boat. Friendships come easy working in such close quarters toward a common goal. By the time the week is over, the crew is usually able to chart a course and set out on its own.

Sailing schools are a wonderful way for singles to visit the Caribbean, as well as scenic ports in the United States.

STEVE AND DORIS COLGATE'S OFFSHORE SAILING SCHOOL

16731 McGregor Boulevard, Fort Myers, FL 33908;
(800) 221–4326 or (941) 454–1700; www.offshore-sailing.com. (E). Three- to seven-day programs, special week for women.

School locations: Jersey City and Barnegat Bay, New Jersey; Stamford and Mystic, Connecticut; Newport, Rhode Island; Captiva Island, Florida; St. Petersburg, Florida; Chicago, Illinois; and Tortola in the Caribbean. Will try to arrange shares—two to five per villa at Captiva Island, two per room in Tortola. Captiva Island offers a special singles unit; single supplement on live-aboard cruises is very small. Meals are included only while cruising.

YEARS IN BUSINESS:	30+
AGE RANGE:	12–75
MOST COMMON AGE:	30s
PERCENT ALONE:	45
NUMBER OF PARTICIPANTS:	60,000 GRADUATES
MALE/FEMALE RATIO:	70/30
YEAR-ROUND	

The seven-day "Learn to Sail" program for beginners is based at a resort and kicks off with a sociable get-acquainted party. Days are divided into morning classes and afternoons on the water. No more than four students are assigned with an instructor to each Olympic-class 27-foot Soling sailboat, and a real bond develops among them. Once the basics are mastered, students can increase their knowledge with more advanced sailing and cruising weeks. A special live-aboard cruising course combines curriculum with a thrilling one-week sail on a 40- to 50-foot boat in some of the world's ultimate sailing destinations—Tortola in the British Virgin Islands and Newport, Rhode Island, depending on the time of year. Graduates can become members of the Offshore Cruising Club, eligible to enjoy cruising vacations in more beautiful locales, and the Offshore Sailing, sailing regularly on club-owned boats at offshore branches.

COMMENTS *Female, 40s: My St. Lucia classmates, numbering just two, were also female—one slightly younger and one slightly older than me, one married and one divorced, all of us from different walks of life and enrolled for vastly different reasons. By the end of the week we enjoyed a very special breed of friendship based on a combination of shared apprehension, excitement, embarrassment, fear, joy, panic, and amazing mutual support.*

Male, 30s: On the last day, like kids, you stay out past the allotted time until, finally, the instructor arrives in his launch to see you home. You wish you could spend a month of sailing days like these.

ANNAPOLIS SAILING SCHOOL

601 SIXTH STREET, P.O. BOX 3334, ANNAPOLIS, MD 21403; (800) 638-9192 OR (410) 267-7205; WWW.USBOAT.COM/ANNAPWAY (M–EE, DEPENDING ON LOCATION; MEALS INCLUDED ONLY ABOARD SHIP)

YEARS IN BUSINESS:	40
AGE RANGE:	16 AND UP
MOST COMMON AGE:	25–35
PERCENT ALONE:	VARIES
NUMBER OF PARTICIPANTS:	3,000 ANNUALLY
MALE/FEMALE RATIO:	VARIES
YEAR-ROUND; BRANCHES IN ST. PETERSBURG, FLORIDA, AND ST. CROIX, U.S. VIRGIN ISLANDS; SEASONAL LOCATIONS IN ANNAPOLIS, MARYLAND, AND THE FLORIDA KEYS; SUITABLE FOR BEGINNERS; WILL TRY TO ARRANGE SHARES	

The nation's largest sailing school boasts 140,200 graduate sailors. The New Sailors Vacation Course includes two days of classroom and on-board instruction and three days of supervised sailing to reinforce new skills in a variety of sailing conditions. Once you've mastered the basics, you can elect to continue with a five-day Flotilla Cruising Course, a cruise vacation at sea that continues your instruction. Sail Away weekends are also offered.

Package arrangements with nearby inns and hotels can be made by the school at each location.

COMMENTS *Female, 20s: I went alone on a two-day program, liked it so much I decided to work there. The age range is about 25 to 50, but most people are in their 20s and 30s and from the Northeast. There are a few couples and many singles, though many are groups of friends who come together.*

Male, 50s: It was a very good experience. The instruction was excellent, and there was no problem being alone. I learned a lot and had fun, though I stayed in a hotel and there was no real socializing at night. Of nineteen people, there was one couple and all the rest were single. They were quite a diverse group of people, but mostly from the Northeast.

Scuba Diving

More Americans every year are descending to discover the eerie beauty at the bottom of the sea. Recent statistics show that around 12 million people now have their diving certification, and with it a kinship that makes it easy to find friends on any diving vacation. If you want to join their numbers, the easiest way is to head for Club Med locations in the Bahamas; Sonora Bay, Mexico; or the Turks and Caicos Islands. Each has a dedicated dive center where you can learn and be certified. Many other Club Meds also offer lessons.

Or you can choose one of the great diving spots—Bonaire in the Dutch West Indies or the Cayman Islands—to gain your certification. For the most current list of courses available, as well as a selection of hotel brochures, contact the island tourist offices at the following addresses/telephones.

BONAIRE GOVERNMENT TOURIST OFFICE

10 ROCKEFELLER PLAZA, SUITE 900; NEW YORK, NY 10020;
(212) 956-5912 OR (800) BONAIRE; WWW.BONAIRE.COM

Diving is what Bonaire is all about, and all major hotels have learning programs. The most luxurious accommodations are at the Harbour Village Beach Resort, where there is a full-service health spa, and the Plaza Resort Bonaire, the newest hotel on the island. Both resorts have fully equipped dive shops offering a variety of courses. The most knowledgeable divers head for the newly renovated Habitat, originally run by Cap'n Don Stewart, an island legend. Ask the tourist office for dive package information and the *Bonaire Adventure Guide*.

CAYMAN ISLANDS DEPARTMENT OF TOURISM

420 LEXINGTON AVENUE, SUITE 2312, NEW YORK, NY 10017;
(212) 682-5582. (OFFICES ARE ALSO IN ATLANTA, CHICAGO,
CORAL GABLES, DALLAS, HOUSTON, LOS ANGELES, TAMPA, AND TORONTO.)

Information packets from the Caymans include a long list of dive packages, many based at resorts and almost all including a certification course for beginners.

Fly-Fishing

Fly-fishing is a sport rapidly gaining fans for the challenge of learning to select and tie the right flies as bait and for the enjoyment of the serene beauty of fishing in remote trout streams.

ORVIS FLY-FISHING SCHOOLS

10 RIVER ROAD, MANCHESTER, VT 05254; (802) 362–3622 OR (800) 235–9763. (I; DOES NOT INCLUDE LODGING)

YEARS IN BUSINESS:	30+
AGE RANGE:	10–80
MOST COMMON AGE:	20s, 50–65
PERCENT ALONE:	30–50
NUMBER OF PARTICIPANTS:	VARIES
MALE/FEMALE RATIO:	3/1

YEAR-ROUND. LOCATIONS ALSO IN EVERGREEN, COLORADO; CAPE COD; THE FLORIDA KEYS; AND MILLBROOK, NEW YORK. SOME CLASSES ARE FOR PARENT-CHILD AND FOR WOMEN ONLY. LODGINGS ARE SUGGESTED, BUT PARTICIPANTS DO THE BOOKING ON THEIR OWN.

This longtime sports outfitter offered the first organized fly-fishing school in the United States and still sets the standard as the sport grows in popularity. The instructors at the two and a half-day course are professionals who give a solid foundation that includes lessons on how to cast, how to make essential knots for tying on flies, how to select the right flies for the right fish, how to read a trout stream, how to wade a stream safely, how to manipulate the lines in tricky currents, and how to play, land, and release a fish. Classes are taught on casting ponds, in an indoor classroom, and on beautiful trout streams.

Kayaking, Canoeing, and White-Water Rafting

Among the many appeals of these water sports is the opportunity to be outdoors on a river in some of America's most beautiful wilderness country. You can learn some of the necessary skills on a regular rafting trip, but these programs focus on instruction.

NANTAHALA OUTDOOR CENTER

13077 Highway, Bryson City, NC 28713;
(888) 662-1662; www.nocweb.com (I–M)

Years in business:	26
Age range:	10–70
Most common age:	20–55
Percent alone:	Majority
Number of participants:	3,200 yearly
Male/female ratio:	More males
Mid-March to October	

Located on a mountainside along the Nantahala River near Great Smoky Mountains National Park, this employee-owned center boasts many paddling champions and is a terrific place to learn water skills. *Esquire* magazine called the center "the Oxford of whitewater canoe schools." Courses in canoeing and kayaking run the gamut from beginner to expert, one day to one week. Participants in longer courses try several rivers. The student/teacher ratio is never more than 5:1.

Lodgings range from vacation cabins to a modern, comfortable dorm-style lodge. Reasonable packages include instruction, room, and meals. Three restaurants include the River's End on the river and Relia's Garden up the hill, where the tasty, fresh-picked vegetables and herbs come from their own garden. Courses are also offered in mountain biking.

COMMENTS *Female, 30s: I've gone half a dozen times alone, and it was great every time. The program is terrific, the instructors world-class—and it's cheap! There are plenty of singles—in my last group, in fact, there was only one couple out of ten people. There are always more men, usually in their 30s and 40s. There is no social pressure; you eat as a group, and it's easy to get to know people. Cabins are lovely, with wooded views from the balcony. The food is very good, all natural and with homemade bread. I definitely recommend it.*
Male, 40s: I've been on lots of kayaking trips, and I think this is the best instruction in the country. I've gone several times, alone and with a friend. You feel at home as soon as you get there. Most people come alone; the majority are from the East Coast, but more seem to be coming from all over. The age range is from 20s to 50s, about 2:1 male. The lodges have beautiful views; the food is so good they put out their own cookbook. And the instruction is great—five students to one instructor, and very patient, understanding teachers.

DVORAK'S WHITEWATER PADDLING SCHOOL

17921 U.S. 285 NATHROP, CO 81236;

(800) 824-3795 OR (719) 539-6851; WWW.DVORAKEXPEDITIONS.COM (I)

The first licensed outfitter in Colorado, this experienced company offers instructional seminars where students begin on flatwater to learn the basic strokes necessary to control a raft, canoe, or kayak, then move down the river to practice their skills in moving water. As skills sharpen, so does the challenge. All of their river trips offer this instruction option. More Dvorak information and participants' comments are on page 114.

Downhill Skiing

Downhill skiing attracts everyone—singles, couples, families—because this is one sport everyone can enjoy. Each ski area has special ski runs reserved for beginners, intermediates, and experts. A lodge at each ski area provides a place for everyone to come together at mealtimes and at day's end. Learning the sport is easier than ever with the new "shaped" skis that make carving turns a snap. Once you learn to ski, you'll actually look forward to winter.

Of all the many types of sports schools available, ski schools are the easiest to find. Almost every slope has midweek five-day learn-to-ski packages at substantial savings over their weekend rates. The most comfortable way to approach this alone is to be part of a package plan by which the group will remain together for the five days; if you simply sign up for individual lessons, you may have different classmates and instructors each day and will have little opportunity to become friendly with those in your class. Ask in advance.

The entire ski-week group generally meets at a welcoming party on arrival, then is divided into smaller groups according to ability. There is the opportunity also for evening get-togethers for ski movies or entertainment. Ski lodges are friendly places anyway, albeit crowded, and it is easy to meet people naturally during the day, at lunch, or at the bar after skiing. Singles are also paired up with other singles in the lift line, though that could as likely mean a ten-year-old child as a possible dinner companion. It's all in the luck of the draw.

Singles' Options

As a rule, more single skiers are found at the big, better-known resorts, such as Vail, Colorado, and Killington, Vermont.

For guaranteed company, there is the **Club Med** at Copper Mountain, Colorado, a modern seven-story lodge at the mountain with a lounge/bar area and a theater/dance floor for mingling. The mountain facilities have been recently upgraded with two new high-speed chairlifts along with greatly improved snowmaking to guarantee good conditions. Rates include skiing Monday through Saturday and daily downhill skiing and snowboarding lessons. Three buffet meals and evening entertainment are part of the package. There is a single supplement for private rooms.

Guests here are graded for ability, then divided into groups of about ten for lessons. A recent participant reports a lot of moral support and encouragement within the group. During her week at the club, adults' ages ranged mostly from 25 to 50, and about a third of the 450 guests were single. Skiers hailed from England, Australia, and France, as well as the United States. Phone (800) CLUB–MED for information.

Ski Club Any Mountain, based in Washington, DC, encourages skiers from other cities to join trips to top North American ski resorts. You'll be with a hosted group of skiers and will be assigned a roommate to avoid single supplement charges. Phone (800) 296–2000 or (703) 979–4300 for upcoming trip schedules.

Moguls Ski & Snowboard Tours organizes an annual Jewish Singles Ski Trip, a sociable way to visit major mountains. This group also holds women's programs and Ski Training vacations for skiers who want to upgrade their skills. The training programs include all-day instruction in groups of six or fewer, group dinners, classroom sessions, video critiques, specialized equipment, and lots of skiing. Courses have been offered at: Whistler/Blackcomb, Big Sky, Kirkwood, Portillo, Chile, and Otztal, Austria. This company also runs an adult Snowboard Camp for those who want to master the art of snowboarding. Phone (800) 666–4857 for details.

Most major ski areas have discovered that females-only ski clinics are popular with women who would rather do their slipping and sliding without a male audience. Contact mountains directly for current schedules.

Lodgings can be informal meeting places as well, with guests gathering in front of the fire for drinks at the end of the day. If you are in your 20s or 30s, dorm-style accommodations are a good place to find other singles. Many ski area lodging offices will steer you to the right places if you ask. Avoid condominium accommodations if you are alone; they limit your sociability.

....

Cross-Country Skiing

Cross-country enthusiasts are growing, lured by the time to enjoy the quiet and beauty of the snow-covered countryside and the lack of lift lines. Almost every major area today offers cross-country trails and instruction; a day or two of practice is all it takes to get started. Local chambers of commerce can point you to inns that have cross-country trails outside the door. But lessons won't necessarily guarantee company. If you are looking for a cross-country group, the best bet is to contact outdoor organizations such as the Appalachian Mountain Club or Colorado Mountain School (see below) or check the winter offerings of the following outdoor trip organizers.

....

Outdoor Skills

The more comfortable and adept you are at outdoor activities, the more you will enjoy and appreciate the outdoors. This kind of enrichment is the goal of these multifaceted programs.

APPALACHIAN MOUNTAIN CLUB

5 JOY STREET, BOSTON, MA 02108;
(617) 523–0636; WWW.OUTDOORS.ORG (I)

At Pinkham Notch Visitor Center in Gorham, New Hampshire, in the heart of the White Mountains, this active club offers year-round weekend workshops for both beginners and advanced outdoor enthusiasts, with 700,000 acres of national forest as a classroom. Among the many topics offered are camping, canoeing, mountain biking, bushwhacking, map and compass reading, nature studies, mushroom hunting, ecology, music, storytelling, drawing, and a host of winter programs from dogsledding to cross-country skiing and snowshoeing

YEARS IN BUSINESS:	120+
AGE RANGE:	UP TO 85
MOST COMMON AGE:	28–55
PERCENT ALONE:	35
NUMBER OF PARTICIPANTS:	80,000 MEMBERS; GROUPS ARE SMALL, VARY IN SIZE
MALE/FEMALE RATIO:	50/50
YEAR-ROUND	

to hawk-watching and nature photography. The lodge is sociable, with many individual hikers staying overnight. Meals are family style. Lectures and slides on outdoor topics are often presented on Saturday evening.

Other AMC lodges with varying seasonal programs include Valley View Lodge in Oliverea, in the Catskill Mountains of New York; the Mohican Outdoor Center in Blairstown, New Jersey, along the Appalachian Trail in the Delaware Water Gap; Bascom Lodge in Adams, in the Berkshire Mountains of Massachusetts; and Mt. Cardigan in New Hampshire.

COMMENTS *E.B.: I'm a longtime AMC member. The lodges are not luxurious, but they are comfortable, the people are outgoing outdoors lovers of all ages, and the club and its program are tops. East Coast singles who love the outdoors should consider joining their local chapters for many congenial activities.*

ADIRONDACK MOUNTAIN CLUB
P.O. BOX 867, LAKE PLACID, NY 12946;
(518) 523-3441; WWW.ADK.ORG (I)

Educational workshops, field trips to see wildflowers or birds, guided hikes, and winter cross-country skiing are among the programs of this venerable club for outdoorsmen

YEARS IN BUSINESS:	120+
AGE RANGE:	2–80
MOST COMMON AGE:	30–50
PERCENT ALONE:	30
NUMBER OF PARTICIPANTS:	46 BEDS IN LODGE
MALE/FEMALE RATIO:	50/50
YEAR-ROUND	

and nature lovers. Classes in outdoor skills include wilderness fishing, paddling, map and compass reading, introductory rock climbing, and basic canoeing and kayaking.

There are also workshops to learn about nature (see also page 119). Accommodations are in the club's comfortable, rustic Adriondak Loj, in private rooms, or coed bunkhouses; family-style, home-cooked meals are served in the pine-paneled dining room.

COMMENTS *Male, 40s: There's lots of diversity because accommodations vary from a dorm for eighteen to family rooms for four to six to private rooms. People come from all over; about half are single, and men outnumber women. There are classes in kayaking and winter sports. A family atmosphere makes it easy to strike up conversations, and everyone is friendly. The staff is wonderful. This attracts outgoing, well-educated people and is great for singles who are into the outdoors.*

Mountain Climbing

Are you up for a challenge? Want to prove you can conquer a mountain? Mountain climbing school can teach you the techniques and the right equipment to get to the top!

COLORADO MOUNTAIN SCHOOL

Box 2062, Estes Park, CO 80517; (970) 586-5758; www.sni.net/homepage/cms (I—does not include lodging)

Years in business:	20+
Age range:	8–60
Most common age:	Late 20s–30s
Percent alone:	40
Number of participants:	3,000 annually
Male/female ratio:	4/1

Located in the shadow of Rocky Mountain National Park, this group offers five- and seven-day Beginning Rock Camps as well as three-day weekends teaching the proper techniques for backpacking, mountaineering, and rock climbing. Longer stays have the advantage of time to hone your skills. Once you've learned the basics, there are intermediate and advanced camps as well as many guided climbs and mountain hikes both in the Rockies and abroad. Lodging in Colorado is your choice of nearby motels or the dorm-style, inexpensive

Climbers Lodge, where there is plenty of company from other climbers and hikers. Meals are not included. In winter the emphasis shifts to skiing, mountaineering, and ice climbing, and once again there are programs for beginner to advanced.

The owners say: "Many people have met and become good friends through these courses and outings. In mountain travel, there is ample opportunity for a tremendous amount of honest, open discussion, and the mountain atmosphere encourages this. Our participants always exchange addresses, et cetera, at the end of trips and stay in contact with each other afterward."

COMMENTS *Female, 40s: I've been once, am going again. It was a lot of fun, there was a lot of instruction, and it was very good. All the participants were from Colorado, and most came alone. I signed up for a more difficult workshop, so there were few women. Ages were 25 to 50.*

Climbing enthusiasts might also consider these other mountaineering schools:

YOSEMITE MOUNTAINEERING SCHOOL
YOSEMITE NATIONAL PARK, CA 95389; (209) 372–1335.

JACKSON HOLE MOUNTAIN GUIDES AND CLIMBING SCHOOL
BOX 7477, JACKSON, WY 83001; (307) 733–4979.

Wilderness Skills

Programs teaching wilderness skills aim to do more than give you techniques for outdoor activities like backpacking, canoeing, or climbing. They present mentally and physically challenging situations meant to stretch your ability to the limit. Success means enhanced self-confidence that will carry over into the rest of your life.

OUTWARD BOUND

ROUTE 9D, R2 BOX 280, GARRISON, NY 10524;
(914) 424–4000 OR (800) 243–8520; WWW.
OUTWARDBOUND.ORG
(I–E, DEPENDING ON LOCATION, INCLUDES FOOD AND CAMPING)
YEAR-ROUND; SPECIAL CLASSES OFFERED FOR WOMEN AND FOR PAR-
ENT AND CHILD

YEARS IN BUSINESS:	30+
AGE RANGE:	14 AND UP
MOST COMMON AGE:	18-25
PERCENT ALONE:	HIGH
NUMBER OF PARTICIPANTS:	10–12 PER GROUP
MALE/FEMALE RATIO:	51/49
SUITABLE FOR BEGINNERS, WILL TRY TO ARRANGE SHARES.	

Outward Bound courses are in a class by themselves. Those who participate, many of them beginners, come to be stretched mentally and emotionally as well as physically—with the wilderness as a classroom. If you want to learn about backpacking, canoeing, mountaineering, rock climbing, mountain biking, white-water rafting, ski mountaineering, dogsledding, snowshoeing, or almost any other outdoor adventure, their five schools in Colorado, North Carolina, Maine, Oregon, and Minnesota and in several urban centers are ready to teach you these skills—and much more. Several courses combine skills such as backpacking, canoeing, and mountain climbing.

Most courses include solo time for reflection. Renewal courses are outdoor experiences specially intended for adults wanting to examine more closely their personal or career goals and renew their energies in an outdoor setting.

The courses usually have five parts. Phase one is a training and physical conditional period, giving instruction in technical skills, safety, first aid, shelter construction, wilderness cooking, environmental awareness and conservation, map and compass reading, et cetera. Next, in phase two, these skills are applied. Groups of eight to twelve are formed, and as participants become more self-reliant, instructors turn the leadership role over to them. The third phase, the solo, is a period of solitude—one to three days in the wilderness alone. Afterward, the group comes together to execute an expedition with a minimum of supervision. Then comes a final event, a last fling with your body that involves running, paddling, cycling, snowshoeing, or skiing—more miles than you may have thought possible. Finally, there is a period of reflection on your experiences, feelings, and personal discoveries during the course.

More than 400,000 alumni, from troubled youths to corporate executives to adults in a period of life transition, testify that meeting the challenges of Outward Bound has helped them to go beyond what they believed they could do and to develop new self-confidence as a result.

NATIONAL OUTDOOR LEADERSHIP SCHOOLS

288 Main Street, Lander, WY 82520;
(307) 332-6973; www.nols.edu (I–E, depending on course)

Formed to train wilderness leaders and educators, NOLS attracts many who are planning a career in wilderness education, but others attend to learn outdoors skills from experts or to learn how to deal with physical and mental challenges. Natural history, horsepacking, backpacking, white-water rafting, mountaineering, rock climbing, sea kayaking, sailing, and winter skiing are among the wide range of pursuits offered.

Years in business:	30+
Age range:	14–75
Most common age:	Each course has a suggested age range, from 17–22 to over 50
Percent single:	High
Male/female ratio:	Varies with the course
Number of participants:	12

Many of these courses run for a month or more. A few are for women only.

Special courses are designed for people who have always wanted to acquire outdoor skills but do not have time for a longer course. Each course specifies the recommended ages; some are designated for a minimum of age 50.

NOLS has certified more than 800 outdoor instructors; typically about 300 of them work for the school each year. Their ages range from 19 to 61.

COMMENTS   *Female, 20s: I learned that almost all the challenges were fun and that living without the so-called conveniences of everyday life is often more pleasant than living with them.*
   Male, 40s: I was blown away by the beauty; I think heaven must look like the Wind Rivers. I will never forget it. These were the best instructors in the world. They engendered confidence in us all. They were confident, and it rubbed off.

Stretch Your Mind

EVER WISHED YOU TOOK BETTER VACATION PICTURES . . . OR could paint a picture? Would you like a better understanding of the stock market . . . or a wine list . . . or what an archaeologist actually does on a dig? What about a yen to try your hand at quilting or carving or playing the fiddle?

Whatever your interest—or your fantasy—you can indulge it on a learning vacation that stretches your mind and talents in scenic surroundings.

In a situation where everyone is learning together, there is automatically a common interest, a natural bond, and a lot of mutual support. Many programs are set up so that the group eats together, but even when meals are optional, students who have shared classes naturally tend to get together for dinner.

The choices are enormous, as is the range of settings. You can learn to paint in Italy, to cook in Provence, or to twang a banjo in the West Virginia hills. Here are some of the many wonderful options.

Learning Vacations

Learning vacations come in many forms, from formal campus settings to research in the field. Besides the programs listed here, most universities also have a week of "Alumni College," and many also welcome non-alums to share the learning.

CORNELL'S ADULT UNIVERSITY
626 THURSTON AVENUE, ITHACA, NY 14850–2490;
(607) 255–6260. (I)

YEARS IN BUSINESS:	20+
AGE RANGE:	30–70
MOST COMMON AGE:	40–60
PERCENT ALONE:	35
NUMBER OF PARTICIPANTS:	150 PER WEEK
MALE/FEMALE RATIO:	VARIES
JULY TO EARLY AUGUST; FOUR 1-WEEK SESSIONS IN ITHACA; LEARNING SESSIONS ALSO YEAR-ROUND IN VARIOUS OFF-CAMPUS LOCATIONS	

"A getaway for nature enthusiasts, armchair philosophers, art and music lovers, romantics and pragmatists of all persuasions," says the brochure, and indeed this largest of all summer university programs offers something for almost every interest. Classes are taught by university faculty; subject matter runs the gamut. Some recent offerings: "The Genie Unleashed: DNA in the Modern World," "What Makes Great Paintings Great? Color, Form and Space in Art," "The Human Mind: Marvels and Mysteries," "Seeing With a Camera; A Photography Workshop," and "Outdoor Skills and Thrills."

This is a "back-to-school" week of dorm living and cafeteria dining with all the many athletic and cultural facilities on campus open to participants. And while there is a large program for young people, which attracts many families, single adults will find plenty of company. The evaluation sheets at the end of each session are enthusiastic: More than 90 percent of the participants say they plan to return.

Cornell also sponsors interesting year-round programs in the United States and abroad. Some examples recently were "Tropical Botany and Coral Reefs" in Tortola, British Virgin Islands; "The Civil War Along the Mississippi River"; and "Mountain and Marine Habitats of Costa Rica."

COMMENTS *E.B.: The Cornell campus is magnificent, in the heart of the Finger Lakes, a region of spectacular natural gorges. I chose "Gorgeous Gorges of the Finger Lakes," a course that offered a daily walk of about 3 miles through the gorges, many of them remote locations tourists would ordinarily miss. It didn't feel like class—the instructor was like a knowledgeable friend who could point out a million interesting things you would never have noticed on your own, from birdcalls to the marks of the last glacier. There were no assignments, but readings were available if we wanted to learn more.*

Our group of a dozen ranged in age from 30 to 80, equally divided between men and women. At least half of the group was on its own during class; even couples at the program tend to choose different subjects. Classmates and dorm mates provide a natural base for making friends. The cafeteria food was so-so, but the setting was another congenial place for meeting people. All you have to do is say, "May I join you?" and set down your tray.

The evening schedule included a wine tasting at a nearby vineyard, a cookout, and a campus concert. If these didn't appeal, there were plenty of activities around campus as a substitute. The week ended with a banquet followed by a "graduation" party. Going to college for a week proved to be a congenial and relaxing vacation. The cost was nominal, and, as a bonus, I learned a lot.

Male, age 39: The combination of camaraderie and intellectual stimulation brought me back twenty years to my days as a student.

Female, 40s: I had a splendid time. Although I came by myself, the program is so well organized, the people so friendly, and your time so full, I never felt at loose ends for a moment.

VACATION COLLEGE

PROGRAM IN THE HUMANITIES AND HUMAN VALUES, COLLEGE OF ARTS AND SCIENCES, CB#3425, 3 BOLIN HEIGHTS, UNIVERSITY OF NORTH CAROLINA, CHAPEL HILL, NC 27599; (919) 962-1544; WWW.UNC.EDU/DEPTS/HUMAN

(I—DOES NOT INCLUDE LODGING OR MOST MEALS)

YEARS IN BUSINESS:	18
AGE RANGE:	15 TO 92
MOST COMMON AGE:	60S
PERCENT ALONE:	50
NUMBER OF PARTICIPANTS:	60–120 PER WEEK
MALE/FEMALE RATIO:	VARIES WITH TOPIC
FROM LATE JUNE TO EARLY AUGUST	

Each summer this lovely campus in Chapel Hill offers a changing series of three- and four-day seminars led by university faculty. A new theme each week means a choice of topics that have recently included "Politics and Health in America," "The Age of Reason," "East Asia," "The Swing Era: Jazz of the Big Bands," and "Literature of the American South."

In addition to alumni, these programs attract many adults looking for a stimulating change of pace, exploring important cultural and social topics. Lodging can be in residence halls or in local motels. An opening dinner gives a chance to get acquainted; after that, classmates often get together to try the many good restaurants in Chapel Hill. Some seminars include a film or two (with popcorn) in the evening.

SUMMER CLASSICS IN SANTA FE

St. John's College,
1160 Camino Cruz Blanca, Santa Fe, NM 87501;
(505) 984-6000; www.sjcsf.edu (M)

Years in business:	9
Age range:	20 to 80
Most common age:	40s
Percent alone:	75
Number of participants:	Maximum of 20 per seminar
Male/female ratio:	40/60
Summer; no single supplement	

Remember those "great books" you were always going to read someday—Shakespeare, Dostoyevsky, or Plato? Each summer, participants in these week-long seminars read and discuss world classics in literature and philosophy. The changing reading list may include such works as the *Bhagavad Gita,* Greek dramas, Plato's *Republic,* or Rousseau's *On the Origin of Inequality.* They also discuss the text of great operas and attend an actual performance by the highly regarded Santa Fe Opera. Participants choose one seminar of the four offered each week and can stay for one or more weeks. Afternoons are left free so that students can explore the historic buildings, archaeological sites, and the many art galleries of Santa Fe. Accommodations are in recently built campus dormitories. Rooms are suite-style, with five individual bedrooms sharing a common living room and a large bathroom, which is partitioned for privacy. The beautiful setting of the college, the lures of Santa Fe, and the unique content combine to give this one of the highest return rates among learning programs.

COMMENTS *Male, 40s: I can't put into words how this program nurtures me and calls all of my intellect into play. It's magic. There are no lectures—tutors begin with a question about the text, and stimulating discussion follows with fascinating people from every walk of life. We develop together and learn from each other. The attractions of Santa Fe greatly add to the experience. I've hiked at Bandolier National Monument and gone to the Chamber Museum Festival and the Santa Fe Opera. It is a total change from my work and home life and has been so rewarding that I've returned three times and this year took a sabbatical to enroll in the college's graduate program.*

Female, 50s: This is a wonderful place because it combines so many things. The classes provoke exciting discussion that one normally does not get at home, important interesting topics, but never stuffy. The people are very bright, the discussion is lively, and you combine one week of reading, another of opera. There's so much available in Santa Fe, and the location of the college in the hills is simply beautiful. It is a marvelous experience.

CHAUTAUQUA INSTITUTION

CHAUTAUQUA, NY 14722;
(716) 357-6200 OR (800) 836-ARTS;
WWW.CHAUTAUGUA-INST.ORG (I–M)

YEARS IN BUSINESS:	120+
AGE RANGE:	2–102
MOST COMMON AGE:	50s
PERCENT ALONE:	25–30
NUMBER OF PARTICIPANTS:	140,000 PER SEASON
MALE/FEMALE RATIO:	40/60
SUMMER	

This is where the idea of learning vacations began. Chautauqua was founded as a training camp for Sunday school teachers and evolved into a nine-week summer feast of arts and education, served up in a period Victorian village. The religious element, while still present, is optional.

The lineup of activities is staggering. Twice-a-day talks by prominent lecturers are on a new theme each week, from arts and humanities to the the economy, science, and politics to sports in American life. The summer school topics include the arts, languages, human relations, public speaking, nutrition, parenting, self-improvement, foreign cultures, and much, much more. Activities such as line dancing, t'ai chi, and aerobics keep the program up to date. Evening entertainment may feature the resident symphony and theater companies, opera, ballet, Shakespeare performances, or guest stars ranging from such jazz greats as Wynton Marsalis to Mary Chapin Carpenter and Johnny Mathis. And for a sporting change of pace by day, golf, tennis, and sailing are available.

Chautauqua lodging includes hotels, inns, guest houses, condominiums, or private homes. The clientele has tended to be on the older side but is changing somewhat as an active children's program has begun to attract young families. For single participants, Joan Fox, director of public information, says, "Chautauqua is a safe haven where cars and cares are outside, a secure gated community where a single vacationer falls in easily with others attending the same lectures, concerts, or classes."

COMMENTS *Female, 40s: I've been alone and with friends; I keep
going back for the intellectual stimulation. The lecturers are great,
and the hotels and food are very good. It's a very special place and is
great for singles . . . people are friendly, and it's easy to meet them.
Female, 50s: Chautauqua has rounded my personality and sharpened
my intellect. How I love it!
Female, 60s: The program is wonderful. You buy a gate ticket and
can participate in any and all activities. You can stay busy all day
long. The group is heavily female and there are many widows, but
many families also come and the age range is wide—from children to
those in their 70s. There is a good number of singles, and it is very
suitable for them. You can stay in a hotel and have meals family style.
People come from all over, but most are from the Northeast. The
place started as a religious institution and is still highly religious for
some, but it doesn't have to be.*

SMITHSONIAN SEMINARS

c/o Smithsonian Study Tours,
1100 Jefferson Drive SW,
Washington, D.C. 20560;
(202) 357-4700 or (202) 357-4800
for catalog; www.si.edu/tsa/sst (E)

YEARS IN BUSINESS:	20+
PERCENT ALONE:	60
MOST COMMON AGE:	45–50
MALE/FEMALE RATIO:	VARIES WITH TOPICS; USUALLY HEAVILY FEMALE BUT MORE MALES FOR SUBJECTS SUCH AS AVIATION.
NUMBER OF PARTICIPANTS:	20–40
YEAR-ROUND; WILL TRY TO ARRANGE SHARES UNLESS SINGLE IS REQUESTED	

Three- to five-day programs for museum associate members (membership is $22) in Washington and at many locations around the country. The variety of topics should please all tastes, from current major art shows to the Civil War, Barrier Island ecology to The National Zoological Park. Programs occupy most of the day. Lodging is in area hotels; seminars may include some meals and a welcome reception.

THE CLEARING

P.O. Box 65, Ellison Bay, WI 54210; (920) 854-4088; www.theclearing.org (I)

Inspired by Danish folk schools for adults that stress teaching, learning, and living together in scenic surroundings, this program calls itself "a unique school of discovery in the arts, nature, and humanities." In a setting meant to provide a clearing of the mind, dozens of courses, from watercolors, weaving, and design to ecology, astronomy, writing, and philosophy are presented. Classes are taught outdoors and in the cathedral-like schoolhouse designed by renowned landscape architect Jens Jensen, located in a wooded setting overlooking the water in Wisconsin's scenic Door County. Participants live in dorms or in charming log-and-stone cabins and enjoy family-style meals at hand-carved wood-plank tables. Inexpensive rates, no bar, hassle-free atmosphere, healthful food, time to meet interesting people, and quiet, contemplative time in unspoiled natural surroundings are part of the experience.

YEARS IN BUSINESS:	62
AGE RANGE:	18–85
MOST COMMON AGE:	55–65
PERCENT ALONE:	75
NUMBER OF PARTICIPANTS:	28
MALE/FEMALE RATIO:	1/3
SPRING THROUGH FALL; WILL TRY TO ARRANGE SHARES	

COMMENTS *Female, 60s: I have been at least twenty times. The Clearing is quiet, serene, a true retreat with time to think and exchange ideas with new people. It's inspiring. Most people are middle-aged and from the Midwest. Accommodations are simple but adequate; meals are not gourmet but good and very social, with lots of lively conversation. The scenery is just beautiful, and you really get to know everyone.*

Male, 60s: I've been with and without my wife. It is easy to be there alone. The group is mostly professionals, many single people, and many women. There is a rule that you can't sit down at the same place twice at meals, so you're almost forced to meet everyone. It is quiet and informal, but with a purpose. I recommend it to anyone, single or not.

STAR ISLAND CONFERENCE CENTER

P.O. BOX 178, PORTSMOUTH, NH, 03802
OFFICES; 110 ARLINGTON STREET, BOSTON, MA 02116;
(617) 426-7988. (I)

The Star Island Corporation, composed of Unitarian Universalist and United Church of Christ constituencies, owns and operates this seasonal religious and educational conference center. Open to all denominations, the center offers discussion/instruction in a variety of weekly themes, such as natural history, art, and international affairs. Outdoor recreation

YEARS IN BUSINESS:	80+
AGE RANGE:	WIDE
MOST COMMON AGE:	VARIES WITH WEEK'S PROGRAM
PERCENT ALONE:	50
MALE/FEMALE RATIO:	MORE FEMALES
NUMBER OF PARTICIPANTS:	180–260
WILL TRY TO ARRANGE SHARES	
JUNE TO SEPTEMBER	

includes swimming, boating, tennis, volleyball, and games. A marine laboratory provides near-natural habitats for native biota, and naturalists lead narrated ecology walks. Evening candlelight services are held in the historic chapel. Living quarters are in a century-old "grand hotel" and a few cottages. Family-style meals and the small size of the island are conducive to meeting other people. A list of the coming year's programs is available by sending a stamped, self-addressed envelope to the Boston office.

COMMENTS *Female, 50s: This is a place to get in touch with your spiritual side. There are more single people than married, more women than men. It is very comfortable to be alone. The programs are very well organized, and I would recommend this to anyone. When you get there, you're not a stranger.*

Male, 40s: I've gone for seven years, sometimes alone, sometimes with a friend. It's an easy group to get to know—meals are family style, everyone wears a name tag, about a quarter are single, but many married people come without their spouses. All activities are optional. Over half choose to go to morning chapel, even more to evening chapel. Workshops are in photography, painting, dance, music, drama, and writing—no experience necessary. Afternoons are free for trips to nearby islands. At night there are guest artists and folk dancing.

Similar Unitarian-sponsored retreats are:

MOUNTAIN HIGHLANDS CAMP AND CONFERENCE CENTER

841 HIGHWAY 1067, HIGHLANDS, NC 28741; (704) 526–5838.

ROWE CAMP AND CONFERENCE CENTER

KINGS HIGHWAY ROAD, BOX 273, ROWE, MA 01367; (413) 339–4954;
WWW.ROWECENTER.ORG

....

Study Vacations Abroad

A number of short-term study and educational tour programs are available abroad, sponsored by U.S. universities in association with colleges in other countries. These offer memorable stays in the ivied surroundings of schools such as Oxford and Cambridge as well as the chance to meet interesting people. Some use dorm facilities on campus; others utilize hotels. The offerings vary from year to year, so it is best to call for current information.

HUMANITIES INSTITUTE

533A PUTNAM AVENUE, CAMBRIDGE, MA 02139;
(617) 497–8665 OR (800) 754–9991.
NO SINGLE SUPPLEMENT ON MOST PROGRAMS; WILL TRY TO
ARRANGE SHARES; SMALL SINGLE SUPPLEMENT IN FLORENCE.
(I PLUS AIR)

YEARS IN BUSINESS:	20+
AGE RANGE:	25–80
MOST COMMON AGE:	40–50
PERCENT ALONE:	80
NUMBER OF PARTICIPANTS:	25
MALE/FEMALE RATIO:	1/3

Education and culture are the focus of this varied program for those who want to learn more about the countries they visit. Some classes are based at such institutions as Cambridge and Dublin's Trinity College, where mornings are devoted to lectures and discussion and afternoons are free for exploring the area. These two- to three-week indepth seminars are equivalent to a short university course and may actually be taken for academic credit. Other noncredit trips are less rigorous, but still education-oriented, concentrating on such topics as the gardens of England, foods of Tuscany, or the art and architecture of Italy. Florentine Renaissance takes in art, architecture, and literature. Each program offers some sight-seeing and evening lectures. About 80 percent of the participants are teachers.

COMMENTS *Female, 50s: I went alone and was very comfortable. There was a diverse group, ages 30 to 65, heavily female. Mornings were spent in class; in the afternoons there were tours of museums or lectures. There was always something to do. The accommodations were not great, but the trip was inexpensive.*

Female, 70s: I've been on several trips alone. It is wonderful, and I always make friends. There is a nice mix of people from all over the U.S., ages 35 to 70, most in their 40s. Many are married but traveling alone. Meals are as a group and there is lots of discussion, making it easy to get to know people. There is always something to do during the week; weekends are free to do whatever you want.

More options:

TRAVEL WITH SCHOLARS, UNIVERSITY OF CALIFORNIA, BERKELEY EXTENSION

MARKETING DEPARTMENT,
1995 UNIVERSITY AVENUE, BERKELEY, CA 94720;
(415) 252–5229. (EE)

The University of California at Berkeley offers two- and three-week travel-study programs in Paris, the south of France, Florence, Sicily, Turkey, Ireland, Oxford University in England and U.S. destinations such as New Orleans. A special program in London with distinguished drama critics gives an in-depth look at the London theater scene.

CAMBRIDGE UNIVERSITY INTERNATIONAL SUMMER SCHOOL

C/O NEW YORK UNIVERSITY SCHOOL OF CONTINUING EDUCATION,
INTERNATIONAL PROGRAMS,
331 SHIMKIN HALL, 50 WEST FOURTH STREET, NEW YORK, NY 10012;
(212) 998–7133. (EE—INCLUDES AIRFARE)

The ivied halls of Cambridge, England, host this two-week annual summer program with a choice of more than twenty courses, from English architecture and art to the history of medicine or twentieth-century British political history. Students select two morning courses; afternoons are free for exploring. The program also includes field trips and evening events organized by NYU faculty.

UNIVERSITY VACATIONS
3660 Bougainvillea Road, Miami, FL 33133;
(800) 792-0100. (E–EE)

This organization sponsors a series of one- and two-week cultural vacations at Oxford and Cambridge universities as well as the Sorbonne and other universities in Dublin, Prague, Budapest, Bologna, Florence, Rome, and London. Lodgings vary from hotels to dorm rooms on campus.

UNIVERSITY OF LONDON
Birkbeck College, Centre for Extra Mural Studies,
26 Russell Square, London, England;
01–71–631–6663; fax, 01–71–631–6683. (I)

This reasonably priced program offers one-week theater study groups for adults, who read three current plays, attend theater productions, and then discuss them. Directors and actors from plays in the series participate in the seminars. Participants live in the college dorms; they are an interesting mix of ages and cultures from many parts of the world. The school also offers many other courses in its summer catalog.

More information on study opportunities for adults abroad can be obtained from:

Transitions Abroad, The Complete Guide to Work, Study & Travel Overseas
Transitions Abroad Publishing, Inc., P.O. Box 1300, Amherst, MA 01004;
(800) 293-0373.

Field Research Volunteer Programs

Assisting scientists and archaeologists in their work is a wonderful way to widen your horizons and get a new perspective on an area. As a side benefit, many of these trips are tax deductible. The cost is considered a donation to underwrite the research.

EARTHWATCH

680 MOUNT AUBURN STREET, BOX 9104,
WATERTOWN, MA 02272;
(617) 926–8200 OR (800) 776–0188;
WWW.EARTHWATCH.ORG (I-EE)

YEARS IN BUSINESS:	28
AGE RANGE:	16–85
MOST COMMON AGE:	35–55
PERCENT ALONE:	50
NUMBER OF PARTICIPANTS:	4,000 PER YEAR, DIVIDED INTO 600+ INDIVIDUAL PROJECTS
MALE/FEMALE RATIO:	40/60

More than 50,000 volunteers have gone out on more than 2,000 Earthwatch vacation-learning experiences in 118 countries and thirty-six states, helping scientists and researchers in field projects ranging from anthropology to zoology. Most participants have college degrees and are a well-traveled lot: professionals, scientists, managers, students, retirees, and teachers.

Would-be volunteers learn about the projects in the annual catalog or by becoming members of Earthwatch. They can send for a more detailed briefing of the projects that interest them. Among the hundreds of possibilities are archaeological excavations; surveys of plants, birds, or animals; underwater and environmental impact studies; and research in agriculture, public health, and art history. Some recent projects: tracking snow leopards in the Himalayas, uncovering aboriginal prehistory in Australia, monitoring wild dolphins in Florida, excavating sites of prehistoric civilizations in Mallorca, studying moose and wolves in Michigan, collecting stories and songs of Dominica, documenting maternal healthcare in Zimbabwe, and helping to census and monitor elephants in Botswana. Costs vary widely, depending on distance, length of stay, and living conditions.

COMMENTS *Female, 50s: For two weeks we lived in splendid isolation studying honey eaters on Australia's Kangaroo Island. I shared a bunkroom with four other women. Just outside my door were kangaroos, koalas, emus, and other creatures people seldom encounter outside a zoo. We did simple but necessary jobs such as hand-pollinating blooms and marking and bagging clusters of flowers for breeding studies. We also observed honey eaters and bees as they collected nectar and pollinated—or failed to pollinate—the plants. We got two days off for sight-seeing. In the evenings, we played games, sang folk songs, talked a lot. The group, ages 25 to 60, had a wide range of occupations. We were a motley and congenial crew.*

Male, 40s: I've gone on six trips, each time alone. It was hard the first time, then became easy. There was about an equal mix of men and women, single and married, from varied backgrounds. How well the program runs depends on the "Principal Investigator," the person in charge. One of my trips was not so well run. I would recommend this type of vacation to other singles, but I would also say that you have to really want to do it. This is not a leisure vacation. There is work involved.

UNIVERSITY RESEARCH EXPEDITIONS PROGRAM (UREP)

UNIVERSITY OF CALIFORNIA,
BERKELEY, 94720;
(510) 642–6586; WWW.MIP.BERKELEY.EDU.UREP
(I–EE)

YEARS IN BUSINESS:	20+
AGE RANGE:	16–75
MOST COMMON AGE:	30–50
PERCENT ALONE:	HIGH
NUMBER OF PARTICIPANTS:	5–10 PER PROJECT
MALE/FEMALE RATIO:	VARIES

Like Earthwatch, UREP programs provide the opportunity to be part of a team doing actual research in the field (this time assisting University of California scholars), while gaining new knowledge, new friends, and insights into another culture. Tax-deductible contributions pay project costs and participants' expenses. Animal-related projects have included studying the birds of the Mayan forest and the monkeys of

Costa Rica. The prehistoric villages of Peru, the castles of County Clare, Ireland, the medieval churches of the Aran Islands, rock art in Baja California and Mexico, and the geology of the Andes are among other recent topics. The only requirements for participation are curiosity about the world and a willingness to invest in learning. For interested participants, UREP holds slide presentations with the chance to talk with past participants in their projects throughout California and in Seattle and New York City; prospective volunteers should phone for upcoming dates.

COMMENTS *Female, 50s: It was a positive and interesting experience that enabled me to see places and have experiences that I probably would not have had traveling with a tour group or alone. It was eye-opening, energy-expending, socially cooperating, native-appreciating, and thoroughly enjoyable—the most highly concentrated two weeks of learning and cultural immersion that I've experienced in many years of travel. The experience exceeded my expectations. It was one of new understanding of another people and of personal growth.*

Male, 40s: I've been on four trips with them, to Easter Island, to the High Sierras twice, and to the Sierra Nevadas—all really great programs because you see things that a tourist would never see. Most people do come alone—couples are rare. The leaders help to get the group to bond together. You have to work together and get along because the trips tend to be in isolated places without bathrooms or other comforts. You get to know one another really well. Everyone has a sincere interest in the project and that brings them together right off the bat. I've met a lot of interesting people, everyone from a physicist to a cop to grad students. It's a great program if you're into learning and being outside in interesting places. But it is work, not for the weak!

Archaeology

Ever fantasized about being an archaeologist and going on a dig? Here's your chance!

CROW CANYON ARCHAEOLOGICAL CENTER

23390 COUNTY ROAD K, CORTEZ, CO 81321;
(800) 422–8975 OR (800) 422–8975;
WWW.CROWCANYON.ORG (I)

YEARS IN BUSINESS:	15
AGE RANGE:	18–75
MOST COMMON AGE:	35–55
PERCENT ALONE:	85
NUMBER OF PARTICIPANTS:	420 PER YEAR
MALE/FEMALE:	30/70

Here in the rugged terrain of the "four corners" where Arizona, New Mexico, Utah, and Colorado meet, adults join archaeologists searching for remains of the ancestral Pueblo culture in the Mesa Verde region of southwestern Colorado. They learn the process of excavation, artifact identification, and interpretation by working on a dig, at the same time gaining firsthand understanding of the environment in which these people thrived. Participants live in round log cabins that resemble Navajo hogans and share hot meals at the lodge and sandwiches in the field. Most stay for one week.

COMMENTS *Female, 40s: I went alone for the first time, have gone back five times, and know a lot of people now. This is the best program I've ever found. The group is warm, with amazing backgrounds and levels of intelligence. The ages range from 18 to 80, about evenly divided between male and female, and last time there were only three couples out of twenty-four people. You have classes in the morning, go to the dig site in the afternoon and early evening, and have lectures after dinner. The food was family style and excellent. This program has caused several people to decide to go back to school for a master's degree.*

Male, 30s: I've been going alone for five years. This is not Club Med, not a summer camp or play time—you are actually contributing to the archaeological work in progress. Accommodations and food are great. It's wonderful for anyone who is into archaeology or Southwestern art.

CENTER FOR AMERICAN ARCHAEOLOGY

DEPT. 75, KAMPSVILLE ARCHAEOLOGICAL CENTER,
KAMPSVILLE, IL 62053;
(618) 653–4316. (I)

YEARS IN BUSINESS:	40+
AGE RANGE:	TEEN TO 65+
MOST COMMON AGE:	20–35
PERCENT ALONE:	80
NUMBER OF PARTICIPANTS:	30 WEEKLY
MALE/FEMALE RATIO:	50/50

An educational and research institution, the CAA offers one- to five-week adult field schools throughout the summer, providing on-site training in archaeological excavation and analysis at a 2,000-year-old Native American village site and at other historic sites in the Illinois River Valley. Newcomers as well as experienced diggers are welcome. Workshops in ancient ceramic and stone tool technologies are also offered in early summer and fall. Evenings are occupied with lectures, classroom activities, ecology hikes, and informal gatherings. Meals are served cafeteria style, and lodging is a dormitory setting.

COMMENTS *Female, 30s: This is mostly doing, not classes. It's an intense, very involving program, working all day with planned activities at night. Accommodations are comfortable though not luxurious; the food was substantial and good.*

PASSPORT IN TIME CLEARINGHOUSE

P.O. BOX 31315, TUCSON, AZ 85751;
(520) 298–7044 OR (800) 281–9176.
NO SET FEES; VOLUNTEERS PAY ONLY THEIR OWN EXPENSES.

No experience is necessary to join this program, which places volunteers as assistants to Forest Service archaeologists and historians in their research on natural forest lands across the nation. Participants have helped to stabilize ancient cliff dwellings in New Mexico, excavate a 10,000-year-old village site in Minnesota, restore a historic lookout tower in Oregon, and clean vandalized rock art in Colorado. Projects vary in length from a weekend to a month, and facilities vary widely. Some projects involve backcountry camping where volunteers are responsible for their own food and gear; others offer meals prepared by a camp cook, often for a small fee. Sometimes volunteers can stay in local hotels and travel to the site each day. There are dozens of interesting opportunities.

To learn about current projects and how to enroll, write or call for the free newsletter published each March and September.

A good source of information on other archaeology vacation opportunities:

Archaeology Fieldwork Opportunities Bulletin

ARCHAEOLOGICAL INSTITUTE OF AMERICA,

675 COMMONWEALTH AVENUE, BOSTON, MA 02215; (617) 353-9361. CALL (800) 228-0810 TO ORDER BOOK. $11 FOR NONMEMBERS.

Nature Volunteer Opportunities

AMERICAN HIKING SOCIETY VOLUNTEER VACATIONS

P.O. BOX 20160

WASHINGTON, D.C. 20041;

(301) 565-6704; WWW.AHS.SIMPLENET.COM

NO FEES EXCEPT A REGISTRATION FEE; VOLUNTEERS PAY THEIR OWN EXPENSES AND TRANSPORTATION.

YEARS IN BUSINESS:	20+
AGE RANGE:	18–65
MOST COMMON AGES:	20–60
PERCENT ALONE:	50
NUMBER OF PARTICIPANTS	300 TOTAL PER YEAR
MALE/FEMALE RATIO:	60/40

The American Hiking Society organizes as many as fifty one- and two-week working Volunteer Vacations into remote and beautiful back country areas in the continental United States, Hawaii, and Alaska. Teams of ten to twelve volunteers armed with shovels and rakes help to renovate and clear existing trails and build new ones. Everyone works hard in the morning, but afternoons are spent relaxing or exploring. Volunteers should be able to hike 5 miles or more a day and supply their own camping equipment.

The **Sierra Club** (see page 90) conducts week-long service trips for volunteers who help maintain trails and preserve the beauty of wilderness locales. **The Nature Conservancy** (see page 121) holds volunteer programs assisting conservation biologists with bird and wildflower inventories or riparian restoration at the Tensleep Conservation Project site in Wyoming.

Sources for additional volunteer suggestions are *Volunteer Vacations,* Chicago Review Press, (800) 888–4741, and *Volunteer! The Comprehensive Guide to Voluntary Service in the U.S. and Abroad,* Council on International Educational Exchange, (800) 349–2433.

Foreign Language Workshops

Learning a new language will allow you to travel abroad with more confidence and may widen your horizons at home as well.

LANGUAGE IMMERSION INSTITUTE

STATE UNIVERSITY OF NEW YORK AT NEW PALTZ,
JFT 916, 75 SOUTH MANHEIM BOULEVARD, NEW PALTZ,
NY 12561; (914) 257–3500;
WWW.EELAB.NEWPALTZ.EDU/LII (I, PROGRAM ONLY)

YEARS IN BUSINESS:	17+
AGE RANGE:	15 TO 80
MOST COMMON AGE:	45
PERCENT ALONE:	75
NUMBER OF PARTICIPANTS:	6–15 PER WORKSHOP GROUP
MALE/FEMALE RATIO:	40/60

This innovative language department sponsors year-round weekend "total immersion" workshops at the New Paltz campus, in New York City, and in Westchester County, plus weekends and a one-week session at the beautiful Mohonk Mountain House resort outside New Paltz. Two-week intensive programs are held in summer at the New Paltz campus.

The approach here is to speak only the new language from day one, perfect for travelers who want to increase their vocabularies and learn conversation quickly. Only enough grammar is taught to give a needed foundation. One to two hundred people may enroll for weekend seminars; they are divided into small groups according to ability. The two-week summer classes include fifty hours of instruction and leave plenty of time for recreation. Twenty languages are offered. Students arrange their own lodging in area motels or inns.

Overseas students can choose homestay, hotel, or apartment accommodations. The LII also sponsors year-round learning vacations in Costa Rica, Mexico, Spain, Italy, and France in conjunction with local language schools.

COMMENTS *E.B.: My weekend at SUNY was a delight. Teachers are chosen for their outgoing personalities as well as language fluency, and they conduct classes with flair and a sense of fun. A typical assignment: "Pick a French character and describe yourself so that the class can guess who you are." Everybody gets into the spirit, and there's lots of laughter as well as learning. The class stayed together at lunch, still speaking French. Most of us chose to have dinner together as well, though we did give ourselves an English break. The approach dredged up every word of my forgotten college French—I was amazed. It left me in much better shape to tackle a trip to France. Male, 50s: It's easy to come to this program alone. Everyone is learning, and we all make mistakes—alone or with a friend, you'd still have to get up in front of everyone and speak a foreign language. Most people do come alone, but everyone bonds quickly in the class. I've also gone on several trips to Costa Rica. I love the homestay program. I've spent an hour at the dinner table with my homestay family after the dishes were cleared, just talking about life in our different countries, family structure, politics—anything. No class can give you that.*

NATIONAL REGISTRATION CENTER FOR STUDY ABROAD (NRCSA)

823 NORTH SECOND STREET, MILWAUKEE, WI 53201;
(414) 278-0631; WWW.NRCSA.COM (I–E)

The NRCSA is a consortium of 125 universities, language institutes, and specialized schools in thirty countries of Latin America, Europe, and Asia that welcome North Americans of any age as well as participants from around the world. They offer hundreds of programs from a week to a year abroad with lodging options from hotels and pensions to family stays. Through this organization, you can learn French in France, Switzerland, or Canada; study Spanish in Mexico, Spain, Costa Rica, Guatemala, or South America; and improve your Italian in Rome, Florence, or Siena. Programs are also available in Japan, Taiwan, Greece, and Russia. Many courses also include art, crafts, cooking, and local history. Contact NRCSA for details on these opportunities.

ECOLE DES TROIS PONTS

c/o EMI International, P.O. Box 640713, Oakland Gardens, NY 11364; (718) 631–0096; (ME). Single rooms are available. Including lessons and all meals.

Years in Business:	10+
Age Range:	20 to 70
Most Common Age:	over 40
Percent Alone:	40
Number of participants:	Maximum of 6 per class
Male/female ratio:	35/65

This is a chance to learn French in the setting of a lovely eighteenth-century chateau where cooking lessons are also offered. The general course consists of nineteen hours of French per week Monday through Friday, with weekends free to explore the area. A holiday course offers fifteen class hours per week, with more time to relax. Those who wish can combine the week with cooking classes (See page 74). This is a total immersion experience, with the chance to speak French constantly in a supportive atmosphere.

Both language and cooking students live, take classes, and dine in the Chateau de Matel in Roanne, a small town on the border of the Beaujolais and Burgundy wine areas that is best known for Troisgros, its three-star restaurant. The chateau, typical of the early 1700s, is set on thirty-two acres of park and woodland. The grounds include a pool and the chance for walks or bike rides along a canal at the foot of the grounds. Hosts are Rene Doral, a Frenchman, and his Australian wife, Margaret O'Loan, both of whom speak English. They get high marks from past participants for their hospitality. Prices seem quite fair for what is offered.

COMMENTS Female, 30s: It was terrific. The setting is lovely, the hosts create a family atmosphere, with everyone dining together, and the food was wonderful. Most of the people had come alone, and I made many friends from around the world, places like Japan and New Zealand. Three years later, we are still in touch. I had lived in France a long time ago, and in one week, I was able to bring back all the French I had known.

Female, 40s: The hosts are wonderful, the food is superlative, and the guests are sophisticated and interesting and come from around the world. The chateau itself is lovely, though guest rooms are simple. Many people come alone. I researched well before I chose this school, and I go back year after year.

Annual listings of language vacations abroad also appear in
Transitions Abroad Magazine
P.O. Box 1300, Amherst, MA 01004; (413) 256–3415; www.transaboard.com

....

Cooking Schools

The opportunity to master the authentic cuisine of France or Italy with instruction from top regional chefs and teachers gives a special dimension to a foreign location and a view of the country most tourists miss. Cooking schools are also a rewarding option for solo travelers in scenic regions of the United States, giving focus to a trip and a chance to learn more about the area. All of these programs include time for sightseeing and opportunities to visit local markets and sample fine cuisine—including some that you will produce yourself. Some cooking programs are quite expensive, but participants say they are wonderful experiences worth saving for!

U.S. Cooking Schools

GOING SOLO IN THE KITCHEN

P.O. Box 123, Apalachicola, FL 32329;
(850) 653–8848. (M)

Years in business:	5
Age range:	20–70
Most common age:	40s
Percent alone:	90
Number of participants:	8–10
Male/female ratio:	1/2

Jane Doerfer, a veteran cooking instructor and author of the book *Going Solo in the Kitchen,* has designed this delightful six-day sojourn explicitly for single cooks. Classes offered periodically from June to October emphasize easy-to-prepare recipes for one and easy meals for entertaining. Sessions are held at the Pelican Inn, a small beachfront hotel on Dog Island, a serene off-shore barrier island. Guests stay at the inn, gather for morning instruction and lunch, and have afternoons free for beaching, boating, sailing, or otherwise relaxing. They regroup in the evening to prepare and enjoy dinner parties together.

COMMENTS *Female, 70s: I'm not a serious cook, but I had the best time and I learned a lot. Jane is a delightful person, and she made it so much fun. There were just four of us, three women and one man, ranging in age from 20s to 70s, from Chicago, New York, Atlanta, and Durham. Everyone came alone. We had very diverse backgrounds, but all were interesting people, and we all got along well. Jane also invited different local people in every night for dinner and that made it livelier than if it had been just the five of us night after night. There was plenty of free time in the afternoon, and I enjoyed Apalachicola because it is off the beaten path, still out of the past and very unspoiled.*

JANE BUTEL'S SOUTHWESTERN COOKING SCHOOL

125 2ND STREET NW, ALBUQUERQUE, NM 87102;
472-8299 OR (505) 243-2622; WWW.JANEBUTEL.COM
(EE)

YEARS IN BUSINESS:	28+
AGE RANGE:	35–65
MOST COMMON AGE:	45–55
PERCENT ALONE:	50
NUMBER OF PARTICIPANTS:	MAXIMUM OF 18
MALE/FEMALE RATIO:	40/60

For chefs who like their menus hot, Jane Butel, the queen of Tex-Mex cuisine and author of fifteen books on Southwestern cookery, shares her secrets in state-of-the-art kitchens with ample room for hands-on learning.

Recipes include regional favorites such as fajitas, tortillas, enchiladas, tacos, and tostados as well as chili stews, tamales, black bean soup, quesadillas, empanadas, and the classic dessert, flan. Students get a taste of Southwest history and food lore along with cooking tips.

Three-hour morning sessions are followed by the lunch that has been prepared in class. Two dinners in local restaurants are included in the weekly rates. Accommodations are in a hotel in nearby Old Town Albuquerque, and afternoons are free to explore the many shops, galleries, and museums of the city. Five-day and weekend sessions are held March through early December.

COMMENTS *Male, 50s: I loved it. I went to the weekend course and enjoyed it so much, I went back for a week. There were sixteen in my week-long group, from late 20s to 50s, from all over the country and the world. Four of us were alone, and there was no problem at all.*

We stayed in the same bed and breakfast; I'm still in touch with one lady from the Netherlands by e-mail. The day starts with Jane explaining things like different types of chiles. Then we paired off to make the dishes of the day, with Jane and her assistants supervising, and we shared the food over lunch. Afternoons were free to explore Albuquerque, which is a beautiful city with lots to do. Old Town is fun just to wander through, and there are great museums nearby. Some nights we got together for dinner. I had a ball and would definitely recommend this to anyone.

LA VARENNE AT THE GREENBRIER

THE GREENBRIER, WHITE SULPHUR SPRINGS, WV 24986;
(800) 228-5049 OR (304) 536-1110. (EE)

YEARS IN BUSINESS:	29
AGE RANGE:	20–80
MOST COMMON AGE:	46
PERCENT ALONE:	75
NUMBER OF PARTICIPANTS:	60
MALE/FEMALE RATIO:	1/3

Anne Willan, the noted founder of Ecole de Cuisine La Varenne in Burgundy, presides over an annual spring cooking series at this luxurious resort. Willan does the three-hour demonstrations on Monday, Wednesday, and Friday. Celebrity guest chefs take over the other two days. All the classes include tastings with specially selected wines. In addition, Greenbrier chefs lead afternoon classes in contemporary American cuisine and offer some hands-on evening sessions. The final night features a champagne reception and the Greenbrier's Gold Service Dinner (black tie optional).

THE NEW ENGLAND CULINARY INSTITUTE

25 CHURCH STREET, BURLINGTON, VT 05401;
(802) 863-5231

Holds six culinary weekends annually at the Inn at Essex outside Burlington, Vermont. Culinary classes and demonstrations are also held regularly at the New England Culinary Institute's Commons restaurant in Burlington. Phone for current offerings.

Cooking Schools Abroad

COOKING WITH FRIENDS IN FRANCE

C/O JACKSON & COMPANY,
29 COMMONWEALTH AVENUE, BOSTON, MA 02116;
(617) 247–1055. (EE)

YEARS IN BUSINESS:	7
AGE RANGE:	21–85
MOST COMMON AGE:	35–55
PERCENT ALONE:	VARIES
NUMBER OF PARTICIPANTS:	8
MALE/FEMALE RATIO:	1/6
GUARANTEED SHARES	

The tile-roofed classic Provencal houses once occupied by Simone Beck and her coauthor Julia Child are shared by students at this six-day program in Provence taught by Kathie Alex, who studied with Beck and other French greats. Up to eight students take part in the program, which offers three morning lessons that culminate in lunch and two days of guided excursions exploring local culture and cuisine.

COMMENTS *Female, late 30s: It was excellent, interesting, fulfilling. There were two couples, two friends, and two single women in our group. Basically you travel and take meals with these people for six days straight—you can't help but get involved. The day is structured until 3: 00 P.M. After that, everyone in the group was very inclusive—always invited everyone to go sight-seeing or share a car to the beach. I was very nervous to get up in front of everyone and try a technique, but the staff made it extremely comfortable, and I felt I had support from the group. The teacher is wonderful, her recipes are great, and her teaching method makes it very easy to learn.*

ITALIAN COUNTRY COOKING

POSITANO, ITALY, C/O E & M ASSOCIATES,
72 MADISON AVENUE, NEW YORK, NY 10016;
(800) 223–9832 OR (212) 252–1818. (E)

YEARS IN BUSINESS:	18+ SINCE 1980
AGE RANGE:	20–60
MOST COMMON AGE:	25–45
PERCENT ALONE:	60
NUMBER OF PARTICIPANTS:	12
MALE/FEMALE RATIO:	60/40

Diana Folonari, of a noted Italian wine family, conducts this one-week program at her home in Positano, a magnificent setting in the cliffs on the Amalfi Drive. The program begins with a reception and a talk on Italian food and wine. Five mornings are spent in class, with students preparing lunches they share. One late-afternoon session features homemade pizza and country dishes. Special sessions on Italian wines are held as well.

Participants stay in a local hotel and have one full day and most afternoons and evenings free for sight-seeing in nearby Amalfi, Ravello, Sorrento, Pompeii, and the Isle of Capri.

COMMENTS *Male, 40s: This is fantastic, one of the best trips I've ever made. I happened to be the only student who enrolled, and Diana and I became great friends. You stay at the best hotel in Positano, with wonderful accommodations. The area is beautiful, the wines delicious, the instruction fantastic. It's expensive but worth it.*

CUISINE INTERNATIONAL

P.O. Box 25228,
Dallas, TX 75225;
(214) 373-1161; www.IGlobal.net/cuisineint (E-EE).
Will try to arrange shares

YEARS IN BUSINESS:	20+
AGE RANGE:	20–80
MOST COMMON AGE:	40–65
PERCENT ALONE:	20
NUMBER OF PARTICIPANTS:	12–18 PER CLASS
MALE/FEMALE RATIO:	1/3

Cuisine International represents cooking schools and culinary tours in Italy and France in a variety of locations, including Venice, Sicily, Umbria, and Provence. Each week-long program offers cooking demonstrations in the mornings and excursions to markets, wineries, and local historical sites in the afternoons. Dinners are in local restaurants and private homes. Accommodations range from converted farmhouses to ancient monasteries to five-star hotels, and are priced accordingly.

COMMENTS *Female, 40s: I did not think that cooking could be made to look so easy or be such fun . . . a most enjoyable week. It was like one long party.*

INTERNATIONAL COOKING SCHOOL OF ITALIAN FOOD AND WINE

c/o Mary Beth Clark,
201 East 28th Street, Suite 15B,
New York, NY 10016;
(212) 779-1921. (EE)

Mary Beth Clark, an experienced American cooking instructor and author of the cookbook *Trattoria*, offers hands-on cooking classes, "The Basics of Great Italian Cooking," in Bologna, one of Italy's culinary centers. Classes are held in a modern kitchen in a stunning sixteenth-century palazzo in the center of the city, and cover dishes from antipasto to "dolce" (desserts). Participants enjoy the meals they have prepared paired with specially selected wines. Two special classes cover the making of pasta and pizza. The week also includes shop-

YEARS IN BUSINESS:	SINCE 1987
AGE RANGES:	20S TO 80S
MOST COMMON AGE:	40S–50S
PERCENT ALONE:	50
NUMBER OF PARTICIPANTS:	10 MAXIMUM
MALE/FEMALE RATIO:	1/3
MAY, JUNE, SEPTEMBER, OCTOBER. WILL TRY TO ARRANGE SHARES.	

ping at local markets, visits to winemakers, and behind-the-scenes demonstration classes and dining in top restaurants. A special October week includes travel and the White Truffle Festival in Alba, where partic-ipants go on their own truffle hunt. Participants can choose first-class or deluxe hotel accommodations.

COMMENTS *Male, 40s: I had a great time. The course was very well organized and everything promised in the brochure really hap-pened. Besides learning to make wonderful dishes and how to pair them with the proper wines, we shopped in local markets and dined in two two-star restaurants. One day was spent in a local pizzeria learning to make a pizza from scratch, and we then enjoyed our cre-ations and wine with the chef. I was the only male in a class of five, ranging in age from 30s to 60s. When it was over, I felt I had made five new friends—my classmates and our teacher, Mary Beth, who was a delight.*

LA VARENNE IN BURGUNDY

c/o ECOLE DE CUISINE LA VARENNE,
P.O. BOX 25574, WASHINGTON, D.C. 20007;
(202) 337–0073 OR (800) 537–6486;
WWW.LAVARENNE.COM (EE, INCLUDES TRANSPORTATION
FROM PARIS)

YEARS IN BUSINESS:	20+
AGE RANGE:	35–60
MOST COMMON AGE:	35–60
PERCENT ALONE:	50
NUMBER OF PARTICIPANTS:	10
MALE/FEMALE RATIO:	VARIES

One-week programs designed by Anne Willan combine cooking in-struction with good living at Willian's lovely seventeenth-century Chateau du Fey in northern Burgundy. Classes are held in June, July, September, and October. Weekly topics vary from fundamentals of

French cooking to French pastry, from traditional French regional cooking to contemporary and French bistro cuisine. Each program is conducted by a talented French chef, with full translation by trained assistants. The goal is to sharpen kitchen skills and convey the gastronomic heritage of France. Each week includes five practical classes, three demonstrations, and a wine tasting. There are excursions to vineyard areas such as Joigny and Chablis, and the week concludes with dinner at a fine country restaurant. The chateau offers a pool, tennis courts, woodlands, and garden paths.

COMMENTS *Male, 40s: This was the most relaxing vacation I've ever had. I left my wife at home and went to enhance my cooking skills. In my group of ten, there was only one couple—everyone else came alone. The instruction was excellent. We had classes in the morning, preparing a lunch. Then we went to local cheese makers or vineyards or had free time to sight-see or relax. Dinner either was prepared by our chef or in a three-star restaurant. We all had a wonderful time.*

Male, 30s: The people were interesting; most were alone and from diverse backgrounds. The trip was special because there was nothing touristy about it . . . cooking was the main focus, and because there were few in the group, you really got to know people. I would highly recommend this to anyone who likes to cook . . . or eat!

LE CORDON BLEU, PARIS AND LONDON
404 AIRPORT EXECUTIVE PARK, NANUET, NY 10954;
(800) 457–CHEF; WWW.CORDONBLEU.NET

While there is no residential program, this world-renowned school offers Paris visitors "Gourmet Sessions," demonstrations, and hands-on classes from a half-day to a month in length, as well as a morning tour of Paris markets with their chefs. A Saturday spent at a soufflé workshop or learning traditional cooking for friends will add a tasty dimension to a Paris visit. All demonstrations are translated into English. Gourmet sessions are also offered in English at the London Le Cordon Bleu school, lasting from three days to one month.

ECOLE DES TROIS PONTS
(see page 66)

Students here can spend six days learning French Provencal cooking or may combine cuisine with lessons in French. The cooking course, offered in English and French, includes six nights' accommodations and all meals, four afternoon cooking classes Monday to Friday, and shopping excursions to local markets. On Friday afternoon there is an excursion to see medieval villages in the countryside.

Classes are no more than eight to ten people. Those who join the language course have five morning classes in French and four afternoons of cooking.

COMMENTS *Female, 40s: Enjoyed the whole week . . . it was a great experience . . . What made the week so special was the way they made me feel at home, a part of the family.*

Cooking classes in many cities in addition to Paris can provide a focus to a solo visit, and a way to make friends. In New York, Peter Kump's School of Culinary Arts (800–522–4610) offers one-week and weekend classes; in San Francisco, Tante Marie's Cooking School (415–788–6699) has similar programs. Both schools also train professional chefs. Check with the visitors bureau in the city you are visiting for local offerings.

For a comprehensive list of cooking schools around the world, order
THE GUIDE TO COOKING SCHOOLS
SHAWGUIDES, P.O. BOX 1295, NEW YORK, NY 10023;
(212) 799–6464 OR (800) 247–6553; WWW.SHAWGUIDES.COM

....

Learn About Wine

GERMAN WINE ACADEMY
C/O GERMAN WINE INFORMATION BUREAU,
79 MADISON AVENUE, NEW YORK, NY 10016;
(212) 213–7036. (E)

Six days of learning about German wines include lectures in English by local experts, travel to grape-growing regions for visits to wine estates and cellars, tastings with winemakers, seminars on wine, and a wide spectrum of tastings of some of the world's classic white wines. Several activities are based at the academy headquarters, a twelfth-century monastery called Kloster Eberbach.

YEARS IN BUSINESS:	24+
AGE RANGE:	21–70
MOST COMMON AGE:	35–50
PERCENT ALONE:	NO RECORDS
NUMBER OF PARTICIPANTS:	MAXIMUM OF 25
MALE/FEMALE RATIO:	60/40
NO SHARES ARRANGED; SMALL SINGLE SUPPLEMENT	

Among the activities are the festive last-night dinner, which includes a blind wine tasting and the presentation of "diplomas." Students are lodged for five nights at the charming Hotel Schwan in Oestrich/Rheingau and spend one day on a Rhine cruise with an overnight stop at the Alte Thorschenke at Cochem, one of Germany's oldest hotels. Areas usually visited include the Mosel Valley, Rheingau, Pfalz, Mittelrhein, and Rheinhessen regions, and the itinerary takes in many picturesque villages. Two tours are usually offered in early September and early October.

COMMENTS *Female, 30s: Some come for business, some for personal interest, but everyone shares the basic interest in wines; several people came alone. Because groups are small and you travel and eat together every day, it's very congenial and you get to know everyone.*

Male, 40s: I came first with a companion, came back alone, returned a third time with my 21-year-old daughter, and always had a ball. About half are couples, the rest come alone, and there was plenty of company even for those in their 20s or 30s. I think this is one of the great bargains of the world—the food is great, and you taste more than 250 wines. As the wine flows, so does the fun. Even on the bus we sang songs and told jokes. It was a constant party.

Photography

Sharpening your ability with a camera not only makes for a rewarding vacation but gives you skills that will enhance your travel pleasure forever after, guaranteeing wonderful personal souvenirs from any trip.

MAINE PHOTOGRAPHIC WORKSHOP

P.O. Box 200, 2 Central Street,
Rockport, ME 04856;
(207) 236–8581; www.meworkshops.com (M)

Years in business:	26
Age range:	14–70
Most common age:	30
Percent alone:	90
Number of participants:	class size, 10 to 18, total weekly, 100 to 200
Male/female ratio:	40/60

With the picture-perfect Maine coast village of Rockport as subject matter and inspiration, one of the nation's leading educational centers for photography offers more than 200 one-week workshops from June to September. The curriculum is designed for serious amateurs as well as professional filmmakers, photographers, storytellers, actors, and writers.

Photography classes range from Photography I and beginning darkroom techniques to master classes in such aspects of the craft as portraits and landscapes, in black-and-white and color. Taught by some of the top people in the field, classes are intensive, all-day experiences aimed to stretch participants to new heights of personal expression, technical excellence, and creative achievement. Workshops also include creative storytelling, feature films, video, and television documentaries.

The home campus in the fishing village of Rockport offers state-of-the-art studios, darkrooms, a theater and gallery, a new digital media center, a production center, dining rooms, housing, and a campus store. The weekly schedule features exhibitions and lectures and screenings by leading photographers and directors. Meals are served in an old New England farmhouse where students dine with the faculty.

Additional workshops are offered in picturesque locations such as Tuscany, Provence, Mexico, and Martha's Vineyard.

COMMENTS *Letters from past students say:*
   "There was such an excitement in the air that I jumped out of bed each morning looking forward to being surrounded by such creative, loving, and interesting photographers."
   "A high-energy, intensely inspirational experience. I have never worked such long hours and had so much fun. Not to mention the fact that I learned in quantum leaps."

More Options

The most comprehensive list of photography workshops is offered by ShawGuides on the World Wide Web at WWW.ShawGuides.com.

Many workshop advertisements are listed in other photography publications such as Modern Photography, 825 Seventh Avenue, New York, NY 10019 (212–265–8360) or Popular Photography, 1515 Broadway, New York, NY 10036 (212-719–6000).

WILDERNESS PHOTOGRAPHIC WORKSHOPS

1017 MARGARET COURT, NOVATO, CA 94947; (415) 382-6604 (M)

YEARS IN BUSINESS:	SINCE 1985
AGE RANGE:	35–70
MOST COMMON AGE:	45–60
PERCENT ALONE:	75
NUMBER OF PARTICIPANTS:	8–12
MALE/FEMALE RATIO:	50/50
YEAR-ROUND; WILL TRY TO ARRANGE SHARES	

Those who already have a basic knowledge of photography will advance their skills in these workshops offered by photographer Brenda Tharp in scenic locales from the Arizona desert to Olympic National Park to Utah's "canyon country." Workshops range from five to sixteen days. Lodging varies with the site but is included; meals may or may not be included.

FRIENDS OF ARIZONA HIGHWAYS PHOTO WORKSHOPS

2039 WEST LEWIS AVENUE, PHOENIX, AZ 85009; (602) 271-5904. (M)

The nonprofit auxiliary of *Arizona Highways,* a magazine known for its quality photography, sponsors more than a dozen three- and four-day workshops in scenic locales around the state, from ghost towns to the Sonoran Desert and Monument Valley, from the Grand Canyon to the

Prescott Rodeo. Trips include houseboating on Lake Powell. Participants are "intensely interested" amateur photographers who have basic knowledge of their cameras. Some workshops are activities trips that may include hiking or rafting, and each is graded for easy to strenuous activity levels.

YEARS IN BUSINESS:	14
AGE RANGE:	20S–70S
MOST COMMON AGE:	VARIES
PERCENT ALONE:	MAJORITY
NUMBER OF PARTICIPANTS:	15–20
MALE/FEMALE RATIO:	60/40
FEBRUARY TO OCTOBER; MODERATE SINGLE SUPPLEMENT	

Beginners may also take several Arizona Photo Sampler tours, which offer five days taking in the most famous and fabulous places in the state, accompanied by an *Arizona Highways* photographer who works with the group and with individuals.

Many local photography centers in attractive resort communities offer one-day photo workshops as well as longer courses. Enrolling in one of these is an excellent way to give an added dimension to an already-planned vacation and to meet new people. A few of the many possibilities are:

CENTER FOR PHOTOGRAPHIC ARTS

P.O. BOX 1100, CARMEL, CA 93921; (408) 625–5181.

MENDOCINO ART CENTER

45200 LITTLE LAKE STREET, P.O. BOX 765, MENDOCINO, CA 95460; (707) 937–5818.

SUN VALLEY CENTER FOR THE ARTS AND HUMANITIES

418 KNOTTINGHAM DRIVE, TWIN FALLS, ID 83301; (800) 574–2839.

NANTUCKET ISLAND SCHOOL OF DESIGN AND THE ARTS

BOX 958, NANTUCKET, MA 02554; (508) 228–9248.

Photography workshops are also ideal ways to enjoy and fully appreciate national parks and wilderness areas that are sometimes difficult to visit on your own. For national park programs including photography, see nature listings beginning on page 119).

....

Art

An art-oriented vacation is more than a chance to develop a lifelong hobby; it means looking at a new locale from a different point of view—with the painter's eye—truly absorbing the details of the landscape and the architecture. The following are among hundreds of art workshops held around this country and abroad each year. For a comprehensive listing, look for the annual directory of art schools and workshops usually published in March in *American Artist* Magazine, 1515 Broadway, New York, NY 10036; (212) 764–7300.

ART WORKSHOP INTERNATIONAL

463 West Street, Apartment 1028H,
New York, NY 10014;
(212) 691–1159 or (800) 835–7454;
www.vacation-inc.com/artworkshop (M)

Years in business:	20+
Age range:	17–80
Most common age:	40–60
Percent alone:	50
Number of participants:	20–30
Male/female ratio:	Majority female
All are assigned roommates unless they specify singles; suitable for beginners.	

Assisi, Italy, a twelfth-century Umbrian hill town, is the inspiring setting for this program offering painting, drawing, and art in a variety of media as well as courses in art history and creative writing and seminars on opera. Fees include hotel accommodations, most meals, studio space, critiques, and lectures.

COMMENTS *Female, 40s: This is an excellent program with no pressure. It was very easy to get to know everyone. My group was all women, ages 16 to 72, half of whom were single, and with all levels of art training. The food and the atmosphere were wonderful. We had painting instruction in the morning, afternoons free, and ate all meals together. A few times each week there were lectures and slide presentations. We went to local concerts or went swimming on our own.*

Female, 50s: A group of very interesting people from all over the U.S. and Europe, mostly women and mostly single, we stayed in a guest house run by nuns with strict rules—you had to dress appropriately for the dining room. But the food was wonderful and the teachers creative. The views were beautiful. Teachers provided a painting theme each day, but you could paint whatever you wanted if you preferred. There was a certain amount of time for peer criticism. We tended to stay together in the afternoon, and the whole group often went out for dinner. It was excellent. I would recommend this to any single person.

LA ROMITA SCHOOL OF ART

1712 Old Town NW, Albuquerque, NM 87104;
(505) 243-1924; www.laromita.org (M)

Years in business:	32
Age range:	30–70
Most common age:	40–55
Percent alone:	60
Number of participants:	10–18
Male/female ratio:	1/8
Shares usually compulsory; suitable for beginners	

Two three-week and three two-week summer programs held in the glorious Italian Umbrian hill country between Rome and Florence give participants a chance to tour as well as paint. Studio days are interspersed with visits to such towns as Spoleto, Assisi, Orvieto, and Perugia. The school is housed in a sixteenth-century monastery with modern facilities. The group includes a leader who is bilingual.

COMMENTS *Female, 40s: On my three-week trip to Italy, many people came on their own. The group is only twenty people, and we were together all the time. People tended to bond together and pair up, but everyone got along really well. It was a pretty diverse group from all over the U.S., ages 40 to 70s, nineteen women and one guy. It seemed that most people did know at least one other person. It was a lovely location, and the side trips were great—we got to see things other tourists would not. Plus, you don't have to worry about the language. It's a very safe way to travel in a foreign country. It was a fabulous trip.*

Female, 60s: I've gone three times alone. A lot of people come by themselves, and it is easy to meet people, as you all have something in common. There are about sixteen to eighteen people in each group, set up by the type of painting you are working on—watercolor, oils, et cetera. There's a mix of skill levels in each group, from painting teachers to people who are just learning. It's a lovely place—I love the owners and how it is run. But you have to want to be painting—it's not just a vacation—it's all about painting.

Art, Crafts, Music, and More

These multifaceted programs have something for almost everyone.

CREATIVE WORKSHOPS AT DILLMAN'S SAND LAKE LODGE

Box 98, Lac du Flambeau, WI 54538; (715) 588-3143; WWW.DILLMANS.COM (I)

YEARS IN BUSINESS:	63
AGE RANGE:	25–80
MOST COMMON AGE:	50
PERCENT ALONE:	30
NUMBER OF PARTICIPANTS:	120
MALE/FEMALE RATIO:	MORE FEMALES
SUITABLE FOR BEGINNERS	

For the past twenty-one years, this family-run resort has offered a weekly roster of workshops under the auspices of the Dillman's Creative Arts Foundation. Running from late May to early October, the courses include more than 100 choices of photography, watercolor and other art courses. The comfortable, rustic lodge is located on a lovely peninsula and offers tennis, lake beaches, canoeing, and miles of hiking and biking trails. This is a family resort, but the workshops draw many guests on their own. Participants are housed in the lodge. Reasonable tuition includes room but not meals.

ARROWMONT SCHOOL OF ARTS AND CRAFTS

P.O. Box 567, Gatlinburg, TN 37738; (423) 436-5860; WWW.ARROWMONT.ORG (I)

YEARS IN BUSINESS:	50+
AGE RANGE:	18–80
MOST COMMON AGE:	30–65
PERCENT ALONE:	20
NUMBER OF PARTICIPANTS:	40–100 PER WEEK
MALE/FEMALE RATIO:	1/3
WILL TRY TO ARRANGE SHARES; SUITABLE FOR BEGINNERS	

Arrowmont is a visual arts complex on seventy wooded acres adjacent to the Great Smoky Mountain National Park. One- and two-week summer workshops draw men and women of all ages and levels of ability who wish to learn both traditional and contemporary crafts. Classes in basketry, quilting, weaving, woodturning, jewelry making, marbling, and enameling as well as painting and drawing and work in clay and fibers are conducted by more than 100 visiting faculty members. Students are housed in simply furnished dormitory rooms in cottage-type buildings. Home-cooked meals are served in a congenial dining room. Having everyone together makes for a warm atmosphere.

COMMENTS *Male, 40s: This is an intense learning experience, the best school of its type. It is fine to be here by yourself, as about half the students come alone. Most are women. People come from all over the world.*
Female, 30s: I had a very pleasant experience. My group was mostly women, and many of the men who did come were with their wives, but it was a great mix of people. People here leave their lives behind. It's like summer camp—easy to become close quickly. The instructors are very well qualified. It's a good place to go alone.

FLETCHER FARM SCHOOL FOR THE ARTS AND CRAFTS

611 ROUTE 103 SOUTH, LUDLOW, VT 05149;
(802) 228-8770;
MEMBERS.AOL.COM/FFCRAFTS/FLETCHD.HTM (I)

YEARS IN BUSINESS:	52
AGE RANGE:	20–70
MOST COMMON AGE:	45–55
PERCENT ALONE:	80
NUMBER OF PARTICIPANTS:	40–80 PER WEEK
MALE/FEMALE RATIO:	1/10
LATE JUNE THROUGH AUGUST; GUARANTEED SHARES;	
SUITABLE FOR BEGINNERS	

The lovely setting in Vermont's Green Mountains adds to the enjoyment of students who come to this school to learn a variety of art forms. Sponsored by the Society of Vermont Craftsmen, the courses include painting, basketry, weaving, rug hooking, tinsmithing, wood carving, quilting, and folk arts such as country tin and theorem painting. Single and double rooms are available in two lodges on campus, with shared bathroom facilities. Meals are family style, and students can use the Farmhouse Lounge/Library for visiting and relaxation.

COMMENTS *Female, 20s: I had been quilting for about a year and wanted to learn new techniques. I researched a bunch of schools, and this is where I chose to go. The instructor was great; the accommodations and food were fine. My class of five was all women. It was open seating at meals so you get to meet people—there were always plenty of people to talk to. Many people do come by themselves.*

Male, 60s: I always travel on my own. I've been going here every year since 1992. I go for wood carving. It's a beautiful spot. I stay in a motel, but I meet people at meals, plus they encourage you to look in on other classes and projects to see what everyone is doing. There are usually eight to ten people in the woodworking class; quite a few come alone. The people are from all over; they range in age from 30s to 80s, and there are usually more women than men. The instructors are very competent. There's always a group of nice outgoing people and a lot of camaraderie.

HAYSTACK MOUNTAIN SCHOOL OF CRAFTS

P.O. Box 518, Deer Isle, ME 04627;
(207) 348-2306. (I)

YEARS IN BUSINESS:	48
AGE RANGE:	18–80
MOST COMMON AGE:	MID-30S
PERCENT ALONE:	30
NUMBER OF PARTICIPANTS:	80
MALE/FEMALE RATIO:	VARIES

Located in a handsome complex in a spectacular setting on the coast of Maine, Haystack attracts many accomplished artisans as well as beginners who want to explore a new medium or begin seriously studying a particular art. Courses in clay, fibers, metals, wood, graphics, and glassblowing are offered.

COMMENTS *Female, 40s: This is a working vacation . . . there's always something to do and you can go from area to area and learn several types of crafts. How structured or loose the course is depends on each instructor. The atmosphere is very warm and people come away extended creatively. Most students are female—some professional women, some retired.*
Female, 30s: There's a cluster of serious art students, and most of the older people are there for vacation. About half are single or came alone. There's a nice balance of public and private time. People come here to have an experience with others who are interested in crafts, and it's not just surface—they form lasting friendships. The food is terrific, very healthy and appetizing. There's something to do all day, and at night there is usually a slide show or a dance or some sort of program.

AUGUSTA HERITAGE CENTER

DAVIS & ELKINS COLLEGE, ELKINS, WV 26241–3996;
(304) 637–1209; WWW.AUGUSTAHERITAGE.COM (I)

YEARS IN BUSINESS:	27
AGE RANGE:	10–75
MOST COMMON AGE:	25–45
PERCENT ALONE:	30–40
NUMBER OF PARTICIPANTS:	ABOUT 500 PER WEEK, DIVIDED INTO SMALL GROUPS
MALE/FEMALE RATIO:	VARIES; ABOUT 50/50 SINGLES MATCHED IN DORM ROOMS

Appalachian arts—from fiddling, blacksmithing, and basketry to whittling and folk painting—are the focus of this excellent five-week summer program. Dance, storytelling, quilting, songwriting, folk carving, clogging, and music from bluegrass to Cajun are also included in the list of 200 workshops, highlighting folk cultures from around the country and around the world. Most workshops run five days, with classes running from morning until late afternoon. Inexpensive housing is available in twin-bed college dorms or in motels off campus. Rates for those staying on campus include most meals. Evening brings many informal jam sessions and get-togethers. The program ends with a three-day folk festival with home cooking and music and dancing that leaves toes tapping for weeks after.

C O M M E N T S   *Female, 30s: It is very easy to meet people, and a great number are alone. It's fairly even male and female. I went for the dancing; the days were strenuous, the instruction very good. The dorm rooms and food are not good, but that's not why you go. It is creative time.*

HORIZONS

THE NEW ENGLAND CRAFT PROGRAM, 5 CLARY ROAD,
WILLIAMSBURG, MA; WRITE TO: 108 NORTH MAIN STREET,
SUNDERLAND, MA 01375; (413) 665–0300;
WWW.HORIZONS-ART.ORG (M)

YEARS IN BUSINESS:	20
AGE RANGE:	18–80
MOST COMMON AGE:	28–55
PERCENT ALONE:	MAJORITY
NUMBER OF PARTICIPANTS:	35–65
MALE/FEMALE RATIO:	30/70
SUITABLE FOR BEGINNERS; PARTICIPANTS PAIRED IN DOUBLE ROOMS.	

Horizons is a center for the visual arts, located minutes from the college communities of Amherst and Northampton in western Massachusetts, a growing center for crafts. The studio and living spaces blend contemporary buildings with historic 1700s farm structures. Workshops include painting, ceramics, metal and jewelry making, hot glass, photography, mosaics, boat building, and more. Small classes are structured to launch beginners as well as to challenge the more advanced. The center takes pride in its home-cooked natural foods.

COMMENTS *Female, 30s: I've been five or six times. The average class has eight to ten people, a real mix of skill levels from professionals to people who want to learn for fun. The one common factor is that they are all really creative people with neat ideas. The staff is excellent—quality instructors and really nice, friendly and helpful. The rooms are rustic; the food is good. I'd recommend it to anyone.*

TAOS INSTITUTE OF ARTS

108 CIVIC PLAZA DRIVE, TAOS, NM 87571;
(505) 758-2793 OR (800) 822-7183;
WWW.TAOSNET.COM/TIA (COURSES ONLY, I)

Intensive workshops in painting, photography, writing and literature, textiles, clay, and jewelry are available in the beautiful setting of Taos, an art colony 7,000 feet high in the Sangre de Cristo Mountains that is deeply influenced by its Pueblo Indian heritage. Classes such as weaving, pottery, mask making, beading, and natural dyeing reflect this Southwestern tradition. Workshops in the traditional clay pottery of the region are held at Taos Pueblo. Courses in contemporary arts are also offered. Tuition for the three- to four-day courses is moderate; students make their own living arrangements, with assistance from the school.

YEARS IN BUSINESS:	11
AGE RANGE:	WIDE
MOST COMMON AGE:	30–55
PERCENT ALONE:	60
NUMBER OF PARTICIPANTS:	400
MALE/FEMALE RATIO:	40/60

TOUCHSTONE CENTER FOR CRAFTS

R.D. 1, BOX 60, FARMINGTON, PA 15437;
(724) 329-1370. (I)

Painting, drawing, weaving, quilting, basketry, pottery, ironworking, pewter making, stained glass, bead making, and woodworking are all on the agenda in five-day workshops in summer and weekend sessions in May and September. Lodging is in rustic log cabins. The center is located 60 miles southeast of Pittsburgh, a drive of about 3½ hours from Cleveland and 4½ hours from Washington, D.C.

YEARS IN BUSINESS:	27
AGE RANGE:	35–65
MOST COMMON AGE:	40–50
PERCENT ALONE:	20
NUMBER OF PARTICIPANTS:	35–65
MALE/FEMALE RATIO:	1/3
GUARANTEED SHARES	

Try Adventure Travel

"**A**dventure travel" is a catchall term for scores of ways to get into uncrowded, unspoiled countryside or untouched wilderness and to be actively involved with the environment and with your fellow travelers. It is an escape from the pressures of urban living as well as a welcome change from passive travel that shows you the world through the windows of a tour bus or a car. Since groups are small and camaraderie between participants is strong, the percentage of single vacationers who choose this kind of vacation is predictably high.

For years, travel labeled "adventure" was considered exotic, limited to hardy backpackers or thrill-seekers who delighted in climbing Mount Everest or careening over dangerous rapids in a rubber raft. But owing to their explosion in popularity over the last decades, adventure trips have become accessible and safe for almost everyone.

Statistics chronicle this boom. In 1949, eighty years after John Wesley Powell completed the first descent of the Colorado River, only 100 people had ever rafted through the Grand Canyon. By 1972, the National Park Service was forced to limit traffic on the river to 17,000 people a year! By now, millions of people have experienced the thrill of exploring the bottom of the canyon by boat. Figures published in 1998 by the Travel Industry of America report that 98 million people have taken an adventure trip in the past five years.

With so many people signing on, the number of operators offering adventure outings has zoomed, and the variety of trips is truly amazing. Just a few of the choices include rafting, backpacking, backcountry skiing, horseback trekking, mountain climbing, and gentler pursuits such as sailing, biking, and walking. Tour operators grade their offerings to suit a wide range of abilities, making it easy for travelers to make a wise choice.

Trips are offered on the seven continents and almost every place on earth, from the subarctic ice floes to the jungles of the equator to the placid countryside of Europe or the United States. You can take your choice of camping out or staying in quarters that are positively plush.

The following pages offer a small sampling of the great selection available. The listing represents some of the longer-established operators or the more unusual adventure choices and runs the gamut from rustic to deluxe. Use the additional references given to find more operators in whatever area interests you most.

The majority of these outdoor trips are priced per person, with no single supplement. When necessary, operators try to arrange shares. Where single supplements do exist, they tend to be low. Luxury trips with a substantial supplement are so indicated.

A warning: More than any other type of trip, adventure travel depends for its success and safety on the experience and skill of the operator, so check references carefully before you make your choice.

There are a few sources for information. Groups operating in national parks must have a permit from the superintendent, so you can write or call to verify the credentials and ask park authorities about the reputation of the company. The American Mountain Guides Association (303–271–0984) in Golden, Colorado, offers accreditation for outfitters and certification for individual guides and will provide names of those who have qualified. The Professional Paddle Sports Association (606–472–2205) in Butler, Kentucky, a trade association for white-water rafting outfits, will provide information about choosing a trip, a list of accredited members, and any information on file on a particular company.

Operators with Trips in Multiple Categories

APPALACHIAN MOUNTAIN CLUB

5 Joy Street, Boston, MA 02108;
(617) 523-0636. (I;E for some foreign excursions)

Choosing an Adventure Trip

There are no standardized requirements for operators of adventure trips or for guides, so choosing a reliable company is important. Here are some questions to ask before you sign on:

- How long has the company been operating? How long have they run this particular trip?
- Can you describe the day-by-day activity and the level of difficulty of this trip? Is there any training or preparation for participants?
- What kind of training is required for guides? How much experience have they had on the route in question?
- Are guides required to know first aid and CPR?
- What kind of insurance does the company carry? (Don't choose any company lacking coverage.)
- On a rafting trip, are life jackets and helmets supplied?
- What do you do in case of serious injury or illness in the wilderness?
- Can you provide names of recent participants on this trip?

Hiking, biking, backpacking, climbing, cross-country skiing, canoeing, snowshoeing, and rafting are among the pursuits of this venerable, conservation-minded club with local chapters throughout the Northeast. In addition to the year-round workshops at its per-

YEARS IN BUSINESS:	120+
AGE RANGE:	5–85
MOST COMMON AGE:	28–55
PERCENT ALONE:	35
NUMBER OF PARTICIPANTS:	80,000 MEMBERS;
	TRIP GROUPS ARE SMALL
MALE/FEMALE RATIO:	60/40

manent lodges (see page 39) AMC sponsors dozens of major excursions throughout North America and abroad. Organized and supervised by volunteer members, these trips range from trekking the Andes to hiking in Norway, from traversing Scotland's Highlands to sailing Maine waters in a windjammer.

SIERRA CLUB OUTING DEPARTMENT

85 Second Street, San Francisco, CA 94105; (415) 977–5630; www.sierraclub.org outings (I)

Years in business:	80+
Age range:	10–80
Most common age:	Not given
Percent alone:	50–75
Number of participants:	10,000 total, 10 to 25 per outing
Male/female ratio:	Not given

Another longtime leader in conserving and appreciating the wilderness, the Sierra Club annually offers about 250 outings to every region of the United States and to foreign countries. Trips range from four days to more than three weeks in length and include backpacking, hiking trips using a single base camp, biking, rafting, canoeing, sea kayaking, and sailing. All are cooperative ventures with volunteer leaders; on camping trips all pitch in with chores and cooking. The club holds special leadership training outings.

The trips require varying degrees of stamina and experience, but the catalog clearly characterizes each outing. Additional brochures available for each trip spell out the details. Base camp trips tend to be easy to moderate and are a good idea for beginners since they allow for taking the day off if you are weary. Highlight Trips are also moderate; they are designed for people who like to hike or walk with only a daypack. International destinations cover the globe—Africa, Asia, Europe, Latin America, New Zealand, even Siberia.

AMERICAN WILDERNESS EXPERIENCE (AWE)

2820-A Wilderness Place, P.O. Box 1486, Boulder, CO 80301; (303) 444–2622 or (800) 444–0099; www.gorp.com/awe (I–M)

Years in business:	28
Age range:	25–65
Most common age:	30–45
Percent alone:	35
Number of participants:	2,500 annually
Male/female ratio:	45/55
Year-round	

Horseback treks, fishing trips, llama trekking, walking, biking, inn-to-inn hiking and canoeing, hiking and backpacking, ranch vacations, canoeing, kayaking, camping, and whale-watching adventures, cattle drives, covered wagon trips, white-water rafting, Alaskan wildlife safaris, and international trips to Peru, Mexico, Belize, Honduras, and the Virgin Islands are among this group's many offerings. Combination trips are made up of riding and rafting. In winter the list grows to include dogsledding, snowmobiling, and trips to warm-weather destinations. There are several trips for singles.

AWE also has a roster of sixty-seven dude ranches; it promises to help vacationers select the right one. Good physical condition is required for these trips—"old enough to get on a horse and young enough to stay on." But they advertise these trips as "The Civilized Way to Rough It" and promise comfort and good food. A third of the participants are repeats.

COMMENTS *Male, 30s: I've taken four trips by myself, found the groups about half singles and even numbers of males and females. Most were in their 20s and 30s, from all walks of life, from all over the country. The program is very well managed. I've recommended it to other single friends.*

Female, 30s: There were mostly families on my ranch stay, with six singles out of nineteen people. The average age was 30s and 40s, but guests ranged from children to one set of grandparents. The accommodations were fine, and each day there was a choice of activities—riding lessons, trail rides, fishing. At night we sat by the fire in the lodge and talked or sang songs. It was a pleasant experience and one I would recommend to singles, especially those with kids.

ADVENTURE DESTINATIONS

23676 Genesee Village Road, Golden, CO 80401; (800) 376–9851 or (303) 526–5734; www.adventuredestinations.com. Will guarantee shares for requests sixty or ninety days in advance, depending on trip. (I–EE)

YEARS IN BUSINESS:	4
AGE RANGE:	21–71
MOST COMMON AGE:	30s–40s
PERCENT ALONE:	100
NUMBER OF PARTICIPANTS:	6 TO 26; AVERAGE GROUPS, 8 TO 16
MALE/FEMALE RATIO;	VARIES

This is an organization devoted to adventure trips specifically for solo travelers. Planning their own trips and using other operators, they offer cycling and hiking plus safaris, Caribbean sailing, snorkeling, skiing, kayaking, canoeing, rafting, horseback riding, rock climbing—almost any outdoor activity you can name. Accommodations range from tents to chateaus. Programs in the United States cover over the West and Southwest, Alaska, and Hawaii. Weekend trips are offered in California. Asian destinations range from Bali to Bangkok, and there are trips in Mexico and Central America and ten European countries. If you want guaranteed single company, this is the place.

WILDLAND ADVENTURES

3516 NE 155TH STREET, SEATTLE, WA 98155; (206) 365-0606 OR (800) 345-4453.

"**O**ff the beaten path cross-cultural experiences," says the literature for this company with interesting itineraries in Peru, the Galápagos, Guatemala, Turkey, Costa Rica, Africa, Alaska, Panama, and

YEARS IN BUSINESS:	13
AGE RANGE:	35–80
MOST COMMON AGE:	40–60; 35–55 ON HIKING TRIPS
PERCENT ALONE:	65
NUMBER OF PARTICIPANTS:	SMALL GROUPS
MALE/FEMALE RATIO:	45/55

TRIPS YEAR-ROUND; SHARE RATES GUARANTEED FOR ADVANCE RESERVATIONS

Belize. The trips combine active exploration with intellectual stimulation. You can choose lodge-based odysseys, yacht voyages, rafting, or hiking-camping trips. Guides provide local history and discussion of contemporary social issues to make the visit more meaningful.

COMMENTS *Female, 30s: It was a very busy itinerary, but we learned a lot and the guides were very knowledgeable. We went to remote places and saw things no tourist would ever see, like a village that can only be accessed by boat or plane. There were about fifteen in the group, only three singles. It was about 50/50 male/female and ages from 30 to 70. The people were pretty outgoing, and most were bird-watchers, so we all had something in common. Also most were world travelers, so they shared a lot of interests. The accommodations and food were wonderful. My only criticism was that the people were too old for me. It was great, and I'd recommend it, but to someone a little older.*

Male, 60s: I went once by myself to Patagonia. It is hard to find a

tour to Patagonia, so when I heard of this one, I signed up. There were only four in the group—one woman and two other men. They all worked at a university together. It was very comfortable being alone. We all got to know each other intimately. Everything worked right with this tour—they're very good at what they do, and the guides are very knowledgeable. I plan to go again, and I'd recommend it to anyone.

OVERSEAS ADVENTURE TRAVEL

625 MOUNT AUBURN STREET, CAMBRIDGE, MA 02138; (800) 353–6262 OR (617) 876–0533. (M–E)

YEARS IN BUSINESS:	20+
AGE RANGE:	45–75
MOST COMMON AGE:	30–50
PERCENT ALONE:	60
NUMBER OF PARTICIPANTS:	TOTAL OF **2,000** PER YEAR; NO MORE THAN **16** PER TRIP
MALE FEMALE RATIO:	37/63
YEAR-ROUND; WILL TRY TO ARRANGE SHARES	

This large outfitter, a division of Grand Circle Corporation (see page 221), offers "soft adventures" on seven continents, geared to somewhat older travelers who want to get off the beaten path and experience the culture of foreign countries with comfortable accommodations. Trip leaders are naturalists, archaeologists, biologists, and explorers who live in the destinations; all are fluent in English. Tented camping safaris, European walking tours, and expedition cruises to the Arctic, the South Pacific, and the Amazon are among the many varied offerings.

COMMENTS *Female, 40s: I've been to Costa Rica and to Jordan with this company, and each time the trip was very well run. There were about twelve people in the group, probably 60/40 women to men on the first trip and 70/30 to Jordan. The trips seem to attract a lot of older women who like to travel both by themselves and with friends. There were a few singles on the trip; they were teamed with roommates. The trips attract very nice, outgoing people. You're with a small group for a fairly long time, so it is easy to get to know everyone. OAT is a great way to do this kind of trip–the itineraries are fairly complicated, and they take care of everything for you.*
Male, 40s: I've been to the Amazon and Galápagos. The trip was

fairly demanding—a certain amount of walking and climbing, but not overly strenuous. We were informed of the type of physical activity before we left. The materials you receive beforehand are excellent— they really tell you what to expect in all aspects. It was an extremely diverse and interesting group—a woman from Alaska, a man who was the Canadian consul to Bolivia. It was mostly couples or friends, just two single women. The staff/tour leaders were top-notch—they really understood the people and culture of Peru. The food was excellent. They caught fresh fish for us each night on the boat. It's a great trip to take by yourself, but you have to be slightly adventurous.

HIMALAYAN TRAVEL, INC.
110 PROSPECT STREET, STAMFORD, CT 06901;
(800) 225-2380 OR (203) 359-3711. (I–M)

YEARS IN BUSINESS:	27
AGE RANGE:	25–70
MOST COMMON AGE:	40
PERCENT ALONE:	50
NUMBER OF PARTICIPANTS:	600
MALE/FEMALE RATIO:	50/50
TRIPS YEAR-ROUND	

As the name suggests, Nepal is the prime focus of this group, but they also offer trekking, wildlife safaris, river rafting, Galápagos cruises, and overland expeditions to Europe, Africa, South America, Turkey, Morocco, Greece, the Alps, and throughout Asia, including India, Tibet, Myanmar (Burma), Thailand, Cambodia, Vietnam, and Indonesia. Many of the Nepal trips can be combined with extensions to other Asian countries.

All trips, including Nepal treks, are graded A to E for difficulty. "A" trips are generally sight-seeing with no sustained walking and with hotel or lodge accommodations. "B" trips, which involve four to six hours daily of trekking, are said to be within the ability of any "weekend athlete."

COMMENTS *Female, 30s: The program is excellent, the equipment they provide is great—a down jacket, sleeping bag, water bottle, pack—everything. The food was delicious. We were up at dawn and trekked all day. You could go at your own pace and didn't have to keep up with anyone. If we were in a town, we stayed in guest houses; if not, we camped. It's very cold at night in Nepal! After dinner we sat around and really talked.*

The group got along very well. The age range was 28 to 66; the majority in their 30s to 40s. Two of us were from the U.S.; the rest were from England. Two guys came together; all others were by themselves; 50/50 male/female. I'd recommend this for anyone who is a little adventurous. If you need to take a shower every day, it's not for you. Male, 40s: I've gone to Nepal twice, alone and with a friend. Neither trip had many Americans. Most were Australian and British, ranging in age from 30s to 50s. On the first trip there was one couple; all the rest had come alone. On the second, there were four couples out of fourteen people. The food was terrific on one trip, terrible on the other. In both groups there were interesting, mature people who became close before the trips were over. The only way to see these views is to walk, so people are willing to put up with a certain degree of discomfort to do it. If you like to hike and rough it a bit, and like mountain scenery, it's for you.

MOUNTAIN TRAVEL–
SOBEK EXPEDITIONS, INC.

6420 FAIRMONT AVENUE, EL CERRITO, CA 94530;
(415) 527-8100 OR (800) 227-2384; WWW.
MTSOBEK.COM (M-E)

YEARS IN BUSINESS:	30+
AGE RANGE:	30–50
MOST COMMON AGE:	35–45
PERCENT ALONE:	60
NUMBER OF PARTICIPANTS:	3,600 ANNUALLY; SMALL INDIVIDUAL GROUPS
MALE/FEMALE RATIO:	60/40
YEAR-ROUND	

The whole world is the territory for these adventure specialists, a merger between two of the oldest and largest outdoor trip operators. Trekking, hiking, rafting, sea kayaking—they cover all the adventure categories, plus cultural tours to exotic locales for the less athletic and inn-to-inn hiking in Europe for those who don't like roughing it. Trips are listed in five categories from easy to strenuous and range from trekking to the base of Mount Everest to canoeing in New Guinea to taking African safaris by van. In addition to the comment below, this group seems to get uniformly high marks from past participants.

COMMENTS *Female, 30s: I went on a rafting trip alone, but I never felt alone. The people were ages 20 to 60, half single, twice as many men, and a very interesting group. The food was great, and the leaders even brought hot coffee to each tent in the morning. We all got along and had a great time. The scenery was spectacular, and the instruction was also great. You could do as much or as little paddling as you wanted.*

More Sources for Adventure Travel

- Adventure Center (1311 63rd Street, Suite 200, Emeryville, CA 94608; 510–654–1879 or 800–227–8747) is an agency representing a number of outfitters offering small-group trips in various categories.
- Wilderness Travel (801 Allston Way, Berkeley, CA 04710; 510–548–0420 or 800–368–2794) publishes a big color catalog listing this organization's 100-plus trips on six continents, from wildlife safaris in Africa to sea kayaking in Fiji to cultural journeys through Japan. Specialty trips, varying from year to year, may focus on special events such as an eclipse, visit archaeologists at work, or concentrate on photography.
- A 72-page Outfitters Directory and Vacation Guide is available from America Outdoors, P.O. Box 10847, Knoxville, TN 37939; (423–524–4814; www.americaoutdoors.org). It includes information on more than 350 professional outfitters.

ALASKA WILDLAND ADVENTURE

P.O. Box 389, Girdwood, AK, 99587;
(907) 783–2130 or (800) 334–8730 or (509) 395–2611; www. alaskawildland.com (E–EE)

YEARS IN BUSINESS:	20+
AGE RANGE:	8–80
MOST COMMON AGE:	AROUND 40
PERCENT ALONE:	40
NUMBER OF PARTICIPANTS:	16 PER TRIP
MALE/FEMALE RATIO:	35/65

June to September; some offerings in March, April, and October and special winter safaris in February and March; will try to arrange shares; very small single supplement.

This group offers seven- to twelve-day adventures, including hiking, rafting, camping, float trips, natural history, cruises, and sportfishing, all in the national parks and refuges of the great Alaskan wilderness. Part of the thrill is close-up views of wildlife such as bald eagles, moose, brown bears, caribou, puffins, and seals. Trips are led by trained guide/naturalists. The operator maintains comfortable backcountry lodges and cabins exclusively for participants on these tours. The itinerary also includes some camping options for the more adventurous. In winter, safaris travel on cross-country skis and snowshoes or via dogsled.

COMMENTS *Female, 60s: Fantastic! I've never been on a better trip. The guides and food were wonderful; there was something new and different to do every day. Most people were in their 40s and 50s, but the range was to 75. There were more women than men, more single than married, brought together by their spirit of adventure. Days were well organized, but there was no regimentation.*

BACKROADS

801 CEDAR STREET, BERKELEY, CA 94710;
(800) 462-2848; (510) 517-1555;
WWW.BACKROADS.COM

YEARS IN BUSINESS:	20
AGE RANGE:	25-65
MOST COMMON AGE:	30-50
PERCENT ALONE:	40
NUMBER OF PARTICIPANTS:	26 MAXIMUM PER TOUR
MALE/FEMALE RATIO:	50/50
YEAR-ROUND; WILL TRY TO ARRANGE SHARES; GUARANTEED SHARE RATES FOR RESERVATIONS SIXTY DAYS IN ADVANCE; TRIPS FOR SINGLES	

Long known as a major operator of bicycle tours, Backroads has expanded to offer 150 active itineraries, including biking, hiking, walking, and multisport adventures in different combinations that mix hiking, biking, kayaking, sailboarding, rock climbing, or in-line skating.

A roster of some ninety destinations includes the Baja peninsula, Hawaii, Thailand, New Zealand, China, Bali, Costa Rica, Turkey, Italy, Switzerland, Austria, Spain, Norway, and the Loire Valley in France. Tours vary greatly in their demands, and are clearly labeled in the catalog for their difficulty. Easy, moderate, or challenging options are always offered each day. Itineraries range from five to thirteen days.

....

Bicycle Tours

Bicycle touring offers an in-depth look at beautiful parts of the United States and the rest of the world with congenial company and plenty of time to explore off the beaten path. Tours are available for intermediate as well as for experienced riders, and all tour operators offer rental bikes, helmets, and other necessary equipment. The tour company maps out a choice of detailed bike routes of varying difficulty. Some bicycle tours camp overnight, but most are "inn-to-inn" with a different comfortable lodging destination each night. Depending on the pace and the choice of routes, you can vary your daily mileage. Everyone is together for breakfast and dinner. Many tours also offer the option of a lunch pool with everyone chipping in and sharing picnics assembled en route by the hosts. Or you may choose to try restaurants along the route. A van accompanies the tour, carrying all the luggage, equipment for repairs, and extra bikes for emergencies. Known as the "sag wagon," the van is also readily available if your legs are weary and you want a ride to the inn.

BACKROADS BICYCLE TOURING
(SEE ADDRESS PAGE 97)

While they have expanded their offerings beyond biking, Backroads remains one of the largest bicycle tour companies, with a 90-page catalog chock full of offerings. They cover the Canadian Rockies, the American west, California wine country, and national parks including Bryce, Zion, Glacier, and the Grand Canyon. A host of farther destinations include Europe, Asia, the Pacific, and Latin America. Some of their itineraries are camping trips, some use comfortable inn accommodations and some destinations offer a choice of either. Tours vary in their difficulty and are clearly labeled in the catalog. Beginners cycle two to five hours daily, advanced tours may cycle five to seven hours a day. Bikers can always choose to take it easy, enjoying the scenery and attractions and picnicking along the way. Trips range from 5 to 13 days. For those who want to test their legs before setting out on a longer route, weekend inn-to-inn tours are available in California.

COMMENTS *Female, 30s: I've done a number of their programs, sometimes alone, sometimes with friends. It is very easy to be alone, as there are often more singles than couples. The people are from all over the world, with equal numbers of men and women from early 20s to 70. I've made many friends that I keep in touch with. The people are highly educated and health-conscious. The best thing about the program is the people who run it. They take care of everything, and you get pampered. The food is amazing, and the hotels are luxury. It's ideal for women alone because it is nonthreatening.*
Male, 30s: I've taken eight tours. The average group is half singles. It is easy to meet people, and you quickly become like a family. About

half the group is from California, the rest from all over the U.S. and the rest of the world. It is an upscale crowd. There are several routes to choose from each day, and you can bike as little or as much as you want. The food is very good, and the accommodations are fine, though not elegant.

BROOKS COUNTRY CYCLING TOURS

140 WEST 83RD STREET, NEW YORK, NY 10024; (212) 874–5151. (M)

Reasonably priced trips from weekends to week-long journeys offer some very appealing destinations. In the U.S., you can tour Florida lake country or cycle scenic Nantucket, Martha's Vineyard, or Block Island.

YEARS IN BUSINESS:	14
AGE RANGE:	OVER 30
MOST COMMON AGE:	LATE 30S, 40
PERCENT ALONE:	75
NUMBER OF PARTICIPANTS:	22
MALE/FEMALE RATIO:	40/60
SPRING THROUGH FALL; A FEW WINTER TRIPS TO FLORIDA; WILL TRY TO ARRANGE SHARES	

Weekend trips take in Cape Cod, Vermont, and the Hudson River Valley. European itineraries include biking and barging in Holland, the Loire Valley, Brittany, Normandy, the Dordogne Valley, and Hungary. Comfortable inns are home base, and days are planned with enough leisure time so that everyone can pedal at his or her own pace and stop and sightsee along the way. Trips average 35 miles per day.

COMMENTS *Male, 40s: This is a first-class organization. I've taken three international trips as well as domestic trips. There is a fairly equal split between couples and singles, male and female. The people are special, and I've made good friends. I would definitely recommend these trips.*

Female, 30s: I've taken many trips with this company and highly recommend it. The accommodations in China were not luxurious, but the trip was very exciting. The group is mostly ages 30 to 45 and is geared to singles who are expected to share rooms, although this is not compulsory. I've also done trips with Butterfield and Robinson of Toronto—more expensive and more couples.

VBT BICYCLING VACATIONS

Box 711, Bristol, VT 05443;
(802) 453-4811 or (800) BIKETOUR;
www.vbt.com (M)

YEARS IN BUSINESS:	28
AGE RANGE:	22–70
MOST COMMON AGE:	35-55
PERCENT ALONE:	50
NUMBER OF PARTICIPANTS:	6,000 ANNUALLY
MALE/FEMALE RATIO:	45/55
APRIL TO OCTOBER, A FEW MARCH AND NOVEMBER DATES; GUARANTEED SHARES	

This outfitter was the originator of the inn-to-inn idea in Vermont, but they have expanded way beyond their home state to cover the U.S., nine European countries, and New Zealand. Along with the choicest New England sites, some forty trips cover the antebellum South in Mississippi, Virginia horse country, the Southwest, California, and the northern Michigan lake country, including Mackinac Island, where no cars are allowed. One of the most popular tours is through the quaint fishing villages of Nova Scotia in the Canadian Maritimes. European destinations include France, Scotland, Italy, England, Ireland, Holland, Spain, and Austria. A winter trip cycles New Zealand. Trips are clearly identified as easy, moderate, or challenging. They range from six to seventeen days and can cover anywhere from 25 to 40 miles per day. Lodging is in country inns.

COMMENTS *Female, 30s: It was really easy to meet everyone on the trip. The staff tried to make sure everyone would get along and pointed out similar interests. The age range was from mid–20s to 70s, pretty even male/female, and a great group, really interesting. There were a few friends, one couple, and four or five singles on my trip, and everyone had a great time. It is very well run; the staff really made the trip. They helped everyone get to know each other, designed excellent routes, and were very nice people.*
Female, 20s: I was very comfortable on a trip to New Zealand alone. There were only two or three married couples. The group ranged in age from 27 to late 50s and came from all over the U.S. We stayed in hotels and always had dinner together. You could do what you wanted each day, pick your routes, and go at your own pace. It was a great trip.

BIKE VERMONT, INC.

P.O. Box 207, Woodstock, VT 05091;
(802) 457–3553 or (800) 257–2226;
www.bikevt.com (M)

Years in business:	20+
Age range:	18–65
Most common age:	30–50
Percent alone:	25–35
Number of participants:	15–20
Male/female ratio:	1/2
May to October; will try to arrange shares	

This operation arranges inn-to-inn bicycle tours in the lovely Vermont and New Hampshire countryside with a new destination every night. Vermont is hilly, but this company's weekend trips and four-to-six-day tours are within the ability of beginning cyclists, and the support van is available when you need a rest. Average runs are 25 to 35 miles a day. Some trips include a day of hiking. This is "a nonthreatening, relaxing vacation," say the organizers. "We don't bike as a group, so everyone is going at his or her own pace. It is easy to make new friends."

COMMENTS *Male, 40s: I've taken several tours. There is good mix of singles and couples, plus children from about age 12. Backgrounds vary, but generally the adults are highly educated professionals. It is easy to make friends.*

Female, 20s: I've done this for six years. When you share a sport, there's automatic camaraderie and all ages mix. You have breakfast together, then set out at your own pace, alone or with others. You meet people along the way, stop together for hot chocolate or a cold drink, and you make friends. I always come home with names and addresses, and often you plan to come back on another trip with these people.

BICYCLE ADVENTURES

P.O. Box 11219, Olympia, WA 98508;
(360) 786–0989 or (800) 443–6060; www.
bicycleadventures.com (M)

Years in business:	15
Age range:	20s to 60s
Most common age:	30–40
Percent alone:	40–50
Number of participants:	13–18
Male/female ratio:	40/60
June to November; winter trips to Hawaii; no single supplement	

The glorious scenery of the Pacific Northwest is the territory for this outfitter. Their signature trip is an eight-day tour of Puget Sound, using ferries to cover five different islands and staying in delightful inns. Two-day stays on Orcas Island and Vancouver Island in Canada allow for extra sight-seeing. In Vancouver, there is the chance to visit world-famous Butchart Gardens and the city of Victoria. Shorter versions of this trip are also available. Other popular destinations are the Olympic Peninsula, the Cascade Mountains, the Oregon coast and the Columbia River Gorge, British Columbia, California wine country, Bryce and Zion National Parks, and Hawaii. Beginner trips can range from 15 to 40 miles daily on easier terrain; intermediate trips cover 30 to 70 miles each day.

COMMENTS *Female, 30s: I would encourage anyone going solo to be adventurous and just do it. The weather, people, food, inns, and scenery were all super. It was the best money I've ever spent on myself.*

Male, 30s: This group is superb——the routes were well planned, the food and inns were wonderful, everything was done professionally. The group was small, one couple and the rest singles in their 30s, all successful professionals, more men than women. Everyone got along well. I've been on more expensive bicycle trips that were nowhere near as good. I also like going with a smaller specialized company; the groups are smaller, and they really know this area.

BUTTERFIELD & ROBINSON

70 Bond Street, Toronto, Ontario, Canada M5B 1X3; (416) 864–1354; in U.S., (800) 387–1147; www.butterfield.com (EE)

YEARS IN BUSINESS:	30+
AGE RANGE:	30–70
MOST COMMON AGE:	45–55
PERCENT ALONE:	30
NUMBER OF PARTICIPANTS:	18–24 PER SMALL GROUP; 5,000 ANNUALLY
MALE/FEMALE RATIO:	40/60
YEAR-ROUND; WILL TRY TO ARRANGE SHARES	

This long-established company has a full roster of luxury biking tours through France, Italy, England, Ireland, Holland, Belgium, Switzerland, Morocco, Spain, and Portugal. Furtherafield, tours take in India, New Zealand, and Vietnam. All feature elegant country accommodations (usually two nights at each stop) and top restaurants, including some Michelin all-stars. There are stops for tastings at regional wineries as well. Routes are rated for difficulty, but cyclists should be able to ride at least three to five hours a day. Several itineraries combine bicycling and walking.

COMMENTS *Female, 40s: This is expensive, but it's the best vacation I ever had and I am going again. About half the group was unattached, equal numbers of men and women, and everyone quickly formed a close-knit group. The couples usually split up at meals and ate with different people. Ages were 25 to 63, interesting folks from the U.S. and Canada. Days were flexible, at your own pace. They take very good care of you, and there are a lot of repeat customers. Female, 30s: I've been several times. There were a lot of people from the East Coast, more couples than singles, usually more women than men. Sometimes we met for activities like wine tasting; sometimes you cycled at your own pace all day. The lodging and food are tops, and most meals are eaten as a group. I'd recommend it to all singles as long as they don't go expecting to meet someone special.*

INTERNATIONAL BICYCLE TOURS

P.O. Box 754, Essex, CT 06426;
(860) 767-7005. (M)

YEARS IN BUSINESS:	20+
AGE RANGE:	7–85
MOST COMMON AGE:	50+
PERCENT ALONE:	50
NUMBER OF PARTICIPANTS:	23 MAXIMUM
MALE/FEMALE RATIO:	1/2
APRIL TO SEPTEMBER; WILL TRY TO ARRANGE SHARES	

Older and novice cyclists are attracted to these leisurely excursions through scenic countryside in the U.S. and abroad. Trips begin at a gentle pace, then gradually increase in daily mileage as everyone becomes more comfortable with cycling. There are periodic stops to relax, share snacks, or take pictures. Destinations include Holland, Denmark, Austria, France, Ireland, and Bermuda. Closer to home, shorter trips are available to Cape Cod, Florida, California's Sonoma Valley, Pennsylvania Dutch country, and along the Chesapeake and Ohio Canal.

COMMENTS *Male, 70s: I've been on six international trips and four domestic. Every trip has been excellent. I always go alone; there are always a number of singles on the trip. They attract an older crowd—about half are over 50. The staff is fabulous; I've been with other*

More Sources for Biking

There are many other tour operators offering biking vacations. Bicycle USA Tour Finder (1612 K Street NW, Suite 401, Washington, DC, 20006; (202) 822-1333; www.bikeleague.org) is a comprehensive directory of more than 150 bicycle tour operators in the United States and abroad, published by the League of American Bicyclists.

companies and they're not even close. The routes and mileage varies by the trip. Unlike other companies that give you a map and you're on your own, you ride as a group so you can't get lost. You have a real sense of security. The trips are paced for someone who doesn't want anything too strenuous. The food is excellent, and the value can't be beat.

Female, 60s: I've been on a dozen trips with IBT, and I'm leaving again in a few weeks. I started out going alone, but I met people on the trips and now we plan to go together. There's always a number of people who go alone. The group is always very congenial and friendly—all very outgoing people. It's a well-run program. They have a unique system with a leader, a corner, and a sweep. The corner stops at an intersection and waves everyone along, and the sweep brings up the rear to make sure no one gets lost or left behind. There are usually a few more women than men, but it varies with the trip. The age range is really 30s to 70s, but I'm bringing my thirteen-year-old-granddaughter on the next trip. The mix of young and old makes it really interesting. You get to know everyone because you ride together all day and sit together for meals. These are great trips.

ROADS LESS TRAVELED

2840 WILDERNESS PLACE, SUITE F,
BOULDER, CO 80301;
(800) 488–8483 OR (303) 413–0938;
WWW.ROADSLESSTRAVELED.COM (I–M)

YEARS IN BUSINESS:	10
AGE RANGE:	35–50
MOST COMMON AGE:	40
PERCENT ALONE:	35
NUMBER OF PARTICIPANTS:	14 MAXIMUM PER GROUP
MALE/FEMALE RATIO:	VARIES
YEAR-ROUND; GUARANTEED SHARES	

"Sampler" and "multisport" adventures combining hiking, mountain biking, horseback riding, rafting, and rock climbing are unique offerings from this group, which also offers separate hiking "ramblers" and "fat tire" mountain biking excursions. Itineraries offer a choice of comfortable inn-to-inn journeys, more rustic hut-to-hut trips, or camping trips. Destinations include Colorado, Utah, Wyoming, Montana, Idaho, New Mexico, and Arizona in the United States as well as Canada. Winter-warm weather escapes take place in Hawaii, Costa Rica, Belize, Australia, and New Zealand. Skiing, snowshoeing, dogsledding, and snowmobiling adventures are available in winter in Colorado or the Grand Tetons. Singles are welcome on all trips and also have their own special trips.

Hiking / Walking

Walking trips with comfortable lodgings awaiting each night are a lovely way to linger through some of America's and Europe's most beautiful areas, far from tourist crowds. There are trips for every ability, from rugged mountain hiking to a relaxed pace in the gentle countryside. A van carries all the gear; walkers need only a light daypack for an extra sweater, a slicker, or snacks. These trips are increasingly popular, and many bicycle touring companies have added walking tours to their offerings.

BUTTERFIELD & ROBINSON

(SEE PAGE 102)

This is a top-of-the-line organization for walking as well as biking tours with luxury accommodations and food. High recommendations are common from past participants. Each person goes at his own pace, and a van is posted at several points so that walks can be shortened if necessary. Areas covered continue to expand. Recent European walking destinations include the Provence, Burgundy, the Amalfi Coast, Tuscany, Austria, Spain, and England. Further explorations on foot take in Turkey, New Zealand and Patagonia. Nepal, South Africa, Chile, Argentina, Belize, Mexico, and Guatemala. A very popular trip combining biking and walking goes into the Atlas mountains of Morocco. Reservationists try to steer solo walkers to trips where they will find company.

COMMENTS *Female, 50s: The Morocco trip was one of the most wonderful experiences I've ever had. They took us to places ordinary tours never get to. We camped out in the desert, rode camels, had fabulous experiences. My group happened to include a group of six married women who had come together, but my most compatible companions were couples. Everyone was friendly, and being alone was perfectly comfortable.*

BACKROADS
(SEE PAGE 97 FOR ADDRESS AND TELEPHONE NUMBER)

Backroads has gone into walking in a big way, with year-round trips for all abilities in scenic locales around the world. Beginner routes cover 3 to 5 miles daily, averaging a gentle two to four hours of walking. Advanced hikers may cover 8 to 12 miles in a day, averaging five to six hours.

THE WAYFARERS
172 BELLEVUE AVENUE, NEWPORT, RI 02840;
(800) 249–4620 OR (401) 849–5087;
WWW.THEWAYFARERS.COM (E)

YEARS IN BUSINESS: 16	
AGE RANGE: 26–72	
MOST COMMON AGE: 50	
PERCENT ALONE: 20	
NUMBER OF PARTICIPANTS: 15 MAXIMUM	
MALE/FEMALE RATIO: 40/60	
WILL TRY TO ARRANGE SHARES	

This British-based company has expanded their original English itineraries to cover Ireland, Scotland, Wales, Italy, France, and Switzerland, always choosing fine country inns as lodgings. Their interesting trips include a garden tour of Dorset, the hills of Tuscany, Ireland's Ring of Kerry, and for hardy walkers, a coast-to-coast route across England. They are the only group offering walks in the Aran Islands of

Ireland. An average day's walk covers 10 miles, with stops for lunch and morning and afternoon coffee or tea breaks. The van is always close by for those who tire or want to take a day off. The group eats all meals together, allowing plenty of time for socializing. The company reports a large number of repeat travelers.

COMMENTS *Female, 50s: I've tried other groups, but I keep coming back to this one because the trips are so well put together and you get so much for your money. Everything is excellent—the leaders, the itineraries, the places we stayed. They are very flexible and go out of their way to see that every single person has a good time. There are mostly couples and single women, not very many single men, but very comfortable for all. I've made friends from Australia and England and planned future trips with people I've walked with in the past. It's a very good choice for singles and the very best way to see a country.*

COUNTRY WALKERS

P.O. Box 180, Waterbury, VT 05676;
(800) 464-9255; www.countrywalkers.com
(I–C; includes breakfast and dinner)

YEARS IN BUSINESS:	20+
AGE RANGE:	30s–70s
MOST COMMON AGE:	40–60
PERCENT ALONE:	60
MALE/FEMALE RATIO:	1/2
NUMBER OF PARTICIPANTS:	AVERAGE 15 PER GROUP
YEAR-ROUND; WILL TRY TO ARRANGE SHARES; SHARE RATE GUARANTEED ON BOOKINGS MADE NINETY DAYS IN ADVANCE	

The coast of Maine, the valleys of Vermont, Nova Scotia, the Arizona desert, beautiful areas in England, Ireland, Scotland, France, Greece, Italy, and Spain and exquisite scenery in Ecuador, Africa, Nepal, New Zealand, Peru, Costa Rica, and Turkey make up the forty-plus far-flung itineraries this company covers on foot. Tours focus on the natural history and culture of the area and are led by knowledgeable local guides. Lodgings are first-class throughout. Hiking options range from 4 to 12 miles a day, and there is always the option to stroll a few miles to a local village, enjoy a cafe lunch, and relax for the afternoon. Everyone gathers for dinner.

COMMENTS *Male, 50s: I've been to Peru and Chile, alone both times. There were nine people on the last trip—two couples, two single women traveling together, and three people traveling alone. I was*

*very impressed with how they ran both programs. The staff that trav-
eled with us and the local guides were excellent and very knowledgeable. They were also there to help if you need a "leg up." We had no
problems because everything was so well planned. The people were
from all over the U.S., and all had traveled fairly extensively so we
had experiences to share and there was never a struggle for conversation. People got along really well and were very helpful to each other.
The room and food was fine. The Peruvian food was interesting—including eating guinea pig! The commonality of interests—liking the
outdoors, traveling, and being active—brought the group together.*

THE ITALIAN CONNECTION (E)
(SEE PAGE 166)

This organization, also listed for its culinary tours, offers nine walking
itineraries in Italy with special emphasis on regional food, often dining in
local homes.

Sailing

Take to the sea for a windswept adventure like no other, with lazy
days of snorkeling and swimming in solitary coves, convivial shipboard fun at night, and stops in picturesque ports where the big ships
can't follow.

WINDJAMMER BAREFOOT CRUISES
P.O. Box 190120, Miami Beach, FL 33139;
(800) 327-2601; www.windjammer.com (M)

"The thought of a tall-ship cruise to a remote island turns people on," says the
captain and founder of this Caribbean fleet that
offers sailing vacations on five classic sailing ships.
The fleet sails from several ports, including

YEARS IN BUSINESS:	40+
AGE RANGE:	25–55
MOST COMMON AGE:	30–40
PERCENT ALONE:	60
NUMBER OF PARTICIPANTS:	66–122
MALE/FEMALE RATIO:	VARIES; ABOUT EQUAL
YEAR-ROUND; WILL TRY TO ARRANGE SHARES	

Tortola, St. Martin, Grenada, and Trinidad. Itineraries in the Western Caribbean leave from Belize City and explore Belize and Honduras. Each week more than fifty islands are visited on six- and thirteen-day outings. In summer, cruises go north to sail the waters of Maine and Nova Scotia.

These are not a luxury cruises but a chances to experience the exhilaration of sailing and to get to small, isolated islands. The cabins are small, but they are air-conditioned and have private toilets and showers. Meals are served buffet style on ship or on picnics ashore. Drinks and wine are plentiful. Dress is always informal, and entertainment can be wacky—toga parties, crab races, steel-drum bands on board.

COMMENTS *Female, 30s: I took this trip with my twelve-year-old son—it is great for both singles and single parents. About half the adults were single, ranging in age from 20s to 50s and 60s, a few more women than men. We were from many parts of the country and with very different backgrounds, but everyone had a wonderful time. The food was fantastic, the cabins comfortable and air-conditioned. We sailed mostly at night and spent days on the islands. The crew is great and tells you the ins and outs of each new port. At night there was always an activity. I made a lot of friends—and I can't wait to go on another trip. It's the best vacation I've ever had.*

Male, 40s: I'm getting ready for my third trip. I've gone with friends and once by myself and I always had a fantastic time. You can let your hair down and relax. There's no pretense, you wear a T-shirt and shorts even for dinner. Everyone is friendly and outgoing, so it's easy to find a group of people you enjoy and go off in port together. The ages were from 20 to 70, but most are 30 or 40, and the 70s are very young at heart. Everyone has fun. You can be alone if you want to, but it's hard not to meet people. The food is very good, but not gourmet. There's only a choice of two entrees at dinner—this is not a luxury liner. But the staff is great and the captain is really accessible. One night he gave an impromptu stargazing class on deck. The itinerary is very special—you meet the local people and see places you can't on a big ship.

MAINE WINDJAMMER ASSOCIATION

P.O. Box 1144P, Blue Hill, ME 04614;
(207) 374-2993 or (800) 807-WIND;
www.midcoast.com/~sailmwa (I)

YEARS IN BUSINESS:	60 +
AGE RANGE:	16–80
MOST COMMON AGE:	30–50
PERCENT ALONE:	25–30
NUMBER OF PARTICIPANTS:	20–37
MALE/FEMALE RATIO:	VARIES, FAIRLY EQUAL
JUNE TO SEPTEMBER	

This fleet of ten nostalgic nineteenth-century two- and three-masted "tall ships" sets sail each summer from Camden, Rockland, or Rockport for Penobscot Bay to explore the evergreen coast and the islands of Maine and to rest in quiet anchorages of unblemished beauty. Ships range from 64 to 132 feet; there are single cabins, or singles may share. The rates are a real bargain. Passengers can help with the halyards and lines, keep a lookout for seals and ospreys, watch the lobstermen setting out traps, or just lie back and soak up the sun. Family-style meals featuring New England chowder, "Down East" lobster bakes, and Maine blueberry pie are not the least of the attractions!

COMMENTS *Male, 30s: I've been twice, and it was great. I was look-ing for something I could do without pressure to find a partner, and this was it. There were a few other singles, but it hardly mattered be-cause with such a small group sharing meals and bath facilities, it was informal and comfortable for everyone. The sailing was terrific, and the food was fantastic.*
Female, 40s: I really enjoyed it and am thinking of going again. There were people from age 30 to one man in his 70s, and nine out of twenty-three of us were single. Everyone got along and enjoyed each other's company.

ECHO: THE WILDERNESS CO, INC.

6529 Telegraph Avenue, Oakland, CA 94609;
(510) 652-1600 or (800) 652-ECHO; www.echotrips.com (EE)
Singles are paired in cabins

Best known for rafting trips, (see page 112) ECHO also runs intimate sailing adventures to Turkey.

Two two-week Turkish trips are aboard a sailing yacht with up to twelve guests plus a Turkish guide. One covers the Turquoise Coast and Anatolia, the other the Aegean Sea; both include exotic historical and archaeological sites and a visit to Istanbul. If you are willing to share a cabin, these are grand excursions.

REMOTE ODYSSEYS WORLDWIDE (R.O.W.)

P.O. BOX 579;
COUER D'ALENE, ID 83816;
(800) 451-6034 OR (208) 765-0841; WWW.ROWINC.COM
SINGLES ARE PAIRED IN CABINS

This is another long-established rafting company (see page 115) that offers adventure cruising, with itineraries in Turkey and along the Dalmatian coast. Turkish cruises are aboard a traditional *gulet,* a 65-to-70-foot handmade Turkish sailing yacht. Two choices are offered, an Aegean cruise and the Lycian shore, both including the famous ruins of Ephesus. Mixing days of walking with sailing on the *Croatian Tapestry,* a modern 95-foot motor/sail vessel. Dubrovnik and Split are among the quaint villages visited.

COMMENTS *Male, 40s: What a fabulous trip to Turkey. I've traveled around the world, and this was the best trip I've ever taken. There were ten of us from mid-30s to early 70s, and we saw things we couldn't see any other way. The crew was excellent and open to suggestions—if we wanted to take a break in a pretty cove to swim, they said fine. There was no problem whatsoever being alone. I was always included as part of the group. I highly recommend it and am going on another cruise with this group next year.*

R a f t i n g

What's so great about running a river? Those who love it call it "River Magic." One longtime operator says he has found that the cooperation required to meet the challenge of the river facilitates relationships, opens lines of communication, enhances personal growth, and helps participants develop lasting friendships more than any other form of outdoor recreation he has ever experienced—which may explain why so many river trips are available and why so many people sign up for them. Maybe Mark Twain said it best "You feel mighty free and easy and comfortable on a raft."

SHERI GRIFFITH EXPEDITIONS INC.

P.O. Box 1324, 2231 South Highway 191, Moab, UT 84532; (800) 332-2439 or (435) 259-8229; WWW.GRIFFITHEXP.COM (L–M)

YEARS IN BUSINESS:	20+
AGE RANGE:	23–60
MOST COMMON AGE:	25–40
PERCENT ALONE:	50
NUMBER OF PARTICIPANTS:	25
MALE/FEMALE RATIO:	50/50
MAY TO SEPTEMBER	

This operator boasts of "Outdoor Adventures with a Touch of Class," priding herself on service of top food on two- to six-day river-running adventures on the Green, Colorado, and Dolores rivers. There are runs for beginners to experts, plus some interesting specialty trips, such as "Expedition in Luxury," a luxurious outing in Canyonlands National Park. Some river trips are combined with mountain biking or hiking on land.

COMMENTS *Male, 30s: To a man, every person on the trip would have jumped at the chance to go again . . . tomorrow, if not sooner. Female, 30s: A well-organized, smooth-running operation with a courteous, knowledgeable, and fun staff. Their ability in the kitchen was unmatched. The trip was a bargain.*

ECHO: THE WILDERNESS CO, INC.

6529 Telegraph Avenue, Oakland, CA 94609; (510) 652–1600 or (800) 652–ECHO. (M)

YEARS IN BUSINESS:	27
AGE RANGE:	7–70
MOST COMMON AGE:	30s–50s
PERCENT ALONE:	VARIES
NUMBER OF PARTICIPANTS:	1.500 PER YEAR
MALE/FEMALE RATIO:	50/50
LATE MAY TO MID-SEPTEMBER	

River-rafting excitement with this group includes special outings with entertainment such as wine tasting, music, and yoga workshops. U.S. rafting trips are held on the Middle Fork and Main Salmon River in Idaho, the Rogue River in Oregon, the Tuolumne river in California.

COMMENTS *Female, 20s: I've gone alone twice and been very comfortable. I was really impressed because I went with a very large group and they handled it beautifully. They were very sensitive about pair-*

ing the guides with the different groups of people and skill levels. The guides are very congenial. They have lots of games and other things in the evening so everyone gets to know each other, and you have to work together in the boats. There is a comfortable mix of men and women (a few more women), and an age range of 15 to 65. The groups are diverse and interesting, and there are plenty of single people.

Female, 40s: I've been going on Echo's trips for fifteen years; I think they are the premier rafting company. I admit that if you go alone you have to be more outgoing—a lot of people do come as a group of friends, and you don't want to intrude. But there are usually one or two singles on each trip and the leaders organize group activities like nature walks and soaking in hot tubs so everyone gets involved. I would definitely recommend these trips to solo travelers. It's a great way to meet people, and I've formed lasting friendships. In fact, I'm planning my next trip with some people I met on an Echo trip.

OUTDOOR ADVENTURE RIVER SPECIALISTS (O.A.R.S.) INC.

P.O. BOX 67, ANGELS CAMP, CA 95222;
(209) 736-4677 OR (800) 346-6277;
WWW.OARS.COM (I-M)

YEARS IN BUSINESS:	28
AGE RANGE:	18–54+
MOST COMMON AGE:	25–45
PERCENT ALONE:	25
NUMBER OF PARTICIPANTS:	16–25
MALE/FEMALE RATIO:	50/50
MAY TO SEPTEMBER; WILL TRY TO ARRANGE SHARES	

With this outfitter you can camp under the stars if sleeping bags are your bag or have the thrill of rafting and the comfort of bed-and-break-fast lodgings at night. Choose the challenge of Class V rapids or gentler trips with an "oar" option, meaning the guide does all the rowing while guests sit back and enjoy the ride. O.A.R.S. offers a wide variety of two- to seventeen-day outings on the American, Kern, Klamath, and Tuolumne Rivers in California; the Rogue River in Oregon; the Salmon and Snake Rivers in Idaho; the Green, San Juan, and Yampa Rivers in Utah; the Colorado River through the Grand Canyon in Arizona; and the Snake River in Wyoming. The catalog ranks each trip for the diffi-culty of the rapids and describes the scenery.

COMMENTS *Female, 30s: I've gone on two trips alone. You can have time to yourself if you want it, but you never have to be alone. My groups ranged from ages 20 to mid-60s; about half were single and two-thirds were male, and they were from all over the country. The people were great, very congenial. You switch boats each day so you get to meet everyone. The food was terrific and we slept under the stars. If you have a spirit of adventure, this is a great experience.*

Male, 30s: I've gone on five trips, alone and with my wife. Many of the people are married but come alone. We were up at sunrise, did everything from running rapids to hiking. You get to know everyone as you switch boats. You can do as much or as little work as you want. There is good food and lots of it. It's a good introduction to rafting—easy, relaxed, and everyone can do it.

DVORAK'S KAYAK & RAFTING EXPEDITIONS

17921-B U.S. 285, Nathrop, CO 81236;
(800) 824-3795 or (719) 539-6851;
WWW.DVORAKEXPEDITIONS.COM (I)

Years in business:	29
Age range:	25–65
Most common age:	25–35
Percent alone:	60
Number of participants:	5,000+ annually; 12 to 25 per trip
Male/female ratio:	50/50
Late May to September in u.s.; November to February abroad	

Dvorak's was the first licensed operator in Colorado. It has grown to offer trips through scenic canyons on ten U.S. rivers and on rivers in Nepal, Mexico, Australia, and New Zealand. Among the states covered are Arkansas, Colorado, Utah, New Mexico, Wyoming, and Texas, where rivers used include the Salt, Dolores, Colorado, and Arkansas. One special offering is a Classical Music River Journey where symphony and Philharmonic artists perform with alpine forests and sandstone canyons as a backdrop.

COMMENTS *Female, 30s: A wonderful experience, the finest thing I've ever done. There were seven of us, all single, age 30s to 50s, about equal numbers of men and women. We stayed in tents, had wonderful, healthful food. The instruction was great—but even less physical people can enjoy this trip, as you don't have to paddle if you don't want to.*

Female, 30s: This was a great thing to do. I went with my ten-year-old son, and although he was the only child, it was no problem—the guides took care of him and were wonderful helping him fish when we hit calm water. We slept in tents, had great food. There was just one couple—from New Zealand—the rest were future guides on their first trip.

RIVER ODYSSEYS WEST (R.O.W.)
(ALSO REMOTE ODDYSSEYS WORLDWIDE)
P.O. BOX 579,
COUER D'ALENE, ID 83816;
(800) 451-6034 OR (208) 765-0841;
WWW.ROWINC.COM

YEARS IN BUSINESS:	19
AGE RANGE OF PARTICIPANTS:	5–86
MOST COMMON AGE:	40
PERCENT ALONE:	18
NUMBER OF PARTICIPANTS:	16
MALE/FEMALE RATIO:	47/53

Idaho is home base for this interesting company, which features rafting on the Snake, Lochsa, Moyie, Owyhee, St. Joe, and Clark Fork Rivers and the Middle Fork of the Salmon River. Many trips offer more than rafting. Some combine rafting and hiking to explore the canyons; others include horseback riding, a stay at a guest ranch or a night at a resort or B&B with warm beds and hot tubs. Special trips are planned for families, men and women only, and for rafters over age 55.

In winter, R.O.W. becomes Remote Odysseys Worldwide. Offerings include adventure cruising (see page 111), and a rafting trip through the mountains and jungles of Ecuador, with time to visit cities and thrills tackling class III and IV rapids.

COMMENTS *Female, 60s: I've gone on two trips, Hells Canyon and the Middle Fork of the Salmon, and loved both. The crew is very professional. The guides are knowledgeable about the nature and history of the area as well as the rivers, and they do a great presentation of food. The group was about sixteen people, a mix of sexes and ages from 20s to 60s. I was the oldest on the last trip, but we all got along and the younger people went out of their way to be friendly and helpful. They make sure everyone gets acquainted the first night. I can't say enough good things about this company.*

NANTAHALA OUTDOOR CENTER ADVENTURE TRAVEL

13077 HIGHWAY 19 WEST, BOX 41, BRYSON CITY, NC 28713;
(828) 488–2176 OR (888) 662–1662; WWW.NOCWEB.COM (I–M)

This top Eastern teaching center (see page 36) also offers a variety of guided white-water and sea kayaking adventures. Rafting locales include not only North Carolina, the southern Appalachians, the Everglades, and the Grand Canyon but exotic destinations such as Costa Rica, Honduras, Corsica, Chile, Turkey, and Nepal.

....

Nepal: The Supreme Adventure

There are many mighty mountains in the world, but the trip to the Himalayas is unique. Since it remains on my dream list, I asked Ben Wallace, who helps organize trips for Himalayan Travel (see page 137) and who has lived in Nepal for three years, to explain why.

The lure of Nepal is the people as much as the mountains, he says. The trails you follow are the only roads in this remote region, the lifeline of the villagers who live here. Every day you are seeing intimately a fascinating and totally different way of life. You can linger, visit homes, and observe how people live, cook, farm, and work. Staying in local homes is an option. Most people come to Nepal thinking the thrill is going to be the big mountains and the view but find instead it is the local life that is the indelible memory.

Ben says that most people once were drawn to Nepal for the physical challenge, but that a higher percentage today are looking for something else, a total change from their life-style and environment. The least strenuous treks usually mean four to eight days on the trail, walking four to six hours a day, with a maximum ascent of about 1,500 feet—within the ability of anyone who does any exercising at home.

Everything is taken care of for you. Someone else puts up and takes down the camp, carries all gear, does all the cooking and cleaning up. You are free to simply soak in the experience. Many people today sign up for the shorter one-week treks, then spend another week sight-seeing or rafting. Ben believes, however, that the longer trips deeper into the mountains are the most rewarding. People who spend the time to really immerse themselves in the culture are hooked—they almost always return.

Ben explains that the degree of difficulty has three components: the duration of time on the trail, how much altitude is gained or lost, and the living conditions. "Someone who is very fit but not used to living in a tent—a jogger for example—may be able to stand up to the physical challenge but not be happy about spending three weeks in a tent.

"Altitude affects people differently—and the same people differently on different days. Above ten or eleven thousand feet, almost everyone feels discomfort, perhaps headaches. A good operator knows this and allows plenty of time for acclimatization."

The food on a trek is a pleasant surprise. A sample menu might include onion soup topped with melted yak cheese, sweet and sour chicken over vegetable fried rice, and cake baked over the campfire. As in any third world country, there may be an occasional stomach bug to contend with. All treks include a medical kit and someone who knows how to use it.

When to come? The trekking season is from late September to May.

More Adventuring Ideas

- Specialty Travel Index (305 San Anselmo Avenue, San Anselmo, CA 94960; 415–455–1643 or 888–624–4030) is a biannual listing of ads from hundreds of operators of adventure and specialty trips of all kinds. It is the source used by many travel agents. Sample index listings: Elephant Ride, Environmental Education, Festival Tours, Film History, Fishing, Foliage Tours, Windjamming, Windsurfing, Winery Tours, Women's Tours. An annual subscription is $10.
- Adventure Center (1311 63rd Street, Suite 200, Emeryville, CA 94608; 510–654–1879 or 800–227–8747) is an agency specializing in adventure travel, offering more than 1,000 annual departures to nearly 100 countries.

Get Back to Nature

You don't have to hike or raft your way into the wilderness in order to enjoy the outdoors. Nature-oriented workshops are available in beautiful and remote settings, and there are wonderful tours and cruises geared to appreciating places where plant, animal, and bird life are abundant.

Many nature-oriented tour operators also offer "soft adventures," such as expedition cruises and safaris to remote places that require no camping or strenuous activity. The choice is rich, from watching penguins and polar bears in Antarctica to viewing moose and elk in Wyoming, from seeing brilliantly colored birds in the jungle to close encounters with giraffes and lions on the African plains.

Vacations that emphasize nature these days often come with a catchy label—"ecotourism." Ecotourism at its best means simply respecting nature. Many operators talk about ecotourism, but do not practice it. Careless, commercial tour operators can drive animals from their habitats and destroy the natural wonders that have drawn visitors. If you choose a vacation emphasizing nature, by all means choose responsible operators and organizations who practice and promote conservation.

Nature Workshops

The nicest thing about nature-oriented workshops is their magnificent settings, where recreation is as appealing as the learning opportunities. These programs aim not only to teach about nature but to inspire appreciation that will carry over into support for conservation when you return home. In that endeavor, the operators often include painting, photography, and writing workshops along with bird and nature walks.

AUDUBON ECOLOGY CAMPS AND WORKSHOP

NATIONAL AUDUBON SOCIETY,
613 RIVERSVILLE ROAD, GREENWICH, CT 06831;
(203) 869–2017. (I)

YEARS IN BUSINESS:	60+
AGE RANGE:	19–80
MOST COMMON AGE:	30s–40s
PERCENT ALONE:	HIGH
NUMBER OF PARTICIPANTS:	55 MAXIMUM, DIVIDED INTO SMALLER FIELD GROUPS
MALE/FEMALE RATIO:	40/60
JULY AND EARLY AUGUST	

Adults from across the country come to the one- and two-week summer sessions held in the society's sanctuaries in Connecticut, off the coast of Maine, and in the Wind River Range of Wyoming.

In these beautiful outdoor settings, adults come to learn, relax, and forge new friendships. Programs focus on field ecology and birding as well as nature photography. One week of nature study explores via kayak. The aim is to reintroduce you to nature, to show how all wildlife is interdependent, and to teach what you can do to protect it. Rustic lodgings are mostly dorm style; meals are buffet. Participants are all ages and backgrounds, from college students and retired senior citizens to teachers and firefighters.

COMMENTS *Female, 30s: A typical day means getting up for an early breakfast and then walking from about 8:30 to 11:30 A.M. with a naturalist who is usually a teacher. The leaders are excellent and really know their stuff. There's time to rest or relax before and after lunch, then there is another program from 2:00 to 5:00 P.M. Depending on the weather and the topic, you might go out by boat instead of on foot. The idea is always hands-on learning. If it rains, classroom talks are held. At night there might be a guest lecturer, square dancing, a slide show, or an evening astronomy walk. The big group is divided into four small groups, and you stay with that group every day for programs, so there's plenty of chance to get to know people. Everyone has an interest in nature, and it's really nice to share that with others. There's a lot of bonding within the group.*

NATIONAL WILDLIFE FEDERATION
CONSERVATION SUMMIT PROGRAM

8925 Leesburg Pike, Vienna, VA 22184;
(703) 790-4363. (I)

Years in business:	27
Age range:	Infants to 70s
Most common age:	30–50
Percent alone:	33
Number of participants:	800 annually
Male/female ratio:	Varies
June and July; will try to arrange shares	

Conservation Summits offer a week of nature education and recreation in beautiful locations that rotate annually. The cost is moderate, and the program is excellent. Depending on the site, activities might include boat excursions to observe whales and sea lions, mountain hikes, or a field trip to a glacier. Nature hikes and outdoor photography are usually featured in all programs, and participants may learn about orienteering, bird watching, geology, and astronomy. Activities are planned to suit all levels of fitness. Lodgings options can vary from rustic lodges to apartment-style suites. All programs serve meals in a central location, either cafeteria or family style. The ambience is relaxed and friendly. Recent sites have included Estes Park, Colorado; Seward, Alaska; and the Adirondack Mountains of New York.

COMMENTS *Female, 40s: The age range is literally infants to senior citizens. You're up early. There are lectures and field trips, yet also plenty of free time. The hiking isn't too strenuous, so anyone can do it. After dinner, there are slide presentations, music, stargazing, or evening wildlife viewing field trips. Accommodations and food vary from fair to excellent depending on location, but the lodgings are always clean and adequate.*

Female, 50s: Summits have been the reason that I've seen most of the United States . . . and also a way to make lasting friendships. I still keep in touch with and visit friends I met at my first Summit fifteen years ago. But most of all, Summits instill in us a love for the earth and each other.

THE NATURE CONSERVANCY

1815 North Lynn Street, Arlington, VA 22209;
(703) 841-5300; Pine Butte information,
(406) 466-2158; www.tng.org (I)
April to September

Another highly respected conservation group, the Nature Conservancy offers weekend and week-long field trips in several scenic locations. Changing activities are set up by local field offices from Virginia's Eastern Shore to the Nebraska sandhills to the coast of Oregon. Other programs take place at permanent Conservancy properties such as Homestead at Hart Prairie in Arizona, where participants are housed in historic cabins beneath the San Francisco Mountains for explorations of peaks and canyons and a chance to work with ecologists on plant surveys or to watch for Arizona's jewel-hued hummingbirds.

Natural History workshops are held at the Pine Butte Guest Ranch in Montana, with lodgings in cozy private cabins at the foot of the Rockies. Home-cooked meals are served in the rustic lodge. There are planned programs for some weeks on topics such as Indians in Life and Legend, Montana Grizzly Bears, Nature Photography, Mammal Tracking, a dinosaur dig or Naturalist Tours of the Rockies, with daily treks into Montana mountains and prairies. This is also a wonderful spot just for the serenity and the chance to hike mountain trails, ride a horse, observe wildlife, or read a good book beside the heated pool. The Tensleep Preserve also offers weeks of family adventures and birding in the Bighorns.

For international "tours" sponsored by the Nature Conservancy, see page 130.

FOUR CORNERS SCHOOL OF OUTDOOR EDUCATION

P.O. Box 1029, Monticello, UT 84535; (435) 587-2156 or (800) 525-4456. (I–M)

This exceptional program offers a variety of backcountry explorations in the beautiful Southwest that includes the chance to learn about archaeology or rock art, to dig for dinosaurs, to track peregrine falcons and bald eagles, to study plants with an herbalist, or to learn Navajo weaving. Some programs include moderate hiking, backpacking,

YEARS IN BUSINESS:	15
AGE RANGE:	15–75
MOST COMMON AGE:	35–55
PERCENT ALONE:	50
NUMBER OF PARTICIPANTS:	375 PER YEAR, DIVIDED INTO SMALL GROUPS
MALE/FEMALE RATIO:	40/60
APRIL TO OCTOBER, PLUS SPECIAL WINTER NATIONAL PARK PROGRAMS FROM MID-JANUARY TO MID-MARCH; GUARANTEED SHARES	

or rafting. Special workshops concentrate on photography and writing. Lodging varies with the program; camping, motels, ranch accommodations, and houseboating on Lake Powell are among the possibilities.

COMMENTS *Female, 40s: I've been on seven trips with them by myself. They're actually responsible for my going back to school and getting my masters in anthropology. I've gone in all four seasons. The groups are small, eight to fifteen, so it's easy to hook up with people and you always get lots of personal attention. Besides the leaders there is always an intern or two who can answer questions or provide extra help if you need it. It's usually 50/50 men and women and ages from 20s to 80s. Many people are by themselves—I always feel comfortable. The food on their river trips is marvelous—I don't know how they do it! The staff are very tuned into the land and the culture of people. They take a very holistic approach to education. I heartily recommend it to anyone and can't wait to go again myself!*
Female, 50s: I've gone on a number of trips, alone and with friends. There are about fourteen in the group, and you're with them all the time so it's easy to get to know everyone. The age range is 20 to 65, slightly more men than women. Most people are by themselves. The program is very well run. The staff are knowledgeable and very helpful about getting people to open up. The guides are chosen very carefully, and they really know their stuff.

OLYMPIC FIELD SEMINARS
OLYMPIC PARK INSTITUTE

111 BARNES POINT ROAD, PORT ANGELES, WA 98363;
(360) 928-3720 OR (800) 775-3720;
WWW.OLYMPUS.NET/OPI (I)

YEARS IN BUSINESS:	11
AGE RANGE:	30–60
MOST COMMON AGE:	40–50
PERCENT ALONE:	70
NUMBER OF PARTICIPANTS:	10–15 PER CLASS
MALE/FEMALE RATIO:	50/50
MAY TO OCTOBER	

The lovely setting on majestic Lake Crescent in the mountains of Olympic National Park adds to the pleasure of these weekend courses covering many aspects of the nature, art, and culture of the region. Nature classes look at birds, butterflies, plants, and marine life. Cultural offerings include Northwest Native American art, traditional plant uses, and hands-on wood carving in the Northwest Coast tradition. Other possibilities explore painting, storytelling, and photography. Participants stay in cabins nestled in a grove of fir trees; each one has a small common area with four adjacent sleeping rooms. Guests are automatically paired. Everyone shares meals at the historic Rosemary Inn, a rustic lodge built by craftsmen at the turn of the century.

COMMENTS *Male, 50s: I've been there many times and I always go alone—it's a very warm and friendly place. Most people are from the Pacific Northwest, but there's always some from all over the country, with diverse backgrounds and a big age range. There are usually eight to twelve in a group, about 25 percent male, and only a third are traveling with someone else, so you never feel like you're the only person there alone. The staff are excellent hosts, making sure everyone feels a part of things. They're also very knowledgeable about the park. The professors who teach the courses are all experts in their fields. I'd definitely recommend this to people traveling alone because you bond with the group almost immediately and become unified. All the people I've encountered are very warm and outgoing.*

Female, 60s: I've gone there seven times, alone all but once, and I always have an excellent experience. I've done programs that are more seminars, and I've done purely travel trips, too. The instructors are experts and have a real interest in the ecology of the area. I feel very safe with all these instructors. I've been on outdoor trips with other operators, and they're not as well run. You feel at home here immediately. The food is all organic and natural and extremely fresh. Everyone cares about the ecosystem of Olympic Park and wants to study and preserve it. I've formed lasting friendships.

Other national parks offer classes similar to the Olympic Park workshops. Among these are:

DENALI INSTITUTE

P.O. Box 67, Denali National Park, AK 99755;
(907) 683–2290. (E)

Guaranteed shares; singles will be matched with roommates on request. Three- and four-day programs for about thirty-six participants are offered each summer, with lodgings at North Face Lodge or Camp Denali, deep in the heart of the park, each with accommodations for 35 to 40 guests. These are the only accommodations from which you can look out at the snow-clad peaks of the Alaska Range and Mount McKinley. Programs include birds, tundra ecology, natural sciences, and nature photography and art as well as guided backcountry hikes, canoeing, cycling, or fishing.

THE YELLOWSTONE INSTITUTE

P.O. Box 117, Yellowstone National Park, WY 82190;
(307) 344-2294. (I)

Workshops emphasizing the wilderness areas of the park are offered year-round. Classes are small (ten to fifteen students) and can run from two to five days. Classrooms are headquartered at many locations in the park, including the historic Buffalo Ranch in the quiet, unpopulated Lamar Valley in the northeast part of the park, where roaming herds of wildlife are so abundant that the area has been nicknamed the "Serengeti of North America." For courses at the Lamar Ranch, lodging is available in heated log sleeping cabins at a nominal fee. There are also a fully equipped central kitchen, bath, and classroom building. For their locations, students arrange their own accommodations in park lodging. Backpacking and horsepackaing seminars are also offered.

YOSEMITE FIELD SEMINARS

Yosemite Association,
P.O. Box 230, El Portal, CA 95318;
(209) 379-2321. (I)

Some 1,000 participants each year attend these seminars, taking in many aspects of the park's ecology and beauty, from studying the stars to tracking wildlife to photography and painting. Backpacking and hiking are also offered. Besides the superb surroundings, directors say people come to meet people, have fun, and to feel safe in a wilderness environment. They add that many people come alone. High-country programs require camping; some programs include reserved lodging in the park and dining; others require making your own arrangements.

ROCKY MOUNTAIN SEMINARS

ROCKY MOUNTAIN NATURE ASSOCIATION,
ROCKY MOUNTAIN NATIONAL PARK, ESTES PARK, CO 80517;
(970) 586–0108. (I)

Eighty-plus one- to three-day workshops include photography, art, geology, tracking mammals, butterflies, and moths, Rocky Mountain flora, mushrooms, herbs, grasses, and other natural and cultural history topics. Students make their own lodging and meal arrangements.

....

N a t u r e   T o u r s

Nature tours offer advantages you could not enjoy on your own. They go to remote areas where getting around can be difficult and where required arrangements often are not easily made from home. The trips have been researched to take advantage of the seasons and make the best use of limited time. They provide the benefit of a knowledgeable guide to answer questions and enrich your experience. And you will also learn from other members of the group, who tend to be interested in and knowledgeable about the natural world. While these tours come with a high price tag, they are often less expensive than trying to duplicate the trip yourself.

Selecting a nature tour involves some of the same issues that you must consider with any tour—the reliability of the company and good references from past participants. But when you choose a tour operator, also remember the issues of ecotourism. Find an operator who has been working for a long time in the country you will be visiting, who knows and cares about the local culture, and who uses local guides and services whenever possible. Find out how guides are trained. Ask about conservation issues and what the company does to minimize its impact on the environment. The background material participants receive often provides a good test of the operator's attitude and sense of responsibility. The best operators send information on cultural traditions and the environment as well as clothing tips and reading lists. Companies listed here have shown their commitment to the environment.

QUESTERS TOURS AND TRAVEL, INC.

381 Park Avenue South,
New York, NY 10016;
(212) 251-1044 or (800) 468-8668; www.questers.com (EE)

This company offers a host of tours accompanied by naturalists whose knowledge of the areas greatly adds to the experience. Culture is part of the focus; at Machu Picchu, for instance, the architecture and the history of the Inca city are studied along with the birds and wildflowers of the area. Other destina-

Years in business:	25
Age range:	25–80
Most common age:	55–70
Percent alone:	45
Number of participants:	varies
Male/female ratio:	20/80
Year-round; will try to arrange shares; if cannot, will absorb the single supplement	

tions include Hawaii, Alaska, the western United States, Mexico, Costa Rica, Belize, South America, Africa, Scotland, Turkey, Australia, New Zealand, the Himalayas, and much of Asia.

COMMENTS *Female, 40s: I've gone on seven trips alone. About half the participants come by themselves. The age range is 20 to 80, and there are more women than men. They are from all over the world. Most come to get away from it all, to get back to nature. On some trips there has been a lot of free time; on others everything is group oriented, but you are always free to do what you want to and pursue whatever aspect of the area interests you. There is a lot of driving through wonderful scenery, but this is definitely not the usual sightseeing tour.*

Female, 70s: I've taken many tours, but these are the best. I've returned ten times and find many people who go again and again. There is a good mix of singles and couples; most of the singles are women. The group is always highly intelligent—this kind of trip does not attract duds—and it is easy to make friends. The tour leaders are excellent and informative.

VICTOR EMANUEL NATURE TOURS, INC.

2525 Wallingwood Drive, Suite 1003,
P.O. Box 33008, Austin, TX 78764;
(512) 328-5221 or (800) 328-8368;
www.ventbird.com

Years in business:	26
Age range:	20–85
Most common age:	55–70
Percent alone:	40
Number of participants:	10–16 per group
Male/female ratio:	40/60
Year-round; will try to arrange shares	

"Some of the best birding experiences of my life have been on Victor Emanuel Nature Tours," said no less an authority than the late Roger Tory Peterson, the author of so many definitive bird and nature guides and a onetime VENT guide. This is the largest company in the world specializing in birding tours, and their trips guarantee compatible company for birders. They cover the globe, from Alaska and Australia to Africa and the Amazon, moving with the seasons to follow the good weather. Rates vary according to destinations, with U.S. trips the least expensive.

COMMENTS *Female, 60s: I went on my first birding trip with this group after my husband died over ten years ago, and the experience was so positive, I've gone back regularly ever since, traveling to wonderful locales including Russia, the Far East, Brazil, and Bhutan. On the last trip there were eight men and four women, lots of them alone. Even many married people come alone because their spouses aren't into birding. Most are over 50. The guides are excellent and I highly recommend this company, but you must be interested in birding—it's almost all we do. We do look at other kinds of nature, but there are no cities or sight-seeing on these trips.*

AMERICAN MUSEUM OF NATURAL HISTORY DISCOVERY TOURS

Central Park West at 79th Street,
New York, NY 10024–5192;
(800) 462-8687 or (212) 769-5700. (EE)

Years in business:	40+
Age range:	depends on program
Most common age:	50 and up
Percent alone:	10–15
Number of participants:	6 to 120
Male/female ratio:	40/60
Year-round; will try to arrange shares	

You need only browse the catalog of this outstanding museum to appreciate the tremendous range of exciting tours available to explore the natural wonders and cultures of the world. Some sixty tours a year cover the greatest wildlife regions and archaeological sites around the globe, always with the finest teams of scientists, educators, and expedition leaders. The choices range from the Seychelles and Madagascar to the South Pole, from Indochina to the Amazon. While cruise and land programs comprise most of their offerings, train trips are also available and include the national parks of the west, the ancient silk road through China and central Asia, and southern Africa by rail. Luxurious African tented safaris are also on the museum's extensive list. Operators are chosen for their proven reputation and commitment to responsible tourism. Though the majority of these trips are expensive, the museum has recently increased its number of affordably priced tours. All are high quality with outstanding educational programs.

COMMENTS *Female, 60s: I've been on five trips. I went to Africa and climbed a mountain to see gorillas, took a fabulous trip to Antarctica, cruised in Asia. I went alone on most of these trips. They are wonderful. There are lectures and daily updates on your itinerary and what you're going to see the next day. You always feel well informed. I love their cruises—it's always open seating at meals, and they'll seat you at a table if you're shy about it—everyone gets to know each other before you're through. All are interesting, wonderful people from all over and all sorts of backgrounds. I'd say a quarter to a third are alone, always more women than men, and an age range from 20s to 80s. It's a relaxed, informal, and easy experience—a great way to travel.*

Other Nature Tours

Other responsible, experienced, nature-oriented tour operators include:

- **The Nature Conservancy,** (see page 121). Worldwide trips to exotic desti-
nations such as Belize, Bolivia, the Galápagos Islands, Indonesia, Mexico,
Panama, and the Sea of Cortez.
- **World Wildlife Fund Travel Program** 1250 24th Street, NW, Washington
DC 20037; (202) 778–9683; www.worldwildlife.org

Tours and voyages to destinations where wildlife viewing is prime, including
Africa, India, Antarctica, Florida's Everglades, whale watching in Baja
California, and viewing winter wildlife in Yellowstone.

- **Geo Expeditions,** P.O. Box 3656, Sonora, CA 95370; (800) 351–5041.
Small groups visit Africa, India, Nepal, Indonesia, South America, or
Australia.
- **Quark Expeditions,** 980 Post Road, Darien, CT 06820; (203–656–0499 or
800–356–5699; www.quark-expeditions.com). A wide variety of tours but
specialists in Arctic and Antarctic travel.
- **Southwind Adventures,** P.O. Box 621057, Littleton, CO 80162;
(303–972–0701; www.southwindadventures.com). Specialists in South
America.

....

Darwin's World: Cruising the Enchanted Galápagos Islands

None of the photographs and none of the shipboard briefings can prepare you for the fantastic reality of the Galápagos, an extraordinary configuration of islands formed by the peaks of million-year-old volcanoes. Isolated some 600 miles off the coast of Ecuador, the Galápagos are unusual in their lava-scarred landscapes as well as their tame wildlife. This is an enchanted world where rare birds and animals that have never been hunted by predators accept human visitors as just one more of nature's species—no more to be feared than a passing bird.

Who lives here? Birds like none you've ever seen. Blue-footed boobies stand a foot and a half high, with feet and legs the color of a clear summer sky. Masked boobies, eyes framed in black, cluck over their tall, fuzzy chicks. Flapping albatrosses, graceful oystercatchers, and exotic lava herons all but pose for the photographers who furiously snap camera shutters in their midst.

In the Galápagos, you'll go swimming with sea lions, step around two-foot-long iguanas, examine bright-red sea crabs, and exclaim at the giant turtles that give the islands their name. Still present are the finches that fascinated Charles Darwin—evolved into thirteen distinct species, each with a beak shaped for most efficiently obtaining its food. Forty-five percent of the plants here are found nowhere else in the world, including the amazing Opuntia cactus that has evolved into a strange and sturdy tree. No matter how much film you bring it won't be enough.

To visit the Galápagos, you must travel to Guayaquil, Ecuador, and board a cruise ship or a sailing yacht. For someone traveling alone, the best bet is the *Santa Cruz,* run by Metropolitan Touring, Ecuador's leading tour company. The most comfortable of the ships, it accommodates ninety passengers. Excursions to the islands are in small boats, each holding only about twenty people, so you will soon be friends with your fellow passengers, marveling together at what you have seen.

As noted in a number of write-ups above, many excellent ecotourism companies schedule cruises to the Galápagos Islands, but the largest company handling this destination (and all of Ecuador) is Metropolitan Touring Galápagos Cruises c/o Adventure Associates, 13150 Coit Road, Suite 110, Dallas, TX 75240; (800) 527–2500 or (972) 907–0414; www.ecuadorable.com.

Sources for Expedition Cruises

One excellent source for a number of expedition cruises is the DISCOVERY Tours program run by the American Museum of Natural History (see page 128). The Nature Conservancy also includes Caribbean and Amazon nature cruises on its travel agenda (see page 130).

Other top operators who run some of the cruises described above as well as a host of others from the Arctic to the Amazon include:

SOCIETY EXPEDITIONS

2001 WESTERN AVENUE, SUITE 300, SEATTLE, WA 98121;
(800) 548-8669 OR (206) 728-9400; WWW.SOCIETYEXPEDITIONS.COM

OCEANIC SOCIETY EXPEDITIONS

FORT MASON CENTER, BUILDING E, SAN FRANCISCO, CA 94123;
(415) 441-1106; (800) 326-7491; WWW.OCEANIC-SOCIETY.ORG

LINDBLAD SPECIAL EXPEDITIONS

720 FIFTH AVENUE, NEW YORK, NY 10019
(800) 397-3348 OR (212) 765-7740; WWW.EXPEDITIONS.COM

ABERCROMBIE AND KENT

1520 KENSINGTON ROAD, OAK BROOK, IL 60523;
(800) 323-7308 OR (630) 954-2944; WWW.ABERCROMBIEANDKENT.COM

SWAN HELLENIC CRUISES, C/O ESPLANADE TOURS

581 BOYLSTON STREET, BOSTON, MA 02116;
(800) 426-5492 OR (617) 266-7465.

OVERSEAS ADVENTURE TRAVEL

(PAGE 93)
HAS A SEPARATE CATALOG DEVOTED TO EXPEDITION CRUISES.

CLIPPER CRUISES, 1ST CULTURAL TOURS and INTRAV

(SEE PAGE 183)
ALSO HAVE NATURE TOURS AMONG THEIR OFFERINGS.

S a f a r i !

Joining a safari to see the big game in East Africa was a longtime dream come true for me—but the reality outdid even my fondest fantasies.

Nothing you've read or seen in picture books can prepare you for the deep emotion that wells up on viewing these magnificent creatures at close range, living in their own environment. It is a jolt of joy and wonder that fills the senses and goes straight to the heart.

Strangers soon become close friends on safari because of this shared emotion and the excitement of the trip. It makes no difference whether you are on your own or with a companion. You are all fellow hunters, intent on prowling the national parks and game preserves, ready to aim your binoculars and shoot on sight with your camera.

The targets are ever-changing. Lightning-swift cheetahs stalk graceful gazelles. A pride of lions sleeps in the sun. Hordes of dizzily striped zebras, big and small, graze in the grasses. Giraffes bat their eyelashes and nibble daintily at the treetops. Thousands of wildebeest stand around like a congregation of bearded old men. Herds of elephants trumpet and splash in a water hole. A family of rhinos stares out like giant, nearsighted Mr. Magoos. Every day, every park holds a new discovery.

The trip is easy for a single traveler because every detail is handled for you. From the moment you are met by a tour representative in your arrival city, you are part of a carefully attended group. There seemed no common denominator for the people who chose this trip, except that they all could afford the high price. The majority of those I met at the lodges were over age 50, but there were younger people as well, and even an occasional family who had brought young children to share the adventure.

While no physical exertion or danger is involved, safaris do mean tiring and difficult travel. The distances between parks are great. Rutted roads are often unpaved, sending up dust or mud, depending on the weather. We were out by 6:30 A.M. many mornings, since the animals are most active just after daybreak, and we often drove for hours searching for the bigger game. No one could stay awake much past 10:00 P.M. The thrill is worth it all.

In Kenya, the best known park is the Masai Mara Game Preserve at the northern tip of the Serengeti Plains, where literally millions of animals graze and hunt. In two days in this park, we spotted more than thirty species of animals and untold numbers of exotic birds.

Other parks have their own specialties. Lake Nakuru is known for huge flocks of pink flamingoes, Amboseli for its large herds of elephants. Samburu Game Reserve, in northern Kenya, has its own species of zebras and giraffes with marking different from those to the south. At Treetops, you stay up late to watch animals congregating outside at a softly lit water hole. At the Mount Kenya Safari Club, the place made famous by the late actor William Holden, you'll have a break—a day spent relaxing in luxury, dining sumptuously, and coming back to find that the logs in the fireplace in your room have been lit for you.

After a fabulous week in Kenya, we were unsure as to what more could possibly be waiting for us in Tanzania. The answer was simply the most spectacular animal watching in the world.

Ngorongoro Crater, an inverted volcano, is one of the wonders of the world, a veritable Noah's ark. In Kenya, we had driven long stretches searching for the elusive big animals. Here, the naturalist guide who drove us down by jeep had only to say, "Now we'll look for the lions," and there they were. Then, "Here's where the rhinos stay"—and there they were.

Serengeti National Park, with its huge numbers of animals, is overwhelming in its beauty and richness. A recent census counted a quarter of a million gazelles, an equal number of zebras, another quarter million of other species including cheetahs, lions, and other predators, and well over a million wildebeests.

Even the smallest of the national parks, Lake Manyara, was rewarding, with its amazing variety of animals owing to the topography that ranges from lush jungle to flat plains. One sight here fills you with amazement—lions that climb the trees in order to nap undisturbed by the park's large herds of elephants.

We were worried about lodging when we crossed the border into Tanzania. Kenya is relatively prosperous and, with over a million visitors a year, has learned how to provide safari guests with creature comforts.

Important Questions to Ask Before You Choose a Safari

- *How long has the company been in the business?*
- *Is Africa their main destination or just one of many?*
- *Are departure dates guaranteed regardless of how many people sign up?*
- *How large is the total group? (More than twenty-five is unwieldy; less than fifteen is ideal.)*
- *Will you be guaranteed a window seat in your van? Will you have a naturalist along in addition to the driver-guide?*
- *Does the company employ local people?*
- *Are its guides and drivers trained by environmental experts?*
- *What airline will you fly and where will you stop en route? (All airlines make a stop in Europe. Changing planes in Amsterdam is an advantage because Schiphol Airport is easy to navigate and it is a quick and inexpensive train ride into town if you have several hours to spend.)*
- *Will you have day rooms during the stopover between Europe and Africa, or simply wait around at the airport?*
- *Where will you stay when you land in Nairobi? (The Norfolk is the great old hotel.)*
- *Is the operator a member of the U.S. Tour Operators Association?*
- *Most important—can they furnish firsthand references from travel agents and recent former passengers?*

Accommodations were not so different from rustic park lodges in the United States. But Tanzania is poor and undeveloped, and we had been warned to expect difficult living conditions.

"Difficult" meant that we lacked hot water at times and the electricity might be turned off from midnight to 6:00 A.M. Still, the beds were comfortable, and every room had a private bath. I've had worse accommodations in Yosemite Park. The striking architecture and scenic locations of the lodges were a wonderful surprise. True, the food left much to be desired, but when the main course did not please, there were plenty of fresh vegetables and rolls to fill in.

For me, the extraordinary animals made a few inconveniences more than worthwhile. In fact, if I could return to only one country, Tanzania is where I would choose to go.

My experiences were in only two countries; safaris are also available in South Africa and several other African nations. Safaris are expensive, but they are a once-in-a-lifetime experience. Start saving.

Choosing a Safari

There are many operators offering safaris that vary in price, from budget trips via open trucks with nights spent in sleeping bags to trips that include comfortable vans and accommodations and the services of skilled guides. Deluxe tours such as those sponsored by the Smithsonian Institution add the services of a naturalist. Some of most luxurious trips are the tented safaris, where the cooks pride themselves on turning out remarkable fare over the campfire.

Wildlife is abundant and weather is mild year-round in East Africa, but the "long rains" period from late March through May is not a good time for animal viewing. The big herds of the Serengeti are in Tanzania in the winter months and in Kenya from mid-July to September.

To compare trip costs, look at the actual days spent on safari. Tours that spend extra days in Nairobi may sound like more time for your money, but bed-and-breakfast accommodations in a city are not the point of an African trip. The most important consideration is a guaranteed window seat in your van.

Among the better-known operators specializing in safaris are:

ABERCROMBIE AND KENT, INTL.

1520 KENSINGTON ROAD, SUITE 111, OAK BROOK, IL 60523;

(800) 323–7308 OR (630) 954–2944; WWW.ABERCROMBIEKENT.COM

YEARS IN BUSINESS: 30+.

A & K MAINTAINS ITS OWN OFFICES AND STAFF IN KENYA AND TANZANIA. (EE)

UNITED TOURING INTERNATIONAL, INC.

1 BALA PLAZA, SUITE 414, BALA CYNWYD, PA 19004;

(610) 617–3300 OR (800) 223–6486; WWW.UNITEDTOUR.COM.

YEARS IN BUSINESS: 50+

THIS NAIROBI-BASED COMPANY IS THE LARGEST TOUR OPERATION IN AFRICA, WITH OFFICES
THROUGHOUT THE CONTINENT AND A WIDE VARIETY OF OFFERINGS. (M–EE)

PARK EAST TOURS

1841 BROADWAY, NEW YORK, NY 10023;

(212) 765–4870 OR (800) 223–6078. WWW.AFRICAPARKEAST.COM (EE)

YEARS IN BUSINESS: 30+

THIS TOUR COMPANY DOES TRIPS FOR THE ASPCA, AN EXCELLENT RECOMMENDATION FOR THEIR
EMPHASIS ON CONSERVATION. OFFERINGS INCLUDE MODERATE AND LUXURY ITINERARIES. SAFARI
PARTICIPANTS RECEIVE A YEAR'S SUBSCRIPTION TO *ECO-TRAVELER* MAGAZINE.

BORN FREE SAFARIS AND TOURS

12504 RIVERSIDE DRIVE, NORTH HOLLYWOOD, CA 91607;

(800) 372–3274; WWW,TRAVELON.COM (E–EE)

YEARS IN BUSINESS: 20+.

A WIDE RANGE OF PRICES, A GUARANTEE OF NO MORE THAN SIX PASSENGERS PER VEHICLE, AND
SOME UNUSUAL OPTIONS SUCH AS A DINE-AROUND PLAN AND SAFARIS THAT INCLUDE WALKING
MAKE THIS OPERATOR WELL WORTH CONSIDERING.

VOYAGERS INTERNATIONAL

(SEE PAGE 167)

SCHEDULES PHOTOGRAPHIC SAFARIS AS WELL AS NATURAL HISTORY SAFARIS.

SAFARICENTRE

3201 NORTH SEPULVEDA BOULEVARD, MANHATTAN BEACH, CA 90266;

(310) 546–4411 OR (800) 223–6046; WWW.SAFARICENTRE.COM

THIS AGENCY SPECIALIZES IN SAFARIS ALL OVER THE WORLD. THEY WILL ADVISE YOU ON APPRO-
PRIATE TRIPS FOR YOUR INTERESTS AND BUDGET.

Get Into Shape: The Spa Vacation

The Spa Philosophy

IMAGE A VACATION THAT SENDS YOU HOME SLIMMER, trimmer, free of stress, and full of energy. That's just what you can expect from a visit to a spa, a healthy vacation experience that is gaining a growing group of advocates from both sexes. Because spas provide a *you*-centered vacation that is dedicated to making you look and feel better, they are perfect for solo travelers, and a large number of guests choose to come alone.

Forget about the old "fat farms." Today's spas are really health resorts, geared as much to the over-stressed as the overweight. Exercise means hiking or tennis as well as calisthenics, and, until you've tried it, you won't believe that a low-calorie diet that can be so satisfying.

A week at a spa is designed to show how quickly the results of regular exercise and healthy eating can be seen in your measurements and morale. And to make up for the ache of unaccustomed exertion, you get wonderful pampering messages and other rewards to ease away the pain.

Spa vacationers pay premium prices for their daily regimen of 1,000 to 1,200 calories and enough exercise to burn them off. Yet advocates declare it is a worthwhile investment. For along with a week or two of healthy living, a good spa aims to give a lifetime bonus—education and inspiration for a healthier life-style when you return home.

At a good spa, guests can learn, often for the first time, exactly how their bodies function—how they react to stress, inactivity, different types of exercise, and different types of food. One of the most important benefits is finding out how to eat well without gaining weight. For those who have talked about exercising without doing anything about it, a spa can be a motivation center, reinforcing good intentions and generating lasting new attitudes and behaviors.

Good-natured sharing of the agonies of sore muscles and longings for forbidden treats creates a common bond among guests that quickly cements friendships. Many guests who meet at spas plan future visits together.

For men who fear that spas are still mainly for overweight women, a pleasant awakening may be in store, since the opposite is often true today. People who come to spas tend to be those who are fit or want to be. They are usually people who take care of their bodies.

Along with exercise, many spas offer stress-control techniques to keep you calm, collected, and better able to stick with your good intentions back home. Many have a holistic slant, including meditation, t'ai chi, and similar techniques. You can take part or not, as you wish.

Most spas will try to match you with a roommate to help hold down the cost.

The Spa Routine

A typical spa day begins with a brisk walk before breakfast. There is a choice of exercise classes, which are spaced throughout the day. The exercises include a balanced mix of aerobics, workouts for body conditioning, and stretching and yoga for both strength and relaxation. Aquatic workouts frequently are part of the routine, turning exercise into fun and games in the pool. Many spas have weight machines and special muscle-building and stretching sessions just for men, accommodating the increasing number of male guests.

Between the workouts come the rewards: soothing messages, relaxing whirlpools, saunas, and steam baths that erase tension and aches. A variety of treatments is offered. Facials, hydrotherapy massage (done in a tub using soothing streams of water), and herbal wraps (mummy-like wrappings of scented moist sheets that draw out body impurities, soften the skin, and relax the muscles) are among the choices. Attendants report that many men whose macho upbringing made them reluctant to try these treatments discover they have been missing out on some of life's nicer luxuries and immediately sign up for repeats.

There is also plenty of time for a leisurely lunch—and a dip in the pool or an hour in the sun with a good book.

Although strong alcohol and fattening hors d'oeuvres are definitely not part of the regimen, some spas do allow a glass of wine at dinner, and many have pleasant pre-dinner "mocktail parties" that offer sociability along with sparkling water, carrot sticks, and surprisingly tasty low-calorie dip. All the food, in fact, is a pleasant surprise. The menus are sophisticated and cleverly served so that every meal has an appetizer, salad, main course, and dessert. While portions are small, wily spa nutritionists know that after four courses most people do not feel deprived.

Evenings include speakers, how-to hints for stress reduction, tips on establishing good health habits at home, or talks and movies just for entertainment. A number of spas now offer workshops in biofeedback and other behavior-modification techniques.

A week's stay is recommended to get the full benefit of a spa. Some warn you when you arrive that day three typically is a day of muscle soreness and doubts for those unaccustomed to exercise. Each day following, however, finds you feeling better—about your body and yourself.

Choosing a Spa

Although the basic programs at spas are similar, the ambience can vary as much as the price range, which runs the gamut from a few-frills $1,000 to a luxury $4,000 a week.

At the top of the scale, and the ultimate spa experience, according to many people, is the Golden Door in Escondido, California, with serene Oriental decor and a staff that outnumbers the guests by 3 to 1. Reflecting current trends, the former all-female spa now offers special weeks for men. Cal-a-Vie is another super-luxury retreat limited to twenty-four guests, each lodged in their own villa-style cottage. Weeks for men only are available here as well.

At the other end of the spa spectrum is the coed Ashram, also in California, described by one recent guest as "a boot camp without food." The raw-food diet and rigorous regimen designed to test guests to the limit of their physical endurance may not be everyone's cup of herbal tea, but those who survive declare it almost an existential experience, and many do return.

Some spas are permissive, leaving it to guests to decide how much or how little activity they want to participate in. Others expect you to maintain a schedule, figuring that if you wanted to loll by the pool, you would have chosen a different vacation.

Locations of spas vary. Some are in the middle of a city; others are in the middle of nowhere. Some are part of a larger resort; others are independent operations. And there are still traditional spas that are for women only.

When you compare costs of spas, be sure to note how many massages and beauty treatments are included; some fees sound inexpensive because you must pay extra for these services.

Spa guest references weren't too helpful, since all were raves. After visits to a number of spas, however, I do have recommendations for best bets for single guests.

Choose a destination spa rather than a resort, where many guests are not part of the spa program and you may be eating spa fare in a dining room where others are enjoying steak and lobster.

Pick-of-the-List Spas

At the top of the list of the best spas for single guests are two coed "fitness resorts"—Rancho la Puerta and Canyon Ranch. Both are well known, and each attracts an active, generally fit, and interesting mix of guests. Here is what each has to offer:

RANCHO LA PUERTA

TECATE, BAJA CALIFORNIA, MEXICO (ABOUT AN HOUR SOUTH OF SAN DIEGO; GUESTS ARE MET AT NO CHARGE AT SAN DIEGO AIRPORT);
RESERVATIONS (800) 443-7565; WWW.RANCHOLAPUERTA.COM;
COED; 150 GUESTS; 30 PERCENT MALE. (E–EE)

This rates my first-place vote for tranquillity, beauty, and value. The 3,000-acre complex, filled with flowers and fountains and ringed

The Right Spa For You

Before you decide on a spa, check current magazines for the latest write-ups or browse through a bookstore or library for more comprehensive coverage. Two good book choices are:

- SPA FINDER *(Spa-Finders Travel Arrangements, Ltd., 91 Fifth Avenue, Suite #301, New York, NY 10003; 212–924–6800 or 800–255–7727; www.spafinders.com). Published by a travel company that specializes in spa vacations, this annual magazine-format catalog of fitness spas has short descriptions of more than 200 spas.*
- FODOR'S HEALTHY ESCAPES, *Fodor's Travel Publications, New York.*

Pick several spas whose approach, location, and rates seem to meet your needs. Write for brochures, which will tell you a lot about the philosophy of the spa and its facilities, schedules, and accommodations. It should also tell you whether massages and other services are included in the fee or are extra. It should describe the menu, the number of calories served, whether larger portions are available if you want them, and whether the emphasis is on a balanced diet or a vegetarian menu.

If you still have questions, phone the spa's fitness director. Ask about the number of single guests or male guests if it is a concern to you. Find out whether someone seats you at meals to be sure you have company when you want it. Spa vacations are expensive, so be sure you make the right choice for your needs.

with boulder-strewn mountains, was born in 1940, long before the fitness boom. It remains a find for any world-weary traveler who wants a rejuvenating getaway in lovely surroundings. Guests stay in Mexican casitas decorated with hand-painted tiles and folk art. Accommodations have no phones or television; many have fireplaces, stacked with wood and ready to be lit each night, and each has its own garden.

You do as much or as little as you please here and eat as much as you want—not as hedonistic as it sounds, since the diet is vegetarian and you can hardly avoid losing weight. Eighty percent of the vegetables are grown in the ranch's own organic gardens, and you've never tasted fresher or better. Fish is served twice a week; otherwise main dishes are pastas, lasagnas, Mexican tortillas and beans, and other dishes that belie their calorie count.

The guests are professionals from all over the United States and Canada. The age range is 25 to 65, but because the Mexican location makes this spa a better buy than many of its American competitors, the average age tends to be younger than at more costly spas, and many trim 20s and 30s are around. Everyone arrives on Saturday, making for a cohesive group. By the time you have hiked, exercised, and dined together for a couple of days, you all feel like old friends. The relaxed, friendly, and low-key atmosphere extends to the health and beauty services. You come here for renewal, not expert pampering.

There six of tennis courts, lit for night play, and five separate pools, some very private gyms are set up to allow indoor and outdoor exercising. Most of the lodgings also offer private decks for sunbathing or stargazing. This is the one spa I could imagine coming to for sheer enjoyment, even if I never went near an exercise class.

CANYON RANCH

8600 EAST ROCKCLIFF ROAD, TUCSON, AZ 85750; (800) 742-9000 OR (602) 749-9000; WWW.CANYONRANCH.COM (EE) COED; 250 GUESTS; 35 PERCENT MALE.

The ambience at this first-class facility is charged with energy, even though higher rates are reflected in a slightly older (and often celebrity-studded) clientele. The gyms and the health center are state of the art; the staff is crackerjack; the menu is varied and delicious; and the beauty treatments are first rate. Single guests have the daily option of joining a group table or dining alone. People who come here love it, but while they may recharge, they don't really escape from the real world. Dress can be a fashion parade of designer leotards and sweat suits. Televisions and telephones are very much part of the hotel-ish guest rooms, and there is a fax machine in the office that gets a lot of use from guests keeping up with business.

Canyon Ranch is blessed with wonderful desert and mountain surroundings, but you must board a van to reach the starting points of the hikes. Some people prefer this because it allows for more variety and is more challenging. Hiking is a big part of the program, and special weeks are devoted to it for those who want a more rigorous schedule.

A Life Enhancement Center is a self-contained part of the spa that focuses on helping participants overcome such habits as smoking or overeating. The Behavioral Health Department of the Center uses all the latest techniques, including private counseling, biofeedback, and hypnotherapy.

CANYON RANCH IN THE BERKSHIRES

BELLEFONTAINE, KEMBLE STREET, LENOX, MA 01240; (413) 637–4100 OR (800) 742–9000. (EE) COED; 240 GUESTS; 25 PERCENT MALE.

The location of this newer (opened in 1990) outpost is 120-acre Bellefontaine, one of the great old Berkshire estates. Although not much of the original complex remains, one of the three buildings in the U-shaped complex is the old mansion house, which retains the original library but is otherwise completely changed. It now houses the dining room, health and healing and medical consultation areas. Exercise facilities are in the new, state-of-the-art fitness complex, which includes tennis, squash, and racquetball courts, an indoor running track, indoor pool, all manner of fitness equipment, and exercise rooms as well as treatment and salon facilities. Another pool and other tennis courts are outdoors. Guests stay in the third area. The rooms, like the dining room, are blandly attractive—like what you'd find in an upscale hotel.

Morning walks may be excursions into the village of Lenox, and hikes and other outdoor activities take advantage of the lovely Berkshire countryside. Summertime guests can take advantage of the wonderful seasonal cultural facilities of the Berkshires, including Boston Symphony concerts at Tanglewood. In winter, cross-country skiing is added to the agenda. The services here are first rate, but given a choice, I still find the Arizona Canyon Ranch and its exquisite desert surroundings a more satisfying experience.

....

L u x u r y   S p a s

When you have the wherewithal ($300 per night and up), you might want to choose these ultimate spa experiences:

THE GOLDEN DOOR

P.O. Box 463057, Escondido, CA 92046;

(800) 443-7565 or (760) 744-4222. THIRTY-NINE GUESTS.

Dating back to 1958, the Golden Door's Oriental ambience and tranquil setting are still considered by many to provide the ultimate serene retreat. A staff of 160 caters to the thirty-nine "treasured guests" with niceties such as a daily one-hour massage in your own room and a nightly before-sleep massage. Most weeks are for women only, but several are scheduled for men and for coed sessions.

GREEN VALLEY SPA AND TENNIS RESORT

1871 West Canyon View Drive, St. George, UT 84770;

(801) 673-4084 or (800) 237-1068; WWW.GREENVALLEYSPA.COM

A beautifully appointed spa with a holistic bent, Green Valley's special bonus is the surrounding Utah red rock country, where hiking in locales such as Zion National Park is a joy. The spa offers relaxation, meditation, and nutrition education along with exercise. Singles get a private bedroom and bath in a two-bedroom condo. Golf and tennis lessons are also available. Special rates are offered for mother-daughter guests.

CAL-A-VIE

2249 Somerset Road, Vista, CA 92084;

(760) 945-2055; WWW.CAL-A-VIE.COM. TWENTY-FOUR GUESTS.

Think of a small village in Provence, and you'll have the picture of this retreat shared by two dozen fortunate guests. Located on 150 acres in a secluded valley north of San Diego, the spa houses guests in Mediterranean style tile-roofed cottages filled with hand-carved furniture and pastel floral chintz. Women's and coed sessions are offered.

Good - Value Spas

Finding spas is no problem. They are mushrooming all over the country—so much so that several books are devoted to describing them. What is not easy is finding reasonable prices. Here are a few suggestions:

THE OAKS AT OJAI

122 EAST OJAI AVENUE, OJAI, CA 93023;
(805) 646-5573 OR (800) 753-6257; WWW.OAKSSPA.COM. COED; EIGHTY GUESTS. (I–M)

Fitness and exercise is the forte of director Sheila Cuff, whose California spas in Ojai and Palm Springs represent good value. With plenty of Cuff's vigorous exercise classes and spa cuisine, guests soon feel healthy and relaxed. The spa opened in 1977 in the center of a quaint arts-oriented town about ninety minutes north of Los Angeles. It attracts many young career women, including starlets from the Los Angeles area. About 20 percent of the guests are male. Some 75 percent of the guests come alone.

THE PALMS AT PALM SPRINGS

572 NORTH INDIAN CANYON DRIVE, PALM SPRINGS, CA 92262;
(760) 325-1111; WWW.PALMSSPA.COM. COED; EIGHTY-THREE GUESTS. (I–M)

This sister to the Oaks has a similar program and a similar clientele. It is equally well priced.

COOLFONT

1777 COLD RUN VALLEY ROAD,
BERKELEY SPRINGS, WV 25411;
(304) 258–4500; WWW.COOLFONT.COM. COED; TWENTY-NINE GUESTS. (I)

Part of a low-key resort on 1,300 secluded wooded acres, the relaxed Coolfont spa program is popular with visitors from the nearby Washington, D.C, area. Spectrum of Wellness programs, available in two-, five- or seven-night packages, include a choice of five fitness classes daily, walks and hikes, weight training and exercise equipment, yoga, t'ai chi, and sessions on stress reduction and relaxation. There is a strong emphasis on wellness and holistic education, with many talks and seminars on these topics. There is a special program for those who want to quit smoking.

Spa guests stay in the comfortable resort lodges and dine at group tables in the modernistic Treetop House dining room, with big, wide windows overlooking the lakefront. The restaurant is known for its generous buffets and its emphasis on healthy, low-fat, and low-calorie choices.

NEW LIFE FITNESS VACATIONS

P.O. BOX 395, KILLINGTON, VT 05751;
(802) 422–4302 OR (800) 228–4676. COED; TWENTY-FIVE GUESTS. (M–E)
RUNS MID-MAY TO EARLY NOVEMBER. VERY SMALL SINGLE SUPPLEMENT.

Set in an attractive hotel, the Inn of the Six Mountains on the slopes of Killington mountain, this active program emphasizes mountain hikes, one of the most pleasant ways to exercise. The program also includes exercise classes, weight training, an indoor pool, and a healthful low-fat, high-fiber, high-carbohydrate diet. Massage is included in the fee. The small size of the group makes for a highly personal program monitored to each guest's needs.

NEW AGE HEALTH SPA

ROUTE 55, NEVERSINK, NY 12765;
(800) 682–4348 OR (914) 985–7600. COED; SEVENTY-FIVE GUESTS. (I–M) YEAR-ROUND.

There is a definite holistic emphasis at this well-priced spa set on 165 acres of rolling hills and woodland in the Catskill Mountains. Along with hikes and classes, there are sessions devoted to yoga, t'ai chi, and meditations. A unique feature here is the Alpine Tower, a climbing tower designed to provide extra challenge. A range of optional health consultations and beauty treatments are available. Menus offer seafood or poultry, many vegetarian dishes, and an open salad bar; guests can choose plans from 600 to 1,200 calories daily. Many of the vegetables and herbs are organically grown in the spa's own greenhouse. Mini-van service to this spa is available directly from New York City for a fee.

LAKE AUSTIN SPA RESORT

1705 SOUTH QUINLAN PARK ROAD, AUSTIN, TX 78732: (512) 372–7300 OR (800) 847–5637; WWW.LAKEAUSTIN.COM. COED; EIGHTY GUESTS. (E)

Set on twelve acres bordering a 23-mile lake, the spa has a full range of exercise equipment plus tennis courts, indoor and outdoor pools, and a bonus—hydro-bikes and sculls to take advantage of the lake. Hiking trails wander the surrounding Texas hill country. Mountain bikes are also available. Besides the usual aerobics, shaping and stretch classes, guests are offered yoga, visualization, and meditation sessions. The dining room has lovely views of the lake and offers many fresh vegetables and fruits from the on-site organic gardens. Nicely decorated guest rooms are in cottages on the grounds.

FRANKLIN QUEST INSTITUTE OF FITNESS

202 NORTH SNOW CANYON ROAD, P.O. BOX 938, IVINS, UT 84738; (800) 407–3002 OR (435) 673–4905. COED; 220 GUESTS. (I–M)

This is one of the best buys around, especially for those who want to take advantage of the extensive hiking program in Utah's majestic red rock country. The hikes are an integral part of the spa's noted weight-loss program. Each guest is tested and assigned to supervised programs according to ability. A low guest-to-staff ratio assures lots of personal attention. Facilities include tennis, a fully equipped gym and weight room, and a spa

Spa Traveling Specialists

The popularity of spas has spawned specialized travel agencies that promise to keep up with the field and suggest the right places for varying tastes and budgets. There is no extra charge for their services; in fact, they often can get you a discount because they are favorite sources of guests. They are:

- Spa-Finders Travel Arrangements Ltd., *91 Fifth Avenue, New York, NY 10003; (212) 924–6800 or (800) 255–7727; www.spafinders.com.*
- Spa Trek International, Inc., *475 Park Avenue South, New York, NY 10016; (212) 779–3480 or (800) 272–3480; www.spatrek.com.*

building offering the full range of beauty treatments. Those willing to share quad rooms will enjoy some of the lowest rates of any spa.

Mexican Spas

Though nowhere near the class of Rancho la Puerta, two additional Mexican spa resorts deserve mention because their rates are so attractive for Americans.

RIO CALIENTE

GUADALAJARA, MEXICO; C/O SPA VACATIONS LTD., P.O. BOX 897, MILLBRAE, CA 94030; (650) 615-9543. COED; EIGHTY GUESTS; NO SHARES ARRANGED; SMALL SINGLE SUPPLEMENT. (I)

Located in a secluded pine forest 18 miles from Guadalajara, this small, casual, very rustic hot-springs resort is a bargain. The program includes hiking and hot mineral-water baths, along with horseback riding, relaxing yoga, and massage. Beauty treatments are available, but they are not stressed here. Meals are vegetarian; many of the foods are grown in their own garden. In keeping with the away-from-it-all feeling, there are no televisions or telephones on the premises.

IXTAPAN HOTEL AND SPA

IXTAPAN DE LA SAL, MEXICO, C/O E & M ASSOCIATES,
72 MADISON AVENUE, NEW YORK, NY 10016;
(800) 223-9832 OR (212) 252-1991.
COED; FIFTY SPA GUESTS; NO SHARES ARRANGED. (I–M)

The weekly package includes six massages, six facials, one manicure, one pedicure, and one scalp treatment. Activities include walks, four aerobics classes, five aquatic exercise classes, two yoga sessions, and three golf or tennis lessons. Guests can use the spa dining room, where meals equal 900 calories a day, or the regular resort dining room. Everyone dresses up at night. Concerts and movies provide after-dinner entertainment. Prices are far below similar offerings in the United States, even after you add on airfare. Cars can be arranged to meet guests in Mexico City for the two-hour drive to the hotel.

Join a Tour

I

F YOU'RE DREAMING OF SEEING THE WORLD, YOU'LL FIND that tour companies are in the dream-fulfillment business. They print up shiny brochures showing the world's wonders, which they will gladly wrap up for you in neat packages.

The Up Side

Tour packages offer many advantages. On a prepaid tour, you can sit back and let somebody else take care of all the details of travel. A tour relieves you of the chores of getting around on your own in unfamiliar cities, choosing hotels, deciding where to eat, making restaurant reservations, or planning every day's sight-seeing. You'll never have to worry about transporting luggage or finding your way to a hotel. And if your luggage does not arrive, it's the tour manager, not you, whose job it is to follow through.

Tour buses generally offer comfortable seats and big windows that give you the best views as you travel. Not the least of the appeal of a tour is the cost. Because of the economies of group buying, tours almost always save money over trying to duplicate the same trip on your own. In peak season, the clout of a tour company often ensures room reservations that an individual cannot wangle.

Some tours also offer roommate-matching services to avoid the single supplement, allowing a big saving for solo travelers. Single sojourners also enjoy the advantage of companionship, especially important at mealtime. Most often, a block of tables is reserved for tour members, and a single person would naturally join the other members of the group.

Tours are a natural for a first trip to Europe or for travel in the Orient or the South Pacific where getting along and getting around may seem more complicated than in the Western world. Tours with a special focus such as art or cuisine may appeal to those who have traveled more widely and done the basic sight-seeing.

The Down Side

Despite the many pros of group travel, however, you should not sign on for a tour without understanding the negative points. In exchange for the advantages, you give up the right to set your own schedule. There's a set time that you must leave your bags outside your hotel room door each morning, as well as a designated hour for breakfast and departure—and those times are likely to be early! The average tour is geared to covering as much ground as possible, so you have little opportunity for browsing or lingering. On a typical "Continental Introduction" grand tour, for example, the highlights in one three-day area might include a canal cruise and a chance to see the Rembrandts at the Rijksmuseum in Amsterdam, Cologne cathedrals, a Rhine cruise, Heidelberg, Nymphenburg Palace in Munich, the Bavarian Alps, and a walking tour of Innsbruck—a lot to take in over a short period of time. You get a sampling, never an in-depth view. And sometimes you get more than you can absorb. You know the old joke—"If this is Tuesday, this must be Belgium." It's easy for everything to become a blur on a whirlwind tour.

And while motor coach travel may sound restful, most tours take a lot of stamina. Besides those early departures, there is a lot of walking. Buses are often prohibited from parking in the center of town and are restricted to coach parks. You will get a good bit of exercise just getting to attractions, climbing hills to castles, and following the guides.

Of course, just because you've paid for the full tour doesn't mean that you must climb every hill or see every sight on the itinerary. It's perfectly okay to decline and meet the group afterward. But when the bus is ready to roll, you'd better be on board.

The size of the group also limits your choice of lodgings and restaurants. Intimate inns and cafes cannot accommodate a busload of tourists. So you'll be staying in larger commercial hotels chosen for their ability to handle a group well, and you will frequently be offered fixed menus in large restaurants, unless you want to pay extra to venture out on your own. Gourmet fare is not the rule, except on deluxe tours. Some hotels and restaurants may be better than you expect; the majority will be quite ordinary. Many tours do not include lunch in order to allow you the chance to visit some local places on your own.

You should also be aware that most motor coach tours tend to attract older travelers. According to the National Tour Association, approximately 70 percent of U.S. motor coach tourists are 50 and older. And the number of travelers by themselves is small, seldom more than four or five per busload. That doesn't mean that couples are not good company, simply that it is not realistic to expect a lot of fellow singles. Budget tours tend to attract more singles as well as a larger number of younger passengers; companies that guarantee shares are also more likely to attract people on their own.

Despite these warnings, the makeup of any one tour is unpredictable, and sometimes you can luck out. One single woman I know reported, "I took a Globus two-week tour of the Orient by myself and to my delight had about eight single people between 30 and 55 for companionship, including a few bachelors and widowers—which the brochure definitely did not guarantee."

What about tours designed exclusively for singles? By all means consider them—many people do (See pages 191–205.) But sign on with the advance knowledge that the greater proportion of the travelers is likely to be female. Not only do single women outnumber single men, but they seem more hesitant about striking out on their own. Choose a singles tour as you would any other—because the destination or itinerary intrigues. And don't be surprised or dismayed at the scarcity of male company.

The one element that makes or breaks a tour is the tour director or escort. It is up to the tour director to see that everyone shows up on time, to appease the inevitable grumblers, and to set a tone of goodwill and fun for the group. Ideally, this person should be all things to all people—friendly, outgoing, humane, intelligent, articulate, witty, well informed, and ever tactful. Directors are usually college educated, and those conducting European tours may speak two to four languages. The better established the tour company, the better the chances that you will have an expert tour director.

···

Choosing a Tour

K nowing both the good and not-so-good points of group tours, a little homework in choosing your tour will ensure a more successful trip.

The first consideration is strictly a monetary one. Tours come in three classifications: budget, first class, and deluxe, based on the type of hotels used. Decide on your price range and compare the offerings within it.

You'll also need to choose between general sight-seeing or special-interest tours. Many varieties of specialized tours concentrate on everything from castles to gardens, Mozart to mushroom hunting. These tours most often are deluxe, but if the itinerary is really exciting to you, it may be worth the splurge. A shared interest helps ensure you will find compatible company.

Most group tours are all-inclusive, meaning that they take care of both air and land arrangements, most meals, and an escort. Local guides may be used in each destination, since it is difficult for a tour escort to be an expert on everything. However, the better operators do have one person who stays with the group throughout even if someone else gives the specialized talks. On trips for special-interest groups, particularly those sponsored by museums and universities, the escort is usually also a well-qualified specialist whose knowledge can add a lot to your trip.

Many escorted tours are available also as land packages only, in case you want to combine them with independent travel. Sometimes you can use the group air arrangements from a package and plan your own itinerary.

There are dozens of tour operators, and since each tour may vary in the number of participants and the expertise of the guides, travel agents who use the companies frequently are your best references. Listed here, as a starting point, are a few reliable, long-established tour operators.

Comparing Tours

To evaluate what makes one general tour more desirable than another, gather a number of brochures covering the areas you want to visit and do a bit of comparison shopping. A good travel agent can supply you with plenty of material to get you started, and can tell you which companies have pleased their clients in the past.

Compare the following areas, then consult your travel agent or the tour operator if you have further questions.

- **Cost:** Figure out the cost of each trip on a daily basis by dividing the total price by the number of nights offered. Days are not a safe guide, because many tours start at noon or dinnertime and end with breakfast. Generally, you get what you pay for—higher prices mean better hotels and restaurants.

- **Food:** How many meals are offered? Do you have a choice of selections or are you limited to a pre-selected menu? Are there dine-around options?

- **Accommodations:** The hotels used by the tour should be noted in the brochure. Look them up in a guidebook to find out how they are rated. If the brochure makes up a name for categories, such as "tourist class," find out what that means. Do all rooms have private baths? Are the hotels centrally located? It's nice to be able to take a walk or visit the shops on your own, not so nice to be stuck miles outside the city.

- **Airline:** Will you travel on a regularly scheduled plane or a special charter flight? If a charter, who runs it? Is departure guaranteed or will your flight be canceled if a sufficient number do not sign up?

- **Pace:** How hectic is the program? Do you have time to rest up from jet lag when you arrive at your destination? Look for tours that spend more than one night in a location. Time to catch your breath during the day and free time for shopping or a bit of sight-seeing on your own will be welcome.

- **Group size:** Will there be one, two, or three buses? How many passengers per bus? When tour groups are too large, there are delays getting into hotels and jams at tourist attractions.

- **Reputation:** There are scores of tour operators—a number of whom cancel unfilled trips—or, worse yet, go bankrupt with your money in the till. You should know how long the company has been in business and whether it belongs to the United States Tour Operators Association. That membership means the company has operated for at least three years and has solid

(continued next page)

references. The association sets stringent requirements on insurance, liability, and financial responsibility. For a list of their members, write to the address at the end of this chapter.

- **Guaranteed rates:** This can be a big advantage on trips abroad in case of extreme fluctuations in the value of the dollar.
- **Guaranteed departures:** This is the operator's pledge to run the tour as promised regardless of how many sign up.
- **Fine print:** Read carefully both tour descriptions and the page at the back of the brochure—the one without the pretty pictures—to find out exactly what is and is not included. There are many kinds of limitations. The brochure should be explicit as to exactly what your tour price covers. Membership fees needed to qualify for the trip, refund regulations, trip cancellation and trip interruption insurance, departure taxes, travel accident insurance, and medical payments are among the items that may or may not be covered.

General Tours

GLOBUS & COSMOS

5301 SOUTH FEDERAL CIRCLE, LITTLETON, CO 80123;
(800) 851-0728, EXT. 7518;
WWW.GLOBUSANDCOSMOS.COM. WORLDWIDE.

YEARS IN BUSINESS:	70+
AGE RANGE:	20s–80s
MOST COMMON AGE:	62
PERCENT ALONE:	30
NUMBER OF PARTICIPANTS:	AVERAGES 36–46
MALE/FEMALE RATIO:	MORE FEMALES
GUARANTEED SHARES ON COSMOS	

This long-established company offers tours on every continent except Antarctica in a choice of price ranges. Globus is first class; Cosmos is more budget-minded and has a slightly younger clientele.

MAYFLOWER TOURS

1225 Warren Avenue, Downers Grove, IL, 60615;
(800) 323-7604.

Moderately priced tours around the United States and Canada, including national parks and hosted holidays in cities such as New York, Washington D.C., and New Orleans.

Years in business:	20+
Age range:	50–75
Most common age:	50–60
Percent alone:	20–40
Number of participants:	35
Male/female ratio:	varies
Guaranteed shares	

MAUPINTOUR

1515 St. Andrews Drive, Lawrence, KS 66047;
(785) 843-1211 or (800) 255-4266;
WWW.MAUPINTOUR.COM

Luxury tours to Europe, Asia, Africa, South Pacific, and United States/Canada.

Years in business:	47
Age range:	varies
Most common age:	50+
Percent alone:	25–30
Number of participants:	averages 25
Male/female ratio:	1:1
Will try to arrange shares	

TRAFALGAR TOURS

11 East 26th Street, Suite 1300, New York, NY 10010;
(212) 689-8977 or (800) 854-0103;
WWW.TRAFALGARTOURS.COM

Specializing in European travel, first class, and cost-saver tours.

Years in business:	50+
Age range:	45–70
Most common age:	51
Percent alone:	10–15
Number of participants:	35–48
Male/female ratio:	38/62
Guaranteed room shares	

TAUCK TOURS

Box 5027, Westport, CT 06881;
(800) 468-2825 or (203) 226-6911;
WWW.TAUCK.COM

A family-owned business, now in its third generation, offering luxury tours in the United States and Canada.

Years in business:	73
Age range:	55–70
Most common age:	55–70
Percent alone:	15–20
Number of participants:	40
Male/female ratio:	Entire group, 40/60; among single passengers, 1:9
Will try to arrange shares	

ABERCROMBIE & KENT INTERNATIONAL, INC.

1520 Kensington Road, Oak Brook,
IL 60523;
(630) 954-2944 or (800) 323-7308;
www.abercrombiekent.com

Years in business:	35
Age range:	WIDE
Most common age:	45-60
Percent alone:	40 in U.S., 33 abroad
Number of participants:	12-20
Male/female ratio:	48/52 U.S.; 38/62 abroad

Probably America's best-known operator of luxury tours worldwide, this firm offers top-of-the-line tours including a wide choice of land tours, plus safaris and expedition cruises.

Special-Interest Tours

There is truly a tour for every interest, whether your love is food, wine, sports, cave art, doll houses, bird-watching, or golfing. Because each of these itineraries is unique, references from past participants are the best way to judge whether you want to sign on. Assume that most special-interest tours will fall into the "very expensive" category, unless otherwise indicated. Here are some of the possibilities:

IST CULTURAL TOURS

225 West 34th Street, Suite 1620,
New York, NY 10122;
(212) 563-1202 or (800) 833-2111;
www.ist-tours.com (EE)

Years in business:	18
Age range:	40-80
Most common age:	50s
Percent alone:	VARIES
Number of participants:	20
Male/female ratio:	40/60

Beginning with itineraries for organizations and special groups, IST has expanded to offer tours to the public, promising to go beyond ordinary sight-seeing to give insight into the culture of destinations in France, Austria, Italy, Greece, Turkey, Egypt, Israel, England, the Czech Republic, Hungary, and China. They also offer an interesting cruise program (see page 183).

ARCHAEOLOGICAL TOURS

271 Madison Avenue, Suite 904,
New York, NY 10016;
(212) 986-3054. (EE)

Years in business:	27
Age range:	30–75
Most common age:	50+
Percent alone:	average 30
Number of participants:	24–30
Male/female ratio:	40/60
Will try to arrange shares	

These luxury tour groups are accompanied by expert scholars who stress the anthropological, archaeological, and historical aspects of destinations that include Italy, Greece, Turkey, Israel, Cyprus, Syria, Jordan, Portugal, Chile, Peru, Bolivia, Egypt, Morocco, France, Spain, Guatemala, China, Indonesia, Thailand, Mali, Ethiopia, Tunisa, Belize, Myanmar, Cambodia, and India.

COMMENTS *Female, 30s: I've been on trips to Turkey, Sicily and Italy, Cypress, and Crete. There were many people traveling alone on all. Most were in their late 40s and 50s, and there were more women than men. The program is excellent and very structured, with most of the time spent at dig sites. The accommodations and food were the best available considering where we were.*
Male, 50s: I've been to Sicily, China, and Yugoslavia alone; all were very good experiences. Though the trips are expensive, the group is not just rich people. Many are the people who save up and take a trip every other year. Most were interesting professionals. The destinations are interesting, the itineraries are meticulously planned, and the days are active. I highly recommend it.

ANNEMARIE VICTORY'S DELUXE GOURMET TOURS

136 East 64th Street, New York, NY 10021;
(212) 486-0353. (EE)

Years in business:	26
Age range:	45–70
Most common age:	55–70
Percent alone:	50
Number of participants:	10
Male/female ratio:	40/60
Will try to arrange shares	

Food lovers will find that even reading this catalog is a delicious experience. These ultraluxury tours, limited to ten people, include Italy, Austria, Switzerland, Belgium, Luxembourg, Ireland, France, and Spain. All focus on the finest dining in each destination, but there is also generous time for sightseeing. Recently very upscale biking and hiking trips have been added to the itinerary, along with a gourmet-wine cruise in the Mediterranean and a luxury cruise to the Galápagos Islands.

COMMENTS *Female, 50s: The best of everything—fine small hotels, wonderful food, flowers in your room, the best guides, plenty of free time, never rushed or hectic. On three trips, the average age was 40s to 65; the biggest number of participants was eight. I was often the only person alone, but you eat together and quickly get to know everyone. I can't say enough good things about these trips.*
Male, 40s: We had just four people, ages 46 to 72. Everything was deluxe, the days were varied, the food was superb. It was a wonderful experience.

MOZART'S EUROPE

c/o NEW VOYAGER TOURS, INC.,
DEER LANE, PAWLET, VT 05761;
(802) 325-3656. (EE)

YEARS IN BUSINESS:	15
AGE RANGE:	32–80
MOST COMMON AGE:	40–60
PERCENT ALONE:	50
NUMBER OF PARTICIPANTS:	26 MAXIMUM
MALE/FEMALE RATIO:	35/65
WILL TRY TO ARRANGE SHARES	

Mozart lovers, here are your dream trips. There are three variations of this deluxe two-week grand tour of Mozart's Europe, all including Salzburg, Mozart's birthplace. One itinerary visits the state operas in Vienna, Prague, and Budapest; another includes summer festivals in Switzerland. The third combines the Vienna and Budapest state operas with the Wurzburg Mozart Festival and the Schubertiade in Hohenems, Austria. A new offering, the Mozart/Bach/ Schubert Grand Tour, includes visits to Eisenach, Weimar, Leipzig, Dresden, and Berlin. Many private concerts and demonstrations are performed on the instruments used by Mozart.

COMMENTS *Female, 50s: This trip exceeded anything I've ever done. My group was older than most —from over 60 to 80—with more women than men and only five or six single people. Still, I made lasting friends, and the tour operators are wonderful people who are always available for companionship. The trip goes to all the pertinent Mozart places, to the opera in Vienna and Salzburg. It is a perfect trip for anyone who loves Mozart.*

*Female, 30s: The trip was a mental adventure, a musical dream
come true. Though most of the group was older and married, it was
still easy to be there alone. The people were interesting, and I never
felt left out. I was sent the name and telephone number of my roommate before the trip, so we had a chance to get to know each other a
little bit even before we left. The leader/owners are especially warm
and were like parents to me. The hotels and food were tops, and there
was plenty of time to do what you wanted. This is for anyone who
likes Europe and music.*

INTERNATIONAL TRAVEL PROGRAM

92ND STREET YMCA, 1395 LEXINGTON AVENUE,
NEW YORK, NY 10128;
(212) 415-5599. (E–EE)

YEARS IN BUSINESS:	17
AGE RANGE:	20s–60s
MOST COMMON AGE:	50s
PERCENT ALONE:	80
NUMBER OF PARTICIPANTS:	25–30
MALE/FEMALE RATIO:	25/75
WILL TRY TO ARRANGE SHARES	

This venerable New York cultural institution has an eclectic and adventurous
international travel program. Some examples: Antarctica and the
Falklands, Legendary Galápagos Islands and Ecuador, Chile's Patagonia
and Easter Island, and Tibet and Bhutan: Mountains, Mystics, and
Kingdoms. Domestic trips have included the Spoleto Festival in
Charleston and Country Music in Branson. These tours have some
unique features. Applicants are personally interviewed before being assigned roommates, making for a better chance of congeniality. A meeting
is held in New York before the trip to talk about the destination and give
everyone a chance to meet. There is a minimum of two nights in each
destination. Dinner is not included in the group itinerary to allow participants to try smaller restaurants in each locale. At the end of the day, the
group leader suggests possibilities in a variety of price ranges and sets up
small groups for each, so that you need never worry about dining alone.

COMMENTS *Female, 30s: Most participants were female and from
the New York area, well educated but not necessarily well traveled.
The art-oriented program in France was wonderful, the guides in
Europe superb, and you were free to leave the group if you wanted. In
Paris, for example, I went off on my own. I've always traveled mostly*

on my own, but I found it so relaxing not to have to worry about details, I will probably do it again—with this group. I learned far more about art than I would ever have done alone.

AMERICAN JEWISH CONGRESS WORLDWIDE TOURS

15 EAST 84TH STREET, NEW YORK, NY 10028;
(800) 221-4694 OR (212) 879-4500. (E–EE)

Tours run by the AJC go to Israel and thirty other countries on six continents. Nile cruises and Far Eastern odysseys, Western and Eastern Europe, and Costa Rica are among the many choices. Tour members have a heritage and an interest in Jewish affairs in common. They often meet Jewish residents in other countries and see sights of special cultural or religious interest.

YEARS IN BUSINESS:	40+
AGE RANGE:	WIDE
MOST COMMON AGE:	50+
PERCENT ALONE:	20
NUMBER OF PARTICIPANTS:	25 AVERAGE PER TOUR
MALE/FEMALE RATIO:	1/4
WILL TRY TO ARRANGE SHARES	

COMMENTS   *Female, late 20s: I've been on two trips alone, to Morocco and on safari in Africa, and to Egypt and Israel. I chose a singles trip, so most people were in their 20s and 30s, though all ages were represented. Women outnumbered men, but everyone seemed to be from similar backgrounds and were fairly successful professionals. Everything was great in Egypt and Israel—guides, food, accommodations. In Africa, the guide left something to be desired and the trip was less structured, meaning you had to do a lot more on your own. I highly recommend the Israel trip but have reservations about Africa.*

Male, 30s: I've been on three trips: singles tours to Israel and to Spain and an "adventure tour" with mostly couples. The singles trips average 130 people, so you can't get to know everybody, but you are divided into tour buses, and you do become very friendly with the people on your bus. Two-thirds of each group was from New York, and women always outnumbered men. I enjoyed the adventure trip because it was less structured than a guided bus tour. These trips aren't like the "love boat"–people are there to travel with others their

*own ages and with similar interests, not to look for a partner. The
group leaders are very good, and I would recommend the tour to
anyone.*

Following is a sampling of other special-interest tours:

ARTS SEMINARS ABROAD
UNIVERSITY OF WISCONSIN–MADISON

610 Langdon Street, Room 721, Madison, WI 53703;
(608) 263–6736; www.dcs.wisc.edu/lsa/travel   (E)

Offered by UW–Madison Department of Liberal Studies and the
Arts in cooperation with UW–Extension, this varied program com-
bines travel abroad with arts-oriented events such as the Edinburgh
Festival or Carnival in Trinidad. Several tours take in U.S. cities, from
New York to Santa Fe. The prices are more reasonable than many univer-
sity-connected programs, but there is a hefty single supplement.

HISTORY AMERICA TOURS

5920 West Plano Parkway, Suite E5, Plano, TX 75093;
(972) 713–7171 or (800) 628–8542; www.visi.net/historyamerica   (I–M)

From the American Revolution to Custer's Last Stand, this group visits
the sites of the greatest moments in American history, with a histo-
rian guide to provide in-depth background to bring the events to life.
Many trips have a low single supplement.

INTERNATIONAL DINING ADVENTURES

106 Lynn Street, Seattle, WA 98109;
(800) 447–6080 or (206) 281–8880. (EE)

Food lovers can learn about as well as sample the cuisines of Spain,
Italy, France, and Thailand or the Cajun cooking of New Orleans.
Singles who book at least ninety days in advance are guaranteed shares.

COOPERSMITH'S ENGLAND

P.O. Box 900, Inverness, CA 94937;
(415) 669–1914. (EE)

Tours of Britain, Europe, and New Zealand, featuring gardens, art and architecture, and lodging in stately homes, castles, and villas.

THE ITALIAN CONNECTION

194–3803 Calgary Trail South, Edmonton, Alberta, T6J 5M8 Canada;
(403) 438–5712; www.italian-connection.com (EE)

Walking, cultural, and culinary tours for small groups, including dinners in the homes of Italian friends.

EXPO GARDEN TOURS

70 Great Oak, Redding, CT 06896;
(800) 448–2685; www.olympus.net/gardens/expotour (EE)

England's Chelsea Flower Show, Holland at Tulip Time, and the world's largest roses in New Zealand are among the destinations sure to appeal to gardeners and flower lovers.

Photography Tours

Tours oriented to photography provide plenty of time and opportunity for bringing home great pictures. Inexperienced photographers setting out on a tour that promises instruction and critiques should be sure that other novices are along. It is also well to know the ratio of participants to tour leaders to be sure you will receive personal attention. You should also get references from people who have traveled with your particular leader. Great photographers may or may not be great travel guides.

CLOSE-UP EXPEDITIONS

858 56th Street, Oakland, CA 94608;
(510) 654–1548 or (800) 457–9553. (EE)

These small-group photographic adventures range from seven to twenty-five days and are paced for good photography. Itineraries are planned to take advantage of best light; early morning and late-day shootings sometimes alter mealtimes or call for picnics in a

YEARS IN BUSINESS:	19
AGE RANGE:	35–75
MOST COMMON AGE:	60s
PERCENT ALONE:	65
NUMBER OF PARTICIPANTS: 5–12	
MALE/FEMALE RATIO:	1:1
WILL TRY TO ARRANGE SHARES; SUITABLE FOR ALL LEVELS	

field. Recent foreign destinations have included Costa Rica, New Zealand, Australia, Burma, Turkey, Venezuela, Guatemala, Paris, Provence, Italy, Switzerland, and England. In the U.S., trips have covered the Southwest, Colorado, Death Valley, Alaska, Yellowstone, and Yosemite.

COMMENTS *Male, 30s: I found the prices a little high and did not consider the leader a good naturalist. However, this was a relaxed holiday, not rushed like other photographic tours I have taken, and the trip was well organized. The group was about equally male and female, with most traveling by themselves.*

Male, 30s: The age range of my group to Costa Rica was from 35 to late 60s and 70s, and about half were single. The program is well run and good for a beginner wanting to learn something new on vacation. The food and accommodations were fine. You have the freedom to do what you want, though it is generally a group situation because of the locale—you can't go off by yourself at night in the Coast Rican rain forest!

VOYAGERS INTERNATIONAL
P.O. Box 915, ITHACA, NY 14851;
(800) 633-0299; WWW.VOYAGERS.COM (M)

YEARS IN BUSINESS:	16
AGE RANGE:	35–70
MOST COMMON AGE:	55+
PERCENT ALONE:	50
NUMBER OF PARTICIPANTS: 11 PER GROUP	
MALE/FEMALE RATIO:	50/50
GUARANTEED SHARES	

"Images of Ireland" is the title of a tour offered eight times annually between April and October to appreciate and capture on film the beauty of western Ireland. The group is led by Ron Rosenstock, who has thirty years of experience as a photography instructor. Voyagers, which plans trips for many universities and museums, also holds photographic and cultural trips to Italy, photographic safaris to Africa, and a variety of other interesting programs, including nature-oriented trips to Indonesia, Africa, Costa Rica, and the Galápagos Islands.

MACRO TOURS AND PHOTO WORKSHOPS

1145 CHURCH STREET, SAN FRANCISCO, CA 94114;
(800) 369-7430 OR (415) 826-1096 (M)

YEARS IN BUSINESS:	16
AGE RANGE:	35–75
MOST COMMON AGE:	40–60
PERCENT ALONE:	90
NUMBER OF PARTICIPANTS:	10–12 PER WORKSHOP
MALE/FEMALE RATIO:	1/3
GUARANTEED SHARES	

From two days in California Wine Country to a week in Maine, Nova Scotia, or Bryce and Zion National Parks, director Bert Banks and his instructors work individually with participants to improve their artistic eye and photo techniques. Their "classrooms" are some of the loveliest parts of America at their most photogenic: California in spring when wildflowers are in bloom, Vermont with foliage in glorious autumn technicolor. Travel is by van; lodging is in motels, inns, or condos. Lunch is often a picnic in the field; everyone joins for dinner at a local restaurant.

COMMENTS *Female, 30s: I've been all over the country with this group, both alone and with friends. All were great trips. They structure the day so that you get to see and photograph things at the peak time for light. The whole trip is a group experience. You eat all your meals together, and you are together all day so you really meet everyone. The groups are about ten to fifteen people, and 90 percent are alone, so it's a very comfortable situation. Ages ranged from 30s to 70s. There are more women than men on most trips, but I've been on one where I was the only woman. It's very safe, and you have the security of the group. Sometimes meals are included, but it is usually just breakfast so the group goes out for lunch and dinner together. Accommodations vary by the trip. The instructors are very good, helpful, and happy to answer all your questions. You get all levels of skill. I'd recommend this to anyone who is interested in seeing and photographing beautiful places at the right time and in the right light!*

There are many photo tour advertisements in photography publications such as **Modern Photography** *or* **Popular Photography,** *and extensive listings can be found on the Internet under www.shawguides.com.*

....

Museum- and University-Sponsored Tours

Some of the best special-interest tours are organized by museums, universities, and college alumni groups. Although generally quite expensive, they are also usually superior and may provide exceptionally knowledgeable escorts. Part of the cost often is considered a tax-deductible contribution.

To find such trips, start with the groups either in your own city or nearby large cities. You may also want to contact some of the following large institutions:

SMITHSONIAN INSTITUTION

c/o SMITHSONIAN STUDY TOURS,
1100 JEFFERSON DRIVE SW, MRC 702, WASHINGTON, D.C. 20560;
(202) 357-4700; WWW.SI.EDU/TSA/SST (EE)

The Smithsonian has a long roster of both U.S. and foreign tours each year, accompanied by experts on nature, folklore, architecture, gardens, wildlife, theater, and many other special interests.

AMERICAN MUSEUM OF NATURAL HISTORY DISCOVERY TOURS

CENTRAL PARK WEST AT 79TH STREET, NEW YORK, NY 10024-5192;
(800) 462-8687 OR (212) 769-5700. (EE)

The museum offers tours of the world's greatest wildlife regions, cultural centers, and archaeological sites, with museum scientists and expert lecturers. (Also listed under nature, page 128.)

NEW YORK BOTANICAL GARDEN, EDUCATION DEPARTMENT

Bronx, NY 10458–5126;

(212) 220–8700. (EE)

Gardens are the focus, but sight-seeing is also included in the tours of this fine organization.

NATIONAL TRUST STUDY TOURS

1785 Massachusetts Avenue N.W.,

Washington, D.C. 20036; (800) 944–6847 or (202) 588–6300.

WWW.TOURSNTHP.ORG (EE)

Tours are to areas around the world known for their well-preserved architecture.

For more information on tours, consult these two organizations:

NATIONAL TOUR ASSOCIATION

546 East Main Street, Lexington, KY 40508;

(606) 226–4444 or (800) 755–TOUR; WWW.NTAONLINE.COM

This group offers free information on packaged travel and a list of more than 630 members in the United States and Canada. They also provide advice on avoiding travel scams.

UNITED STATES TOUR OPERATORS ASSOCIATION

342 Madison Avenue, Suite 1522, New York, NY 10173;

(212) 599–6599; WWW.USTOA.COM

This group issues a free list of its member companies, including details of programs and destinations. It also offers pamphlets on how to read a tour brochure and select a package tour.

Avoiding Travel Scams

The National Tour Association urges travelers to be wary of unreliable or dishonest tour operators. Here are some of the group's tips on playing it safe.

- If you work with a tour operator, make sure that the company offers a consumer protection plan.
- Use a credit card to purchase tickets, and if cash must be used, always get a receipt—everything must be in writing.
- Verify that the tour company has errors and omissions, professional liability insurance—all professional tour companies have this coverage.
- Ask for a reference from a client with whom you are familiar.
- Avoid high-pressure sales tactics with a limited time to evaluate the offer.
- Beware of companies sending a courier for a check, requesting a direct bank deposit, or demanding a certified check.
- Decline offers requiring a property sales presentation.
- Prior to payment, review complete details about any trip in writing.
- Request specific hotel and airline names, addresses, and phone numbers—broad terms such as "all major hotels" and "all major airlines" are a warning flag.
- Insist on a local phone number if given a toll-free number—this will establish that the tour company or travel agency has a central office from which it operates.
- Never use 900 numbers.
- If you receive a vacation certificate in the mail, take it to a respectable tour operator or travel agent who can evaluate it.
- Call the National Fraud Information Center (800–876–7060), or local and state consumer protection agencies to report all incidences of travel-related fraud.

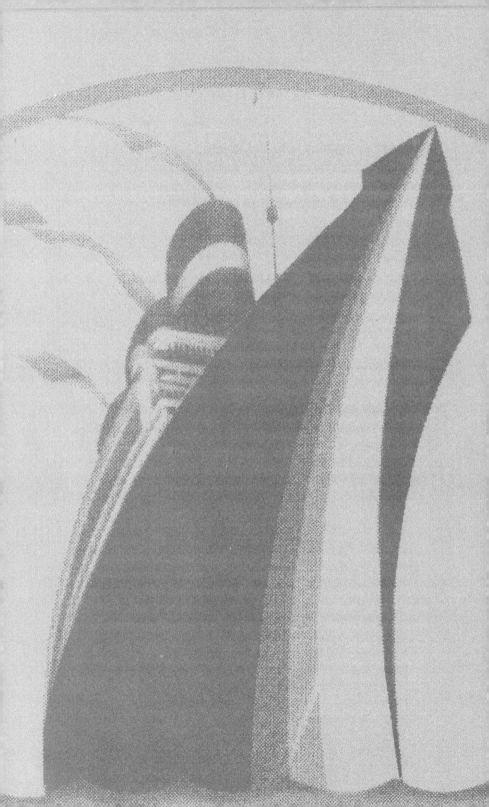

Go to Sea

AYBE YOU DON'T WANT AN ACTIVE VACATION AT ALL.
Maybe what you'd really like to do is lie back and soak up
some sun. Or maybe you can't decide. You'd like to relax,
but you'd also like the excitement of seeing new places.

Cruises offer the best of two worlds—the chance to travel while you
enjoy the pleasures of resort life at sea. The new superliners really are
floating resorts, with a lineup of activities ranging from exercise classes
and trapshooting to lectures, dance lessons, contests, and the chance to
strike it rich in the casino. And few resorts can match the menus on a
cruise ship, where something is being served almost nonstop from 7:00
A.M. until that fabled midnight buffet.

Best of all, these are resorts where you will never lack for company at
dinner.

Ship travel is also safe, easy, and convenient. Accommodations, activities, entertainment, and lavish meals are all part of one package price,
often even including transportation to the port of departure. And you can
travel to a number of new places on one vacation without the hassles of
making plane connections or dealing with luggage. No matter how many
ports you visit, once you unpack, you need never face a suitcase again
until you head home.

Recent changes in the cruise industry offer more good news for single
people. No longer catering only to the wealthy or to older travelers, many
cruise lines have updated their facilities and programs, shortened their
itineraries, widened their offerings, and whittled their costs to appeal to a
much wider audience—including singles. According to statistics from
Cruise Lines International Association, single passengers represented 25
percent of the passengers signing on for cruises between 1993 and 1998.

A Singular Dilemma

It is only fair to warn, however, that a cruise vacation by yourself does present some special challenges. In spite of the increase in numbers, singles remain a definite minority on most cruises. On a recent sailing aboard one of Carnival Cruise Line's "fun ships," which attract more single passengers than many other lines, the number who showed up for a get-acquainted singles mixer was less than 150 out of about 1,400 people on board—and the women outnumbered the men 10 to 1. Only a few other cruise lines, including Royal Caribbean and Norwegian, make the effort to hold an event for singles on board.

The overabundance of females may be welcome news if you are a male, but therein lies the dilemma for women. After dinner, couples naturally couple up. Evenings on shipboard are romantic, particularly on the nights when everyone dresses up for dinner, and it isn't much fun to be alone. Yet that's exactly what you may be, and you should know it in advance. If you are a female who will feel like a wallflower without a dancing partner, don't go on a cruise by yourself. If, however, you can enjoy the pleasures of days at sea and be content to watch the evening's entertainment and then maybe read a good book at night, cruising is for you.

Meeting and Mingling

With all those couples around, cruising is a situation where you really want to find compatible single company, even just a good buddy of your own sex. The new cruise liners keep getting bigger and bigger, and it is harder to meet people on an enormous ship. On a large ship, it takes a little luck and a lot of effort because it is easy to feel lost on ships with more than 1,000 passengers.

The only people you see regularly each day are those at your dinner table, so your seating assignment is crucial. Ask to be placed at one of the largest tables, which usually seats eight, to increase your chances of meeting people you'll want to spend time with. And request the second, or later, seating. The first seating tends to attract those who are early to bed, and because the dining room must be cleared ahead for the next sitting, there is little time for lingering over conversation.

If you are not happy with your table, ask to have it changed—and do it right away.

Persistence and an outgoing attitude are needed to search out the other unattached passengers on board a big ship. Even on ships that hold a singles mixer, if you don't connect at that early gathering, there are no set places afterward to meet the other single passengers on board. To better your odds of meeting people, sign up for lots of daytime activities. Women should not be afraid to try the bar, which is easy and comfortable to do on a ship. A piano bar is often a particularly pleasant gathering place.

Florence Lemkowitz, a veteran cruise writer, suggests that it is a mistake to go to bed early the first night at sea if you want to meet people, since that's just when other solo travelers are probably checking the scene with the same thought in mind. The first night is the best night to visit the ship's lounges and bars, she says, before people give up on them because nobody seems to be around. She also recommends telling the social director that you want to make friends, putting him or her to work on your behalf.

One regular cruiser I know makes up little cards with her name and cabin number. These are not meant to serve as invitations to drop in. Ships' cabins have telephones, and, on a large ship a card ensures that the new acquaintances will know where to call if they want to get together. You can't just assume you will run into one another again.

Recognizing the lack of dance partners, several lines have gone out of their way to make things pleasanter for single women at night. "Gentleman hosts" are now provided by a growing number of cruise lines, including American Hawaii, Celebrity, Commodore, Norwegian, Premiere, Regal, Royal Olympic, and Silversea. Congenial single men in their 50s and 60s are invited to come along as hosts to dance with unaccompanied women, attend cocktail parties, act as a fourth for bridge or a partner in dance class, or sometimes just serve as someone to talk to. These men, mostly retired, are carefully screened for both sociability and dancing ability. Forget about romance, however; they receive explicit instructions to mingle, with no favoritism allowed to any one passenger or group.

If you are a male who would like to apply, contact the employment office of the cruise line that interests you. Just remember this isn't a restful vacation; dancing every dance takes a lot of energy.

One solution to the cruising dilemma is to go with a group. A company that makes this possible is Majestic Sun Tours, 5975 South University Drive, Davie, FL 33328; (954) 252–8888 or (800) 995–7245 (www.majesticsun.com). This company organizes some two dozen cruises for singles each year, booking blocks of space aboard regularly scheduled sailings on lines such as Carnival, Royal Caribbean, and Celebrity. Each group has its own tour director, dines together, enjoys separate activities as well as participating in the ship's recreation, and does its own shore excursions. Group members are paired to avoid the single supplement. This solves the problem of single company, but not the male/female ratio, since women make up the majority of these groups.

Boarding the Right Ship

If the lack of romance does not deter you, you can concentrate on the other pleasures of being at sea. And these are plentiful. There's nothing quite like the sense of freedom you feel standing on a breezy deck and gazing at the limitless horizon—or the excitement of watching a new port loom ever closer into view.

With a group or on your own, your first decision when planning a cruise should be based on which ports you most want to visit, and that depends a lot on the season. In winter, the Caribbean is by far the most popular destination. The eastern ports of the Bahamas, Puerto Rico, St. Thomas, and St. Martin are the most frequently chosen because they are easily reached on seven-day cruises from Florida. Close seconds are Jamaica, Cozumel, and Grand Cayman. Cruises out of San Juan go farther afield to western Caribbean islands such as Barbados, Guadeloupe, Martinique, St. Lucia, or Antigua. These harbors are less crowded with cruise ships and for that very reason are more appealing to many people. These itineraries are particularly appealing when the fare to San Juan is included in the price. Hawaiian cruises are also popular with single cruisers.

In summer, Bermuda is a convenient port of call in the east, while

Alaska's Inside Passage, with its ice-blue glaciers and some of the continent's greatest scenery, makes for an unforgettable and increasingly popular cruise in the West. Unlike many trips where you see very little from port to port, the views of Alaska from shipboard are often so engrossing that many passengers need no other daytime entertainment than watching the show from their deck chairs.

If you have the time and the fare, there are also wonderful itineraries to South America, the Mediterranean, the Greek Islands and Turkey, the South Seas, and Asia, and a number of exciting and exotic expeditions to remote regions of the world. In fact, there's almost no place on earth you cannot happily explore on a cruise.

One problem you rarely have to consider any longer is seasickness. Today's giant ships are remarkably stable, and there are plenty of over-the-counter remedies such as Dramamine available as an extra safeguard. Choose a cabin close to amidships and near the waterline for the least amount of motion. And relax, knowing that if all else fails, the ship's doctor is ready with an injection that will quickly put you back on an even keel.

Getting the Best Deal

Once you have decided where you want to go, your next dilemma is choosing among the many companies offering similar itineraries. The makeup of passengers will vary from week to week, but here are a few general guidelines.

Your age may narrow your choices. Generally, longer and more luxurious cruises attract older passengers and many retired people. Three- and four-day cruises to the Bahamas and Freeport from the East Coast and to Baja California from the West Coast tend to attract younger passengers. Seven-day Caribbean trips are perfect winter vacations for all, and they get a good mix of people.

If you are worried about gaining weight from the nonstop meals on a cruise ship, you can choose from many ships with extensive fitness centers and daily exercise classes. Some even offer spa cuisine.

Theme cruises are a boon for single passengers because they have a focus. These are regular sailings with the customary itinerary of ports, but with special guests and entertainment on board to provide a drawing card. The singles percentages on these cruises may be no higher, but the chances of meeting people who share your interests probably will be.

Knowledgeable travel agents and cruise specialists will know about these offerings, which vary each year. Some of the specialty choices in the past have included jazz festivals, guest Cordon Bleu chefs, photography instructors, and themes from natural history to soap operas to sports. There are now cruises aimed at golfers, bridge players, wine and art connoisseurs, opera and film lovers, and Civil War buffs.

The nationality of the crew can affect the ambience of the ship. Greek cruise line operators such as Royal Olympic are known for warmth, for example. Individual ships in a company's fleet may differ in size as well as personality. Read a comprehensive guidebook to cruises to learn more about specific vessels you are considering.

The best guide I've seen is Kay Showker's *Unofficial Guide to Cruises*. She not only describes the good and bad points of each cruise line but tells you the kind of passengers you are likely to find aboard. And she gives in-depth descriptions of accommodations and amenities on each ship in the line.

For singles, Showker recommends smaller ships: "It is easier to mix, and the staff takes greater care to ensure that you are part of the ship's social life," she says. Among smaller ships, she advises that expedition and educational cruises are the best choices. "A camaraderie develops quickly among passengers who share common interests and a certain sense of adventure," she points out. "For single women, the number of unattached men is likely to be higher than on traditional cruises."

The Single Supplement

One of the big deterrents to cruise travel for singles is cost. Cruise lines impose surcharges anywhere from 110 to 200 percent of the double rate if you want to occupy a cabin alone. The policy for singles is always stated in the ship's brochure, but pricing varies considerably on each line according to the season. Special deals for singles may be offered when a cruise is not fully booked, another good reason to use a cruise specialist who is up-to-date on pricing.

Some companies do give more of a break to solo passengers. Here are some of the more favorable options.

Guaranteed rates

A guaranteed single rate means you pay a set price, usually with a modest added supplement, and the cruise line assigns your cabin at the time of departure. You don't get a choice of rooms, but you do have privacy. You could wind up in the least desirable cabins, but since the cheapest and the most expensive cabins usually sell out first, your chances are good of getting a decent mid-range accommodation. If you don't travel in high seasons, such as winter in the Caribbean, you may even luck out with a nice outside cabin.

Below are cruise lines offering a guaranteed fare at press time; be sure to check current information since policies do change. Other lines may offer these rates for cruises with light bookings even if the catalog does not say so, so be sure to ask.

NORWEGIAN CRUISE LINES

95 MERRICK WAY, CORAL GABLES, FL 33134; 800–327–7030; WWW.NCL.COM

Popular-priced cruises to the eastern and western Caribbean, the Bahamas, Mexico, South America, the Panama Canal and Hawaii, Europe, Bermuda, New England, Canada, and Alaska. Many theme cruises focus on music—jazz, country & western, magic, big bands, and rock—and sports, including basketball, hockey, baseball, and football.

ROYAL CARIBBEAN CRUISE LINE

9035 SOUTH AMERICA WAY, MIAMI, FL 33132; 305–379–2601.

Popular-priced cruises to the Caribbean, Bermuda, Alaska, and the Mexican Riviera.

SEABOURN CRUISE LINE

55 SAN FRANCISCO STREET, SAN FRANCISCO, CA 94133, 415–391–7444 OR 800–527–0999.

Small, luxurious ships with understated elegance; no tipping allowed, you can even have twenty-four-hour room service. Itineraries include Southeast Asia, the Panama Canal, the Caribbean, South America, the Mediterranean, the Baltic, Alaska, Africa, New England, and Canada.

Single supplements can be as low as 10 percent on certain cruises, and the line is said to take special care of solo passengers. You'll be paying top dollar, but little penalty for being single.

SILVERSEA CRUISES

110 East Broward Boulevard, Fort Lauderdale, FL 33301, 800-722-9955.

Small, ultra-luxurious ships, all suites with ocean views, wine and drinks included in the fare, offering cruises to Europe, the Mediterranean, South Africa, South America, Canada, America's East Coast, the Caribbean, the Far East, and the South Pacific. On some sailings suites are available for 110% of the double rate.

HOLLAND AMERICA LINES

300 Elliott Avenue W., Seattle, WA 98119; 206-281-3535 or 800-426-0327.

Upscale cruises to the Caribbean, the Panama Canal, Alaska, the Mediterranean, Northern and Western Europe.

Comparing Rates

To compare prices of similar cruises, divide the total cost by the number of full days on board. Arriving in home port at 8:00 A.M. hardly counts as a day at sea. In calculating the cost of any cruise, remember that you must figure at least $7.50 per day for tips. The recommended sums are $3.00 per day for room stewards and waiters, $1.50 for busboys. If you order drinks or use the barber shop or beauty salon, figure a 15 percent tip on each tab. Tips for shipboard personnel who provide special services are at your own discretion.

If you plan to take group tours ashore, be sure to include that cost in your calculations, as it can be considerable. The more ports, the more added expense.

To save money booking a cruise, you are better off reserving very early or very late. Early birds get advance booking discounts. Since the advent of so many new mega-ships with huge capacities, some lines are offering better pricing for single passengers who are willing to wait until 30 to 60 days before the sailing date for confirmation. And some offer standby fares for those who will take unfilled space close to the sailing date.

For this reason, passengers are wise to deal with a travel agent who specializes in cruises and is up-to-date on all the current possibilities. Larger cruise specialists also can frequently offer their own discounts, passing along the reductions they get from the cruise lines for being favored customers who buy space in bulk.

Dealing with someone who is familiar with the industry will also give you an edge in choosing a ship where you will be happy, regardless of the price. Single passengers come in all demographics and tastes, as do any other cruise passengers. A company such as Carnival has become the largest afloat by going after first-time cruisers who may have little travel experience. They offer lots of participatory activities and costume parties (such as male beauty contests for husbands wearing their wives' nightgowns). These are right on target for many of their passengers, who thoroughly enjoy the high jinks. But sophisticated travelers may prefer a more conservative ambience, even if the tab is higher. Paying extra usually means getting better food as well.

Among the knowledgeable agencies that specialize in cruise travel and also offer discounts are:

WORLD WIDE CRUISES

8059 WEST McNAB ROAD, FORT LAUDERDALE, FL 33321;
(954) 720-9000 OR (800) 882-9000; WWW.WWCRUISES.COM

A good bet for solo travelers, this company has a special Singles Desk and a computerized roommate-matching service devoted to serving single passengers.

THE CRUISE LINE INC.

150 NW 168TH STREET, NORTH MIAMI, FL 33169;
(800) 777-0707; WWW.CRUISELINE.COM

This company publishes a free magazine, *World of Cruising*, with cruise news, tips, and listings of current discount offerings.

CRUISES, INC

5000 CAMPUSWOOD DRIVE, EAST SYRACUSE, NY 13057
(800) 854-0500; WWW.CRUISESINC.COM

Another cruise specialist, this company publishes *The Cruise Directory*, with descriptions of ships and listings of special discount rates.

Agencies offering discounts on late bookings are:

- SPUR OF THE MOMENT CRUISES, (800) 343-1991 OR (310) 521-1070.
- POST HASTE TRAVEL; (800) 881-7690 OR (954) 966-7690.

Whichever cruise you choose, you are putting out a sizable sum, so don't fail to protect yourself with travel insurance. Read the regulations carefully: The two important things to cover are the cost of your fare if you must cancel or the cruise is interrupted, and the potentially large cost of major medical expenses away from home, especially in an emergency that would require evacuation from the ship. Almost all cruise lines offer insurance, as do travel agencies and independent insurance companies, so compare prices.

If you are traveling to an area that your own health insurance does not cover, you may need supplemental medical insurance as well. You will find more on travel insurance on page 314.

Kay Showker offers another word of warning: Always pay for a cruise with a credit card. If you go through a travel agency, see that the charge is run through the cruise line's account rather than the agent's, protecting you in case the agency should go under with your money in the till. Paying with a credit card also allows you to cancel payment if the cruise is not provided as promised.

Other Cruises

Large cruise ships are not the only way to go to sea. Check out the interesting and offbeat itineraries offered by smaller ships sailing scenic waters at home and abroad.

CLIPPER CRUISE LINE

7711 Bonhomme Avenue, St. Louis, MO 63105,

(800) 325-0010; www.clippercruise.com

Clipper's three ships, the *Yorktown Clipper* (138 passengers), the *Nantucket Clipper* (100 passengers), and the *Clipper Adventurer* (122 passengers) cover a wide range of territory. Destinations include the Caribbean, Costa Rica,. Panama, South America, Prince Edward Island, Alaska's Inside Passage, Mexico's Sea of Cortez, Western Europe, Antarctica, the Baltic, Scandinavia, the British Isles, Greenland, the Northwest Territories, and closer to home, Florida and the Great Lakes. Onboard naturalists and historians play an important role in enhancing the enjoyment of the places visited.

INTRAV

7711 Bonhomme Avenue, St. Louis, MO 63105; (800) 456-8100 or (314) 727-0500; www.intrav.com.

The owners of the Clipper Cruise Line detailed above, INTRAV also publishes a catalog, *Special Editions,* detailing upscale small ship cruises offered on chartered ships from other lines. Destinations range from the Baltic to the Sea of Cortez in Mexico. River cruises run the gamut from the Nile and the Rhine to China's Yangtze. Many can be combined with land tours. Historians and naturalists are on board to enhance the experience.

IST CULTURAL TOURS

(See page 160)

The company publishes a separate catalog, *Beyond Cruising,* detailing small-ship voyages on sailboats, riverboats, and barges. The ships charge a flat rate for singles. You may pay more than the double rate, but you have a choice of cabins and guaranteed privacy. The owners report that many singles, especially older women, are frequent passengers, enjoying the informal and inclusive atmosphere of the ships.

DELTA QUEEN STEAMBOAT COMPANY

30 ROBIN STREET WHARF, 1380 PORT OF NEW ORLEANS PLACE, NEW ORLEANS, LA 70130;
(800) 543–1949 OR (504) 586–0631.

This line keeps alive the 150-year-old tradition of cruising the Mississippi River through the heartland of America on picturesque steam-powered paddle wheelers. The 138-passenger *Delta Queen* is listed on the National Register of Historic Places. Her sister ships, the *Mississippi Queen* and *American Queen,* are larger, accommodating more than 400 passengers. Three- to fourteen-day cruises sail from New Orleans, Memphis, St. Louis, and St. Paul on the Mississippi River; from Louisville, Cincinnati, and Pittsburgh on the Ohio River; from Nashville on the Cumberland River; Chattanooga on the Tennessee River; and Galveston on the Intracoastal Waterway. This is a nostalgia trip, offering an ambience of homespun, old-fashioned Americana. Though the average passenger is over 50, all ages seem to enjoy these leisurely, relaxed journeys. Old-fashioned entertainment such as Dixieland jazz and barbershop quartets and many festive special events (such as the Great Steamboat Race, the Kentucky Derby cruise, or Cajun Christmas celebrations) keep things lively. The line offers a guaranteed share program and has gentlemen hosts to keep the ladies happy on the dance floor.

KD RIVER CRUISES OF EUROPE

2500 WESTCHESTER AVENUE, PURCHASE, NY 10577;
(914) 696–3600 OR (800) 346–6525 IN THE EAST
AND (800) 858–8587 IN THE WEST; WWW.RIVERCRUISES.COM   (E–EE)

Small ships of about 100 passengers sail the Rhine, the Moselle, the Seine, the Danube, and other beautiful European rivers from April to November. Daily stops are in the great cities of the continent as well as smaller towns and countryside you might otherwise miss. Rates are reduced by 15 percent in April and May and 10 percent in July, which can be delightful times to travel. KD has a 25 percent supplement in many room categories.

EUROPEAN WATERWAYS

140 EAST 56TH STREET, NEW YORK, NY 10022;
(212) 688–9538 OR (800) 217–4447; WWW.EUROPEANWATERWAYS.COM

A placid, comfortable way to see Europe is along its waterways, with congenial small groups and plenty of time to sightsee at each stop. The barges cruise at about 4 miles per hour, so it's easy to get off and bicycle, walk, or jog along towpaths or go into nearby villages and catch up with the ship at its next stop.

The company arranges trips on rivers and canals in France, Holland, England, and Ireland.

Freighter Cruises

If you have the time for long voyages, freighter travel is an adventurous way to visit foreign ports at a reasonable cost and in surprising comfort. Many retired people and teachers and others with long vacations sign on. Trips may range from twenty to seventy days.

Most cargo vessels accommodate no more than twelve passengers, so the experience is very personal. Staterooms are spacious and have views, and, unlike cruise liners, many freighters have large, single cabins. This is travel for the self-sufficient, for there are no shipboard activities and evening entertainment usually means conversations, cards, and games. Rates may average as little as $100 a day, including meals shared with the ship's officers. Passengers may also use the lounge and deck. Possible destinations include Australia and New Zealand, the Norwegian coast, South America, the South Pacific, Africa, Europe, and the Orient.

To learn about freighter travel, contact

TRAVELTIPS CRUISE AND FREIGHTER TRAVEL ASSOCIATION

163–07 DEPOT ROAD, P.O. BOX 580188, FLUSHING, NY 11358;
(800) 872–8584 OR (718) 939–2400.

A modest membership fee is credited toward the first voyage. Members receive the *TravLtips* magazine, which includes firsthand accounts of other members' journeys. These stories provide great armchair adventures. There is also a listing of upcoming freighter itineraries as well as discounts on special-value regular cruises. A free pamphlet is available, answering many questions about freighter voyages.

Sailing Cruises

The best bet if you are looking for single company on a ship is to board a sociable, no-frills windjammer sailing cruise, where many passengers are unattached. (See page 108 under Adventure Vacations for more details.) A more luxurious option is

WINDSTAR CRUISES
300 ELLIOTT AVENUE WEST, SEATTLE, WA 98119;
(206) 281-3535 OR (800) 258-7245; WWW.WINDSTARCRUISES.COM

The beautiful tall-masted luxury sailing yachts of this company accommodate 148 passengers and attract sophisticated, active individuals ages 25 to 65. Destinations include the Caribbean, the Mediterranean, Costa Rica, the Greek Isles, and Italy's Amalfi coast. These trips are less expensive than you might expect, but singles do pay a 150 percent supplement.

Also note that Club Med now has its own sailing ship—the world's largest.

Cruise Expeditions

Small ships that are able to get off the beaten path to such exotic locales as Antarctica, Africa, Polynesia, Micronesia, Melanesia, and Indonesia offer exciting excursions for adventure-minded travelers. These trips are expensive, but they are also once-in-a-lifetime experiences. Since the numbers of passengers are small and the visits are thrilling, the groups quickly become close, making these seemingly remote excursions very easy to enjoy on your own. Some of my most memorable travel experiences have been on expedition cruises. Operators report that many passengers come by themselves.

The following are among the great expedition cruises I can personally recommend:

Cruising the Nile

A trip on the Nile is an unforgettable experience, offering a chance to see life on the banks of the river and to visit the astonishing ruins and the tombs of the pharaohs with expert guides. The narrow ribbon of gentle river allows a close-up view of village life while at the same time providing a graphic illustration of the Nile's importance—beyond the border of green irrigated by the river, barren desert begins.

Longer cruises begin in Cairo; shorter ones begin in Luxor or Aswan (reached by plane from Cairo). The major sights lie between the cities. Sight-seeing stops include the Temple of Luxor and the awesome ruins of the Temple of Karnak as well as the Valley of the Kings, where the tombs of Tutankhamen and other pharaohs were found; you will also see the Valley of the Queens and the Tombs of the Nobles, which contain some of the most important art of ancient Egypt.

Besides the many international expedition cruise companies, a number of local Egyptian operators run cruises, as do the major Cairo hotels. Among the most popular operators for Americans are familiar names such as Sheraton and Sonesta. The best source for current Nile options is MISR Travel, 630 Fifth Avenue, New York, NY 10111; (212) 332–2600 or (800) 223–4978.

The Coastal Express: Cruising the Fjords of Norway

The ads call this "The World's Most Beautiful Voyage," and it's hard to argue as you cruise along Norway's breathtaking coastline. Wending into steep and narrow fjords, gliding past glaciers, farms, and fishing villages and crossing the Arctic Circle, the Coastal Express fleet goes where larger cruisers cannot venture. Although cabins are comfortable and newer ships in the fleet are a bit more luxurious, these are not ordinary cruise ships. They are working cargo ships, the vital lifeline for the hardy fishermen and farmers in the more remote northern villages along the coast. As they pick up and deliver mail, supplies, and passengers at thirty-five towns and villages along the way, the ships provide a true close-up look at local life. Talks on board tell a lot about the country and its people.

The sail is all the more fascinating because the panoramas change daily on the way to "the top of the world." From the home port of Bergen to Kirkenes at the end of the line, trees give way to Arctic tundra, mountains to flats, and depending on the season, the light may change from night and day to all night or all day. The music of Edvard Grieg on the loudspeaker announces the most dramatic entry into the narrow, steep-walled Trollfjord, where mountains loom almost close enough to touch.

Tromsø, the gateway to the Arctic, and Trondheim, Norway's third largest city and one of the oldest, are major stops with many sights to see. Other ports are so tiny it takes no more than five minute to walk the town, but often there is a pleasant surprise—a whimsical statue, a little park, or simply the chance to watch fishing boats and people going about their daily routines. The final stop in Bergen is best of all. Cradled by steep mountains, filled with cobbled lanes and quaint wooden houses, Bergen delights everyone.

There are no floor shows on the Bergen Line and no midnight buffets. Meals are not extravaganzas, but they do feature absolutely delicious fresh seafood. Don't sign on if you want the usual cruise ship experience; do come aboard for the experience of a lifetime. If you can't spend the entire twelve days, fly to Tromsø and take the homeward voyage to Bergen.

For information, contact Bergen Line, Inc., 405 Park Avenue, New York, NY 10022; (212) 319–1300 or (800) 323–7436.

Cruising the Sepik River, Papua New Guinea

Papua New Guinea is like nowhere else on earth, a fantastically varied island, a bird and flower lover's paradise still widely unblemished by humans. The country's finest native art, such as masks, carvings, and bark paintings, can be found in villages along the Sepik River. This route is served by two modern and comfortable small boats, the *Melanesian Discoverer*, a catamaran accommodating forty-eight passengers that departs from the port of Madang, and the *Sepik Spirit,* an eighteen-passenger vessel that leaves from the art-filled Karawari Lodge, the country's oldest and best-known tourist lodging.

The serpentine Sepik River provides the only route of transportation in this region. Its twists and turns provide a new vista around every bend—exotic birds, luxuriant vegetation, families traveling by dugout canoe, and thatched-hut villages where you can go ashore to see traditional ceremonies.

While Papua New Guinea is remote, it is a perfect add-on to a visit to Australia and a truly unforgettable travel experience. It is one of the few remaining places on earth where you can see tribes living as they have since the Stone Age. In many areas, they have had contact with the Western world for less than fifty years. The cruise can be combined with a land package for further exploration in the beautiful highlands.

The best source of current tour and cruise information is Papua New Guinea Tourism at 5000 Birch Street, Suite 3000, West Tower, Newport Beach, CA 92660; (714) 752–5440; www.paradiselive.org.pg or www.airniugini.com.pg.

Finally, cruising the Galápagos Islands is one of the ultimate travel experiences. Read about it under Nature, page 130.

Expedition cruise operators

Better-known cruise companies that roam the globe from the Arctic to the Amazon using smaller ships are listed on page 132.

Cruise References:

The Unofficial Guide to Cruises: 1999 Edition
Kay Showker, Bob Sehlinger, Macmillan General Reference, New York.

Berlitz 1998 Complete Guide to Cruising and Cruise Ships
Douglas Ward, Berlitz Publishing, Oxford, England.

Adventure Cruising: The Complete Guide to Specialty and Small Ship Cruises
Don W. Martin, 1996, Pine Cone Press.

HEY! Want to
make friends easily?
Let 'em know you're
connected with
AVIATION!

The Singles Scene

With the number of single travelers growing so rapidly, it is only natural that enterprising folks will find ways to serve them. This chapter is a potpourri of advice, events, and services of interest to singles—tours and resorts where singles mingle, publications aimed to help the single traveler, and ideas for finding a compatible roommate to beat the high cost of traveling solo.

Because younger travelers might prefer the company of their contemporaries, there is a section on age-specific programs for the 20–35 age group that get a high percentage of single participants. The growing number of trips and services just for women is detailed in the next chapter, followed by a survey of the scene for seniors—a burgeoning list of possibilities for those over age 50.

Let's look at some of the possibilities for all ages.

Newsletters

The best way to keep track of current special opportunities for solo travel is with a newsletter. Subscription rates change, so be sure to inquire about current prices before sending a check!

Travel Companions, published bimonthly by the Travel Companion Exchange (see page 193), is valuable even if you have no interest in finding travel partners. It is chock-full of travel news and bargains, including special deals for singles, and good advice on traveling alone and on travel in general. Annual subscriptions are $48; a sample copy is $6, applied to the full price if you subscribe.

Connecting: Solo Travel News (1996 West Broadway, P.O. Box 29088, Vancouver V6J 5C2, BC Canada; 604–737–7791) is one of the most valuable resources for single travelers. Published by Diane Redfern, a Canadian, the twenty-page, bimonthly newsletter is packed with up-to-the-minute information on upcoming tours in the United States, Canada, and worldwide, divided into sections labeled "just for singles" and "single-friendly." Readers share their firsthand travel experiences and finds, suggest singles-friendly lodgings, and post ads seeking travel companions or offering hospitality to visitors.

The most unique service from *Connecting* is the annual *Single-Friendly Travel Directory,* listing descriptions for every tour operator, resort, or cruise line with special offerings for solo travelers. The directory is in looseleaf form to allow for regular updates, which appear in the newsletter. The directory is free to subscribers, or can be ordered separately for $7.95. Annual subscriptions to *Connecting* are $25; sample issues, $5.

Singular Travel (150 River Street, Hackensack, NJ 07601; 201–646–9678) is an eight-page bimonthly published by staff members of the Bergen *Record* newspaper in Northern New Jersey. The pages include experiences from single readers, rosters of singles tour operators nationwide, lists of upcoming trips, and features such as book reviews. Readers can place ads looking for travel partners. Subscribers in New York and New Jersey will find listings for local singles travel groups and singles social clubs. Subscriptions are $12.

Solo Dining Savvy (P.O. Box 1025, South Pasadena, CA 91031; 800–299–1079; 323–257–0026) is a bimonthly eight-page newsletter begun in 1997 by editor Marya Charles Alexander, devoted to "taking the bite out of eating alone." She offers tips on dining alone comfortably and features solo-friendly restaurants in different cities, resources to be filed for future travels. Readers also contribute their finds. Subscriptions are $29 yearly.

Single Traveler (P.O. Box 682, Ross, CA 94957; 415–389–0227) is a bimonthly publication with good information on singles-friendly destinations, lodgings that give singles a break, and the latest news on trips for singles. Subscribers can also join Single Travel Connections, a network for meeting other single travelers of all ages. When they feature tour operators, this newsletter gives information much like the charts in this book, with group size, age range, percentage of singles, and male/female ratios. Subscriptions are $29.

Travel Companions

For many solo travelers, one of the most useful resources is The Travel Companion Exchange (Box 833, Amityville, NY 11701; 516–454–0880 or 800–392–1256; www.whytravelalone.com). An organization started in 1982 and dedicated to pairing travel-minded single people. The goal is to avoid the discriminatory supplement for singles while meeting new friends at the same time. Members are also resources for homestays for travelers. A six-month membership is $99 and includes a subscription to the TCE newsletter mentioned in the last section.

Founder Jens Jurgen says the organization has served more than 13,000 members across the United States and Canada and has current members representing every state. There are other matching services (some listed below), but none comes close to the numbers or reliability of this group. Most members are age 40 or over, but ages can range from 20 all the way to 85. There are slightly more females, but a good number of males, Jurgen reports.

The Exchange provides information; members do their own contact work. Applicants fill out a profile form describing themselves and their travel interests, then place a free listings in a newsletter that is circulated to all members, with an abbreviated description, including age, and where they hope to travel. Those who are interested can send for the longer profile, and, if the interest remains, can contact the person directly for a meeting before deciding to make travel plans.

Even if the vibes are good, Jurgen recommends spending time together on a weekend or short trip before setting off on a long excursion. Since the listings specify where the person lives, you can look for someone close enough to meet before you make further plans.

While some members wish to be matched with members of their own sex, many are equally interested in meeting partners of the opposite sex, and Jurgen reports that many compatible traveling mates have turned into lifetime companions. Here are samples of recent listings:

Ted: 41, 5'11", SWM [single white male], NS [nonsmoker]. Quiet, practical professional w/sense of humor. Enjoy most fine arts, current events, good food, learning about other cultures. Seek FTC [female traveling companion] 30-40. Considering trip to Mideast or North Africa, but flexible. Home: So. California.

Marie: 32, 5'4", 140, SWF, NS. Banker. Easygoing, good sense of humor, well-traveled, love European sight-seeing, museums, castles, dining. Other int: tennis, reading, classical music, making new friends, weekend trips. Home: Philadelphia.

"L": 65, 5'10", 148 DWM [divorced white male], NS. Enjoy tennis, reading, hiking. Seek F/MTC 40–70, college grad with enthusiasm for life. Good conversational skills a must. Pix. Home: Grosse Pointe, MI.

There is also a shorter listing in this newsletter for specific travel plans. These are recent examples:

DWF, 45, NS. Seek MTC 50–65 to explore Spain/Portugal, rent condo and use as home base. No. California.

SWM, 51, NS. Like hosting FTC 34–52, smoker ok, wkds for Tanglewood concerts, also NYC, Cape Cod & fall in New Engl. CT

For a women-only matching service, see page 211.

....

Trips for Singles

One way to ensure meeting other single people is to sign up for a tour designed expressly for singles. These offerings change from year to year, and many singles tour operators listed in the first edition of this book are no longer in business. This list is limited to those who have been operating for some time. Many are operators listed in other sections of the book but who offer, in addition to other programs, special trips designated for singles. All of these groups will try to arrange for shares, but there may be a surcharge if you request single occupancy. Here are some of the possibilities:

THE SINGLE GOURMET

133 EAST 58TH STREET, NEW YORK, NY 10022;
(212) 980–8788. (EE)

This nationwide organization dedicated to good eating and sociability started in 1982 and now has chapters in more than a dozen U.S. locations, three Canadian cities, and London. Restaurant outings are arranged regularly in each city, and a few trips are offered to all members each year. The trips include a full sight-seeing agenda but concentrate on dining, visiting the very top restaurants in each location. Lodgings are also deluxe. Recent trips included San Francisco and the Napa Valley, New Orleans, and a New Year's Eve journey to Spain. Travelers are paired at no charge. Members may attend dinners in other member cities when they travel. The age range of membership is from 20 to 60, with most age 40 or older. Women outnumber men 5 to 2. Many of the trip participants are from the Northeast, but there is a representation from all the chapters. Members say the trips are well run and sociable, and the days are flexible enough to allow for free time. Chapters are found in New York and its suburbs; Chicago; Philadelphia; Minneapolis/St. Paul; Denver; Ft. Lauderdale; Houston; Phoenix; Philadelphia; Norfolk and Richmond, Virginia; San Francisco, San Diego, Orange County, and Los Angeles, in California; and more cities to come.

AMERICAN JEWISH CONGRESS
(SEE PAGE 164)
The highly respected cultural organization offers several tours for singles only to Israel and other destinations. Some tours are designated for travelers under age 49.

MAJESTIC SUN TOURS
(PAGE 176)
Schedules "singles only" groups on regularly scheduled cruises, guaranteeing a roommate and congenial company.

AMERICAN WILDERNESS EXPERIENCE
(PAGE 90)
Among the many adventure offerings of this large outfitter are a number of camping, inn-to-inn hiking, and inn-to-inn canoeing trips expressly for "singles and solos." Included are winter biking, hiking, and snorkeling trips to Mexico. Their Old West Dude Ranch vacations (see page 28) include special rates for single adults at a number of ranches.

ADVENTURE DESTINATIONS
(PAGE 91)

This group's adventures are all for singles, and they cover much of the globe.

BACKROADS
(PAGE 97)

Offers many walking and biking trips for singles in the U.S., Europe, Asia, and the Pacific. The itineraries are identical to regular offerings and offer a choice of camping or inn stays.

ROADS LESS TRAVELED
(PAGE 105)

Combines biking and hiking with rafting and horseback riding on singles trips to the Colorado Rockies and the Southwest. Singles tours attract younger participants, with 35 the most common age.

NANTAHALA OUTDOOR CENTER
(PAGE 36)

Holds a three-day singles weekend focused on sociability and fun for kayakers and canoeists of all levels. Things start off with a welcome party. The next day the group divides on the river according to skills but comes together for meals and evening sessions.

WINDJAMMER BAREFOOT CRUISES
(PAGE 108)

Sets aside several cruises each year for singles. They cut off registration when one gender reaches 50 percent, so there's always an even mix.

TENNIS CAMPS LTD.
(PAGE 12)

Offers special weeks for singles, as does **Topnotch at Stowe** (page 13).

Singles Tour Specialists

O Solo Mio, 640 Los Altos Rancho, Los Altos, CA 94024; (800) 959–8568 or (650) 917–0817; www.osolomio.com. Formed in 1991, this company arranges singles tours and arranges for roommates, eliminating the single supplement. Groups are divided into mid-30s and younger, mid-30s and older, and all ages. Trips have included safaris, cruises, fall foliage in Canada, and tours in Spain, Portugal, England, Italy, Australia, New Zealand, Belize, Greece, Israel, and the Riviera. You can be on the mailing list for notice of coming trips by phoning. A detailed quarterly newsletter describing future trips is $20 annually.

Solo Flights 10 Taits Mill Road, Trumbull, CT 06111; (203) 445–0107 or (800) 266–1566 outside Connecticut. Well past its twentieth birthday, this travel center for singles offers a variety of tours in Costa Rica, Europe, and the United States, as well as cruises and Club Med vacations. They try to arrange shares.

Wilson & Lake International, (800) 227–5550, specializing in trips to Britain, offers trips from London for singles organized in England by HF Holidays. Recent choices have included a stay on the Isle of Jersey and a walking tour in Portgual. There is no single supplement.

For Young Singles

The following tours for younger travelers report that at least half of their participants are traveling solo. Both tours will arrange shares.

CONTIKI HOLIDAYS

300 PLAZA ALICANTE #900, GARDEN GROVE, CA 92840; (800) 266–8454 OR (714) 740–0808; WWW.CONTIKI.COM (I)

For more than thirty years, Contiki has served adventure-minded passengers ages 18 to 35 with trips to Europe, Africa, Australia, New Zealand, the continental United States, and Hawaii. Most participants are in their 20s; 70 percent are single, and they come from English-speaking countries all over the world. The average male/female ratio is 40/60, but according to one insider, males outnumber females on many U.S. and South Pacific tours, while European trips tend to be more heavily female. The trips are by motor coach. For trips labeled "Superior," accommodations are in hotels and resorts. Budget travelers stay in Contiki-owned chalets and villas, cabins, and hotels, sometimes four to a room. All rooms have private baths. Said one young woman recently returned from her first trip to Europe: "I can't think of a better way to go."

CLUB 21–35, TRAFALGAR TOURS

21 EAST 26TH STREET, NEW YORK, NY 10010;
(800) 457-6891 OR (212) 689-8977; WWW.TRAFALGALTOURS.COM (I)

"Fast-paced coach tours through Europe for younger travelers who want to see as much as possible on a budget," say the managers of this program, which has offices around the world, providing an international mix to the group. Itineraries to Europe range from twenty to thirty days, with lodgings in hotels.

....

Resorts Recommended for Singles

CLUB MED

This is still the first place that comes to mind when you ask a travel agent to suggest a solo vacation, though Club Med is far from the "swinging singles" scene of a few decades ago. The original guests have grown up and so has the club. Turkoise and Cancun are the only clubs still designated "for adults only." Families are courted, honeymooners are welcomed, and seniors get special discounts. Increasingly, Club Med is promoting more exotic locations such as Bora Bora or the Algarve coast of Portugal. And for this pioneer in all-inclusive resorts, competition from an increasing number of newer resorts means upgraded rooms and lower rates, good news for the many loyal fans of Club Med.

Does that mean Club Med is no longer a good choice for solo vacationers? Not at all. The greatest appeal of Club Med remains. The first resorts to cater to singles remain beach vacations where you can be absolutely comfortable by yourself and never have to dine alone. Singles still make up a big percentage of the membership, and many of them welcome the fact that the social pressure at many clubs is less than it used to be.

Those who knew the Club Meds of old will be pleasantly surprised at new and remodeled clubs with larger and better-appointed rooms. Columbus Isle in the Bahamas is the most lavish of the new breed, filled with fabulous folk art and antiques; it even offers TV and telephones in the rooms, a far cry from the spartan original Club Meds. Paradise Island, Cancun, Sandpiper, and St. Lucia clubs have also had multi-million-dollar renovations. Eventually sixty villages worldwide will be updated.

Many clubs have kept up with the times by offering aerobics classes and fitness centers with the latest in exercise equipment. You can have a massage at many clubs. And you can learn anything from sailing, scuba diving, and windsurfing to tennis and skiing to circus skills such as juggling, acrobatics on a trampoline, or tricks on a trapeze. With the exception of scuba diving, horseback riding, and golf, sports instruction is included in one all-inclusive price, along with three lavish meals a day and wine or beer for lunch and dinner.

While many guests still prefer to save by having a roommate assigned, single rooms are now available with an added supplement; this can be a modest 10 to 20 percent off season. The Paradise Island makeover includes many single-occupancy rooms with full-size beds.

The best deal at Club Med is to take your chances with the Wild Card option. You pick the week for a set, money-saving price; they pick the place. Vacationers reap the benefits of allowing Club Med to even the numbers at its various resorts. Singles are never sent to family-oriented clubs.

Because Club Med is such a well-known choice for single vacationers, it deserves special space and description, pro and con.

Life at Club Med

Life at Club Med villages is meant to be carefree. There's no cash to worry about. You are given a card when you arrive that allows you to charge any expenses and settle up at the end of your stay, so your money can go into the safe until you leave. Rooms usually aren't provided with clocks, so old hands know to bring a watch and an alarm clock. Lessons are scheduled at specified times, and if you don't get there on time, you'll miss out.

With the many activities offered, days can be jam packed—or you can ignore all the activities and find a quiet spot on the beach. Meals are all-you-can-eat extravaganzas with dozens of choices. Some dishes are better than others, but if you don't like your first selections, you can always go back and find reliable alternatives, such as roast beef, lamb, or turkey served from carving stations.

A hostess seats everyone at big round tables, making it very easy to meet people. You can then make reservations to dine together with your new friends in the smaller specialty dining rooms.

But Club Med is not for everyone. If you hated summer camp and you are not turned on by the idea of group lessons, line dancing, and the "Hands Up" song with hand motions, you may not be Club Med material. "Olympics Day" is really a grown-up version of a "color war"—everyone is divided into teams for competitions that include everything from basketball to beer drinking.

In all fairness, though, no one forces you to do anything. You can stay under a palm tree with a book if you like and go for a walk on the beach after dinner, but you can't avoid the music and activity around you or the sound of the loudspeaker announcing daily in English and in French contests such as volleyball and water polo tournaments.

The voice belongs to a GO (*gentil organisateur*), one of the bouncy, good-looking young men and women who do everything they can to make their enthusiasm contagious to their flock of GMs (*gentils members*). The GOs work hard, giving sports instruction, being sociable, lead-

Club Med
Locations for Adults

**Clubs open to all ages, but with
no special facilities for children:**
- Buccaneer's Creek, Martinique
- Columbus Isle, Bahamas
- Paradise Island, Bahamas
- Magic Isle, Haiti
- Sonora Bay, Mexico

- Bora Bora, French Polynesia
- Moorea, French Polynesia
- Da Balaia, Portugal

Adults over age 18 only:
- Turquoise, Turks, and Caicos
- Cancun, Mexico

ing trivia contests before dinner and group dances afterward (no partner necessary). Then they put on the evening entertainment, which can be surprisingly good for amateurs. Sophisticated? Not really, but you have to admire their energy. After the show the disco opens, and dancing goes on well into the night.

Choosing a Club

If you decide to give Club Med a try and look at their big catalog, you'll see plenty of tempting properties. After all, two of the club's main attractions are great locations and interesting architecture. Management makes it easier by pointing out which clubs are primarily geared to families, which to adults, and which are open to all ages but have no special facilities for children, which discourages families with younger kids.

If you have a particular sport or activity in mind, one way to ensure that you'll enjoy the week is to choose Club Med villages with a specialty. Intensive tennis and horseback instruction are offered at Sonora Bay, and dedicated diving centers are found at Columbus Isle, Turquoise, and Sonora Bay. Golf is available at half a dozen locations at an added fee, and some clubs offer free instruction. Sandpiper hosts an Intensive Golf Academy taught by PGA professionals. The club has two eighteen-hole courses and one nine-hole, par 3 course that is free for guests. Turquoise has the most complete circus program. You'll find more current offerings in the catalog.

One final bit of personal advice: Don't choose a club with a location that requires several plane changes or long bus rides. The journeys are tiring and expensive and use up valuable vacation time. Check travel time carefully when you make your plans; times from the airport are listed in the catalog. Club Med one-week packages via charters save time and money; you'll probably save even if you have to pay for an overnight in the departure city in order to make connections.

The ambience at the various clubs depends entirely on the current crop of GOs (they shift assignments every six months) and the makeup of the guests, which changes from one week to the next. Like any vacation, you take your chances on whom you will meet when you choose a Club Med location—but judging from the enormous number of people who return time and again, the chances are good that you will make friends. The club reports that more than 40 percent of their guests are repeaters.

To enroll in any Club Med, you must pay a one-time initiation fee, and there is an annual fee thereafter. The travel sections of major newspapers frequently carry ads from tour operators who buy space in bulk and promise discounts on rates, so check before you reserve.

For more information and a catalog, contact any travel agent or Club Med direct at (800) CLUB–MED.

COMMENTS: EB: I recently spent a week at Club Med Turquoise, wanting to see firsthand the changes since my last visit to a Club Med several years ago. This remains the best beach vacation I know for a single person. The general atmosphere is very friendly; by the time you've had a few meals and taken part in a few activities, you know a number of people. Many of them are interesting and have diverse professions, and since Club Med is international, guests come from all over the United States, Canada, and Europe.

Turquoise attracts many singles in their 20s and early 30s, but the age range went well into the 60s when I was there, so no one needed to worry about feeling out of place. Some of the younger guests were intent on drinking and partying, but other than creating a few noisy tables in the dining room, they didn't affect the other guests.

Undoubtedly, those who get the most from the Club Med experience are the sociable, fun-loving types who enjoy the line dancing and group songs and who take advantage of the many sports available. But there was ample room to escape on one of the loveliest beaches in the Caribbean, and even a section of quieter beach where classical music was piped in each afternoon.

The most positive change I found was the food. The choices were really impressive. At every lunch and dinner, there were half a dozen meat and poultry entrees, two kinds of pasta, and nearly twenty kinds of vegetables. Each night featured a different theme—French, Italian, Caribbean, and Tex-Mex, to name a few. Seafood night brought caviar, smoked salmon, crab legs, and tons of shrimp—and these were just the appetizers! Every meal offered bountiful fruit and cheese displays, a tempting array of desserts, and breads so delicious, they were a peril to the waistline.

The entertainment was also better than I remembered, thanks to a clever choreographer who knew how to make the most of his amateur cast. Some of the most exciting entertainment came on the night when guests showed off what they had learned at the circus workshop, displaying high-wire balancing and acrobatic feats that were nothing short of amazing. The circus emphasis adds to the spirit of fun at this particular club; wherever you go, you find people practicing juggling and other tricks.

I had only one criticism: Drinks between meals priced around $5 seemed quite expensive, and excursions were also pricey, anywhere from $40 to $75. The excursion prices are listed in the catalog, so take a look before you go, and come prepared to spend a bit if you want these extras. Remember also to add in the cost of departure taxes and transfers from the airport to the club.

Most of the people I met had been to several clubs and planned to come back again. Why do they keep returning? Here were some of the comments:

"No surprises. I know the food will be good and the staff will be great."

"I come for the diving. It is much more reasonable than at other resorts, and since I don't do it often, I like the fact that I am so well supervised."

"I like meeting people from all over."

"I like having so many sports options without having to worry about what they cost."

"So easy to meet people, so friendly."

....

SuperClubs

SuperClubs operates seven adults-only, all-inclusive resorts in Jamaica and one in the Bahamas. All welcome singles, but two, Hedonism and Breezes, attract the largest numbers.

Beautifully located in Negril, Jamaica, along a 7-mile swath of beach, Hedonism II has attractions similar to those offered by Club Med—rates that include all meals, plus tennis, sailing, water-skiing, windsurfing, volleyball, a Nautilus gym, squash, snorkeling, scuba diving, bicycling, horseback riding, aerobics, and arts and crafts classes. In addition, they offer an open bar all day and night and nighttime entertainment that includes top local bands and performers. The long beach at Negril is shared by several hotels, convenient if you want to take a walk into town or sample the local nightlife.

Hedonism's unique lure is the freewheeling Jamaican spirit and contagious reggae beat that permeate the island. "Let's party" is the motto, right from the rum punch you are handed as you arrive. All this attracts a young crowd, averaging between 21 and 35 and about 65 percent single. There is a nude beach and a "prude" beach. One observer noted with surprise that it was the young who tended to be covered; older guests, who ranged into their 60s, seemed to be on the nude beach, unconcerned with appearances. Much of the food is grown locally, and menus feature a lot of native fruits and vegetables.

Breezes Golf and Beach Resort on Jamaica's North Coast has a more sophisticated ambience and strong emphasis on sports, including golf, tennis, and scuba instruction. For more information, contact SuperClubs, (800) 859–7873 or (954) 925–0925 (www.superclubs. com).

More singles-friendly resorts

Several other all-inclusive resorts in the Caribbean encourage solo guests, though their programs vary from year to year and current offerings need to be verified.

Clubs International (800–777–1250) has daily activities for singles who want to mix and mingle, including a weekly "get acquainted" cocktail party at Club St. Lucia. The resort charges a single supplement.

Sun Swept Resorts (800–544–2883) usually waives single supplements at its luxury resorts and spas, La Source in Grenada (www.lasourcegrenada.com) and Le Sport in St. Lucia (www.lesport.com.lc), during the low season from mid-April through October. The single supplement is quite low the rest of the year. In addition to the usual resort facilities, these all-inclusives include massages, facials, and other excellent spa treatments, fitness classes, sessions with a personal trainer, and instruction in yoga, meditation, and stress management. There may be a table in the dining room set aside for single guests.

For Women Only

ONE OF THE MOST NOTICEABLE TRENDS IN TRAVEL IS THE growth of activities for women only. There have always been spas for women, and as mentioned, almost every major ski area has begun offering special ski weeks for women. But the desire for comfortable, noncompetitive, nonpressured travel has spawned a dramatic increase in options for women, and there are more publications and organizations than ever to encourage women to take to the road. There's even a mail-order company, Christine Columbus, that specializes in travel gear for women.

The most popular women-only trips fall into the active, adventure category. These trips are challenging, but they supply a supportive atmosphere and eliminate the need to keep up with macho males. The companionship and sharing on strictly female trips is another major lure; participants report firm friendships that last long after the trip ends, a big plus for participants whether single or not.

Carole Jacobs of *Shape* magazine aptly describes the appeal of these journeys. "Women-only adventure travel is more than a girl's night out . . . There's no better place to find yourself than on top of a mountain, no better time than when you're climbing a cliff to discover that your better half is not the one you left behind, but the one you found within."

Here are some of the varied resources and trips available for women:

Publications for Women Travelers

Maiden Voyages (109 Minna Street, Suite 240, San Francisco, CA 94105, (510) 528–8425; www.maiden-voyages.com) is an attractive and useful quarterly magazine "for women who live to travel or dream about travel." There are many first-person accounts as well as features on topics from natural hot springs to gourmet rail adventures. Topics covered range from safety to book reviews and from trips for women to special lodgings. Free listings are offered for women looking for travel partners. Subscriptions are $16 per year.

Journeywoman magazine www.journeywoman.com, a free on-line quarterly, describes itself as a networking magazine for female travel enthusiasts. Subscribers come from all over North America and from as far afield as Europe, Hong Kong, Israel, Vietnam, and Turkey, making for a wonderful exchange of travel tips and stories. For those with access to the Internet, this magazine is chock-full of valuable information and resources, from hotels welcoming singles to tours for women. Many of the advertisers are American. An article on "Safe and Solo in Turkey" includes suggestions on dining, names a Turkish bath reserved for women only titled Tuesdays, and reminds that women must cover their heads on entering a mosque. A story on Tucson tells of a women-only golf instruction program, social hikes for those over 50, and women-led desert walks.

Female Traveling Companions and Hostesses

SHARED ADVENTURES—A WOMAN'S TRAVEL NETWORK

c/o Viking Travel Service
610 North Washington Street, Naperville, IL 60563;
(708) 983–1766

Shared Adventures has a new agency affiliation, but Carol Napper, who founded the service in 1987, is still at the helm, and the aim is still to help women find compatible traveling companions. The agency keeps files on members, and when one requests a travel partner, a "network alert" goes out in the form of postcards and direct calls to those who have already indicated interest in the destination. Viking Travel Service also keeps tabs on current trip offerings for women only, described in a newsletter to members. They can help locate a tour to suit individual interests, even if they cannot locate a roommate. Recent offerings have ranged from Caribbean cruises to cooking school in Italy to a tour of historic homes in Charleston. Women of all ages have enrolled; the majority are between 30 and 55, and the majority are from the Chicago area.

WOMEN WELCOME WOMEN

c/o Betty Sobel, USA Trustee,
10 Taits Mill Road, Trumbull, CT 06611;
(203) 445-0141

This organization was formed in 1984 to foster international friendships by enabling women of different nations to visit one another. There are some 1,600 participants from sixty countries, ages 16 to 90. Each new member fills out a form asking to be a hostess, a traveler, or both. Questions on the form include age, occupation, religion, politics, and languages spoken. Details from these applications are included on a world-wide membership list, divided by countries. Visits are arranged individually, initiated by travelers writing to prospective hostesses. The organization recommends continued correspondence to become acquainted a bit before an actual visit and suggests that the first stay be short, in case expectations are not met.

Members also sometimes arrange to get together. Thirteen women from the United States, England, Australia, Scotland, Holland, and Belgium gathered a few years ago in Westport, Connecticut, with each woman housed in a volunteer's home. Such gatherings are publicized in a newsletter published three times a year with news of forthcoming events, reports of members' travels, and requests for touring companions.

This is purely a voluntary organization, funded by its members' dues and donations. Minimum dues are $30.

Women's Tour Operators

As with any program, before you sign on to one of these tours, ask for reference names and numbers of former participants.

THE WOMEN'S TRAVEL CLUB

21401 NE 38TH AVENUE, AVENTURA, FL 33180;
(305) 936-9669 OR (800) 480-4448

With more than 1,000 members nationally, ages 30s to 70s, this club offers at least one small-group trip per month with room shares guaranteed to destinations from Paris, India, Italy, and Mexico. U.S. trips are also on the agenda, including spa holidays. Membership is $35, which includes a monthly newsletter.

ISIS WOMEN'S TRAVEL ASSOCIATION

C/O EMPRESS TRAVEL HEADQUARTERS, 465 SMITH STREET, FARMINGDALE, NY 11735; (800) 284-0022, EXT. 2191; WWW.EMPRESSTRVL.COM

Founded in 1996, ISIS consists of local clubs that meet in various cities. Trips for the group are organized by Empress Travel and include cruises and destinations from Jamaica resorts to South African tours. Roommate matching is one of the benefits of membership. A U.S. trip is planned each year to allow members from different cities to meet. Dues, which include a newsletter, are $49 per year. To find a club near you, contact Empress headquarters.

Women-Only Adventure Travel

WOMANTREK

1411 EAST OLIVE WAY, P.O. BOX 20643, SEATTLE, WA 98102;
(206) 325-4772 AND (800) 477-TREK. (I-E)

Off-the-beaten-path adventures for small groups of women only (with female guides) run the gamut from biking, rafting, sea kayaking, trekking, skiing, llama pack trips, and leadership courses to deluxe tours. Ages range from

YEARS IN BUSINESS:	12
AGE RANGE:	22–80
MOST COMMON AGE:	35–65
PERCENT ALONE:	75
NUMBER OF PARTICIPANTS:	300 PER YEAR
MALE/FEMALE RATIO:	ALL FEMALE

the 30s to the 70s. Destinations include Peru, India, Nepal, Greece, China, Nova Scotia, Africa, Mexico, Thailand, the Galápagos Islands, and Tibet. Ski trips are in Washington and New Mexico. The organization offers camaraderie and the opportunity of a lifetime for women who are looking for experiences of personal importance and who wish to see the world, says the brochure. Some white-water trips include workshops on management, leadership, and personal renewal.

COMMENTS *Female, 40s: I've gone on three trips, alone and with a friend. The groups were made up of very intelligent people, and I formed lasting friendships with women from age 20 to 60. The guides are knowledgeable and the programs first-rate.*
Female, 60s: I went on a safari alone and it was fine. The groups were small, only seven on my tour. The women's ages ranged from the 30s to 60s, but most were in their 40s and single, and mainly from the West Coast. Everyone got along well. It was a wonderful experience.

ADVENTURE WOMEN

15033 KELLY CANYON ROAD, BOZEMAN, MT 59715;
(406) 587-3883 OR (800) 804-8686; WWW.ADVENTUREWOMEN.COM (M–E)

Worldwide adventures for women over 30 range from one-week U.S. trips to three-week world journeys. Trips are rated easy, moderate, or high energy. Many trips are designed for beginners who want to enjoy adventure travel within a supportive and noncompetitive environment. Activities include river-rafting, horseback treks, hiking, and fly-fishing in the western United States plus safaris in Africa, trekking in Nepal, and high adventure such as rafting in Chile or Gorilla trekking in Uganda.

COMMENTS *Female, 40s: I've gone hiking in the U.K., staying in small family hotels and sharing rooms. I've also gone cross-country skiing in Wisconsin and camping on a glacier in Alaska. The women have diverse backgrounds, but share a love for adventure. They come from all over the U.S., but predominantly from Illinois and Wisconsin. Good organization; will go again.*

YEARS IN BUSINESS:	17
AGE RANGE:	30–79
MOST COMMON AGE:	LATE 40S, EARLY 50S
PERCENT ALONE:	ALL WOMEN; OWNER SAYS THE MAJORITY ARE OR HAVE BEEN MARRIED AND HAVE CHILDREN
NUMBER OF PARTICIPANTS:	10–20
MALE/FEMALE RATIO:	ALL FEMALE
NO SINGLE SUPPLEMENTS	

Female, 70s: I've taken four trips, including hiking and canal boating in England. The trips are well organized, and I've always made good friends with women of all ages.

SHERRI GRIFFITH EXPEDITIONS

(SEE PAGE 112)

This group offers sojourns into nature with spectacular scenery to quiet the soul and white water for excitement. The adventure is described as a supportive, noncompetitive setting to learn outdoor skills taught by well-trained and personable riverwomen.

Other adventure groups to investigate include:

WOMANSHIP

THE BOATHOUSE, 410 SEVERN AVENUE, ANNAPOLIS, MD 21401; (800) 342-9295

Provides sailing instruction and sailing cruises on Chesapeake Bay and in San Diego, New England, the Pacific Northwest, the Great Lakes, Florida, the Caribbean, Greece, Ireland, and other destinations.

WOODSWOMEN

25 WEST DIAMOND LAKE ROAD, MINNEAPOLIS, MN 55419;
(612) 822–3809 OR (800) 279–0555; WWW.WOODSWOMEN.MN.ORG

This organization is devoted to supportive and challenging learning opportunities. It sponsors many outdoor travel adventures, from dogsledding to backpacking, bicycling, walking, sea kayaking, canoeing, and other outdoor endeavors. Members get a quarterly newsletter.

ADVENTURE ASSOCIATES

P.O. BOX 16304, SEATTLE, WA 98116;
(206) 932–8352

Organizes trips from Nepal to Bali to the Greek Isles.

WOMAN TOURS

P.O. BOX 68, COLEMAN FALLS, VA 24536;
(800) 247–1444 OR (804) 299–6199; WWW.WOMANTOURS.COM

Biking tours for women in New England, the Blue Ridge Mountains, Southwest Canyons, California Vineyards, the Canadian Rockies, and New Zealand.

WOMANPOWER ENTERPRISES

2551 SUMAC CIRCLE, ST. PAUL, MN 55110;
(612) 773–0937 OR (800) 879–1696

Provides in-depth, women-only safaris to Kenya.

Women's Travel Gear

Christine Columbus (www.christinecolumbus.com; 800–280–4775) addresses the special needs of women travelers with an on-line catalog. Along with handy safety items and handsome accessories, this catalog features items you won't find in other places. For instance, a half-slip with zippered pockets keeps jewelry and money secure and her chic leather tote bag has a hidden compartment in the bottom to stash sneakers and double as a hideaway for wallet and passport.

TRAVE

The Golden Age: 50 and Over

HY A SPECIAL CHAPTER FOR OLDER TRAVELERS? Age is no deterrent on the great majority of the group trips mentioned in this book, and adventurous seniors in their 80s are happily roaming the globe on their own right this minute. So what's so special about the older traveler?

To begin with, there are more of them. With those much-publicized baby boomers entering their fifties, the number of so-called seniors is mushrooming and everybody wants their attention. The *New York Times* in 1996 reported that the 55-to-74-year-old age group accounts for 39.9 percent of the population; by 2006, it is expected to be nearly 50 percent.

These are people who tend to have more disposable income and more time to spend it, so it isn't surprising that many people want to tap into that market early. No longer do you have to be 65 to reap discounts. Age 50 has become the "golden age" for many travel benefits.

The American Association of Retired Persons has lowered its age requirement to 50, opening a whole range of travel discounts to those who reach the mid-century mark. Learning opportunities geared to older adults are growing rapidly. Elderhostel, the wonderful educational program for seniors, has lowered its age limit from 60 to 55—with companions as young as 50. Interhostel offers educational experiences abroad for travelers age 50 and older.

On an active trip, sometimes even the fittest traveler of a certain age may welcome a gentler pace and the comforting knowledge that you don't have to keep up with thirty-year-olds. A growing number of operators are meeting this need with "soft adventures" geared to healthy, active over-50s.

For many older singles, especially once-married individuals who find themselves considering solo travel for the first time in their later years, the company of contemporaries may seem reassuring. Numerous group tours labeled "over 50" may be of interest to these travelers.

So a special chapter for the over-50 generation seems in order just to recap all the privileges that come with age! Let's look at some of the trips that you can't take unless you're over 50!

ELDERHOSTEL

75 FEDERAL STREET, BOSTON, MA 02110;
(617) 426-8056. (I) YEAR-ROUND

Since 1975, this remarkable program has provided intellectual stimulation and good company for adults over age 55 and their companions of any age who want to continue to expand their horizons. It offers inexpensive, short-term academic programs at educational institutions around the world. The topics? Cicero to computers . . . politics to poetry. More than 2,000 institutions participate, providing programs in every American state and Canadian province and seventy other countries. Some 250,000 travelers take part each year; about 40 percent of them single. Typical U.S. programs offer three courses that meet daily for sixty to 90 minutes each. Living/dining accommodations are in dormitories, conferences centers, or hotels, and participants have the use of the campus or hotel recreational facilities. The charge for many programs in the U.S. is under $400. Besides classroom courses, programs include bicycling trips, cross-country skiing, stays in country houses and private homes, trips to other countries, and study cruises, all at reasonable rates. Put yourself on the mailing list, and three times each year you'll get a 150-page newspaper-sized catalog crammed with possibilities. A land-sea program in Alaska, a stay at Trinity College in Wales, a spring sojourn in the Great Smoky Mountains, a jazz course in New Orleans, or a stay in New Delhi—it's enough to make younger folks want to hurry up and age!

SENIOR VENTURES

CENTRAL WASHINGTON UNIVERSITY, 400 EAST 8TH AVENUE; ELLENSBURG, WA 98926;
(800) 752-4380; WWW.CWU.EDU/~CONTEDHP/SENPROG
YEAR-ROUND

Does the term "beyond baby boomer" describe you better than "senior citizen"? asks the brochure of this ambitious program now in its second decade and made to order for adults who want to keep learning and exploring. Some fifty classes are offered during the summer in two-week segments; participants can take any or all. Participants stay in dorm rooms with private baths, and there is an entire residence hall designated "single occupancy only." Transportation for the two-hour ride from the Seattle airport is provided on the starting dates of each session.

Further afield, the school sponsors activities such as "scholar-ship" learning cruises to Alaska and travel opportunities all over the world for adult learners, from Antarctica to Africa, escorted by college faculty and in-country specialists.

SENIOR VENTURES

SOUTHERN OREGON UNIVERSITY, 1250 SISKIYOU BOULEVARD, ASHLAND, OR 97520
(800) 257-0577 OR (541) 552-6285

Southern Oregon pioneered the Senior Ventures concept in the Northwest in 1983. Their emphasis is on the well-known Oregon Shakespeare Festival in Ashland, with classes on the theatre taught by OSF company professionals and tickets to the plays included in the tuition. Courses run four nights to two weeks. Some programs include other subjects; one popular combination features bridge classes. Participants live on campus.

INTERHOSTEL

UNIVERSITY OF NEW HAMPSHIRE DIVISION OF CONTINUING EDUCATION
6 GARRISON AVENUE, DURHAM, NH 03824;
(603) 862-1147 OR (800) 773-9753; WWW.LEARN.UNH.EDU (E-EE)
YEAR-ROUND

Another education-oriented group operating since 1979, Interhostel study tours for adults over age 50 (and companions 40 or older) are held in many countries abroad, in conjunction with local sponsoring host universities and educational institutions. More expensive than Elderhostel, these trips still are good value, with rooms usually in comfortable hotels and all meals and airfare included in the fee. Several programs feature Christmas abroad. The most recent catalog lists more than fifty options, from Paris to Florence, Prague to Beijing. Faculty of schools in each city give insight into the history, politics, natural environment, and culture of the region. Excursions to sites of historic or cultural significance supplement classroom learning, and the itinerary includes social activities. Special programs include Christmas in Paris or in Mexico.

Interhostel tries to find roommates, but if no share can be found, there is a single supplement, often no more than to 15 percent more than the double rate.

SENIORS ABROAD

12533 PACATO CIRCLE NORTH, SAN DIEGO, CA 92129;
(619) 485–1696.

This is an international exchange program for adults over age 50, much like those that young people enjoy. Participants stay with families in New Zealand, Australia, and Japan. Those who wish may provide hospitality in their own homes for travelers to the United States. A typical tour includes short homestays in several locations around the country; some tours may also intersperse a few days at hotels or B&Bs. These are not bargain tours—the cost of administration of a program like this is high—but they are reasonable and do provide a unique opportunity for an in-depth look at another culture, an ideal option for single travelers who want companionship and the opportunity to meet contemporaries in other lands. Some 3,500 people have participated since the program began in 1984.

MOUNT ROBSON ADVENTURE HOLIDAYS

BOX 687, VALEMOUNT BOE 2ZO, BRITISH COLUMBIA, CANADA;
(250) 566–4386; WWW.MOUNTROBSON.COM
MAY TO SEPTEMBER

Travelers who want a comfortable taste of adventure in the Canadian Rockies will enjoy this company's "Fifty Plus Adventure," four days and five nights of guided activities at a gentle pace, including hiking, canoeing, and rafting floats to view birds and wildlife, waterfalls, and exceptional mountain scenery. Lodgings are in cozy cabins; all meals are included.

Seniors also are welcome on all of Mount Robson's "gentle adventures."

ELDERTREKS

597 Markham Street, Toronto M6G 2L7, Ontario, Canada;
(416) 588-5000 or (800) 741-7956; www.eldertreks.com
(I-E, plus airfare)
Year-round; guaranteed shares

Promising "exotic adventure for the young at heart," these in-depth programs take small groups to Sumatra, Bali, Thailand, Nepal, Laos, Morocco, Ecuador, Turkey, New Zealand, and many other fabulous destinations, exploring local culture, nature, and scenery on foot and by boat. There is always emphasis on meeting local people.

WALKING THE WORLD:
OUTDOOR ADVENTURES FOR PEOPLE 50 AND OVER

P.O. Box 1186, Fort Collins, CO 80522;
(970) 498-0500 or (800) 340-9255. (M-E)
Will try to arrange shares

Name a beautiful place and chances are this group will take you hiking there. Designed for active, outdoors-oriented older travelers, this group, founded in 1987, features eclectic worldwide destinations including Asia, Costa Rica, Switzerland and New Foundland, New Zealand and Ireland, Tuscany and the Scottish Highlands, Banff and Jasper National Parks in Canada, Hawaii, Wales, and the Devon Coast. Closer to home, walking tours range from the coast of Maine to Arches National Park in Utah. Hiking is not difficult but does cover some high elevations. Trips are from eight to twenty-one days; distances covered daily range from 5 to 8 miles on some trips to 7 to 10 miles on others. Depending on the destination, accommodations may be bed and breakfasts, hotels, motels, or country inns; a few trips involve camping, with shared responsibilities for setting up camp and cooking.

OVERSEAS ADVENTURE TRAVEL

(SEE PAGE 93)

In 1995 Grand Circle Travel, one of the over-50 tour operators (page 221), purchased this company in response to growing interest among clients for adventure travel. They now feature an entire catalog of comfortable worldwide adventures designed for travelers over 50.

ALASKA WILDLAND ADVENTURE

(SEE PAGE 96)

Senior Safaris, eight-day, seven-night itineraries, promise all the thrills of Alaska's national parks and wildlife refuges—and in-room bathroom facilities. June through August. (EE)

ADVENTURE DESTINATIONS

(PAGE 91)

This specialist in adventure tours for singles also offers walking tours for travelers over age 50, reporting that 60 percent of the participants are solo travelers. Destinations include Colorado, Maine, Washington state, Hawaii, and Canada, along with Central and South America, Europe, and Asia. Lodgings are in comfortable inns.

INTERNATIONAL BICYCLE TOURS

(PAGE 103)

Easy, picturesque terrain and a leisurely pace characterize this companies tours to Holland, Italy, and Austria, which attract many older bicyclers.

BALLROOM DANCERS WITHOUT PARTNERS

c/o LUXURY WORLDWIDE CRUISES AND TOURS,
1449 N.W. 15TH STREET, MIAMI, FL 33125 ;
(800) 778-7953 OR (561) 361-9384; WWW.VACATIONSPLUS.COM

This Miami travel agency caters to single men and women over 50 who enjoy dancing. It offers dance-oriented cruises on ships on major cruise lines and on the *Delta Queen*. The programs, open to beginners to advanced dancers, include instruction. At least one man is signed on for every five women; if enough men don't sign up, gentlemen hosts are added. Cost depends on the cruise selected. Share rates are guaranteed.

....

Tour Operators Serving Seniors

If you want to see the world with fellow travelers in your own age group, consider these tours aimed at those who have passed their fiftieth birthdays. (Also note that the majority of travelers on many tours listed on pages 215–22 are over age 50).

GRAND CIRCLE TRAVEL

347 Congress Street, Boston, MA 02210;
(800) 955–1042 or (617) 350–7500; www.gct.com (M–E)
Single supplements vary; many are low and they are waived entirely
on some departures and several cruises.

Begun in 1958 to serve members of the AARP, Grand Circle opened its trips to all in 1980 and boasts that 95 percent of their passengers say they will travel with them again. Tours take in the U.S., Mexico, all of Europe, Egypt, Israel, South Africa, Austrialia, New Zealand, and parts of Asia, including cruises and safaris.

SAGA INTERNATIONAL HOLIDAYS

222 Berkeley Street, Boston, MA 02116;
(800) 343–0273; cruises, (800) 952–9570; Road Scholar Programs,
(800) 621–2151; www.sagaholidays.com (M)
Will try to arrange shares; No single supplement on many tours

Taking Advantage
of Senior Discounts

- Join the American Association of Retired Persons as soon as you turn 50. AARP dues are small, and membership entitles you to many benefits, including discounts at every major hotel, motel, and car rental chain in America.
- Even if you don't belong to an organization, always ask hotels if they offer senior discounts. They won't bring it up unless you do; they have no way to know your age.
- Ask for the discount when you make your reservation; many places won't honor it later. At hotels, remind the clerk of your discount when you check in.
- Carry your driver's license or other proof of age when you check in, just in case you are asked.
- Compare rates. Sometimes special promotions at hotels are a better deal than the senior discount.
- Check with your auto insurance company; many companies offer a discount on car insurance after you pass your fiftieth birthday. Ditto for banks and retailers like Sears.
- Ask tour operators and resorts whether they offer a senior discount. Among the many who do are Club Med (page 198) and American Wilderness Experience (page 90).
- Are you a skier? Recognizing that older skiers are good business, almost every area now offers discounts, with the qualifying ages ranging anywhere from 50 to 60.

More Perks at 62

Getting a bit older definitely has its advantages:

- When you reach age 62, you are entitled to a 10 percent discount on airlines—all you have to do is ask! Also check with major airlines about money-saving coupon books and other good deals available to senior passengers.
- Amtrak takes off 15 percent of its lowest fares for passengers 62 and over.
- For $10, you can buy a Golden Age Passport that admits you to all the national parks, forests, refuges, and monuments free for life. Seniors get half off on fees for camping, parking, and tours, as well. Passports are sold at all parks. For details write to the National Park Service, P.O. Box 37127, Washington, D.C. 20013.

Established in the United States in 1981, this leader in tours for mature travelers offers an extensive catalog of trips across the United States, Canada, Mexico, Europe, and Latin America. "Road Scholar" programs are partnerships with local museums and universities to make these tours an in-depth learning experience. Several tours are cosponsored with the Smithsonian Odyssey program. The catalog assures that they will go out of their way to make singles feel welcome and part of the group.

MATURE TOURS

10 TAITS MILL ROAD, TRUMBULL, CT, 06111;
(800) 266-2566 OR (203) 445-0107. (I-M PLUS AIRFARE)
WILL TRY TO ARRANGE SHARES

This is a sister company to long-established Solo Flights (page 197) concentrating on "youthful spirits over 50." Cruises on the Panama Canal and the Mississippi River; escorted trips to London, Israel, Spain, Costa Rica, and New York City; and New England fall foliage tours are among the recent offerings.

For more senior savings, see these books:

- *The Mature Traveler's Book of Deals,* Adele and Gene Malott, 1998, GEM Publishing Group, and
- *Unbelievably Good Deals and Great Adventures That You Absolutely Can't Get Unless You're Over 50,* Joan Rattner Heilman, 1998, NTC/Contemporary Publishing.

Section Two

Solo TRAVEL Know-How

SOUTHERN LINES PACIFIC

going av

Some General Advice

f I'd traveled with a group or even another person, I wonder what memories I'd have missed. Would the man with the box of pigeons at his feet on the Polish train have offered to show me his town? The man at the tiny restaurant in Switzerland probably wouldn't have invited me to polka, and I am quite certain the hotel owner in Saba wouldn't have joined me for dinner, his treat.

—Letters to the Editor, *Travel Holiday*

Group vacations may provide great experiences and wonderful companionship, but many independent souls still prefer to set their own pace and agenda. If you've always wanted to see the Statue of Liberty or the Eiffel Tower or the Duomo in Florence, there's absolutely no reason why you cannot blaze your own path, design your dream trip, and happily do and see exactly what you please. One of the special privileges of solo travel is being able to tailor a trip to your own special likes and dislikes. Sleep as late or get up as early as you please. If you love antiques or bookshops or offbeat museums away from the main tourist track, you can indulge to your heart's content. If you want to savor a sunset, no one will say "Let's go." If you hate cathedrals, you need see nary a one!

It will take more planning to go your own way, yes—but often that very planning is a part of the fun of travel. Advance research is the best way to start learning about your destination. The more you know beforehand, the more you will get out of your trip.

Will you meet people on your travels? Probably more than if you were with a partner. You'll try a little harder to make friends than if you had a built-in companion, and you will be more approachable than if you were deep in conversation with your friend or spouse.

What are the best destinations for a first trip on your own? Whenever anyone asks me that question, my answer is, "Head for a city." Every great city has its own intriguing rhythms and personality, and often you can actually sense these best when you are alone, when you have no distractions and plenty of time to stroll, eyes wide open and antennae turned on high. Staying in one place also gives you a chance to get your bearings and begin to feel confident about getting around.

The best time to plan a city trip alone is during warm weather, when sociable outdoor cafes are in high gear. But, if you can avoid it, don't travel alone during the peak vacation season in July and August. Hotels and restaurants are least happy to see single guests during these months because this is when they are busiest and best able to fill tables and rooms with two or more instead of one. All the sights you want to see are also most crowded in high season. Late May, June, September, and early October are the ideal times to enjoy good weather without encountering hordes of tourists.

Pick your city carefully. Don't go alone to places like Los Angeles where you must drive unfamiliar streets or freeways to get around. Choose towns with a vital, walkable center and plenty of intriguing neighborhoods that can be explored on foot, plus an efficient and inexpensive public transportation system to get you from one place to another so that you won't need a car. Cities fitting this description usually meet another important criterion that makes for easier travel on your own— they have large single populations and many informal neighborhood restaurants to serve them.

Among the cities in the United States that meet these qualifications well are Boston, New York, Philadelphia, Chicago, Seattle, and San Francisco. Charming historic smaller cities like Charleston, Savannah, and New Orleans are also easy to cover on foot. The best bets in Canada are Montreal, Toronto, and Vancouver. Almost any major city in Europe is a likely candidate, though places where English is spoken are probably the best choices for a first foreign venture. This doesn't mean you must limit yourself to London, wonderful city though it is. Think also of Dublin or Edinburgh, where English comes with a delightful brogue; Amsterdam, where the multilingual Dutch will welcome you in your own tongue; or Copenhagen, where English is the second language. I'll zero in on some of my favorite cities in the next chapter, but first let me share some techniques that work for me when I get ready to visit any new town.

Sizing Up a City

If you allow yourself to arrive alone in a new city without specific plans, you can feel lost and confused. To feel in control, your days should be mapped in advance. Start at home by contacting the local tourist office for information and maps of city streets and transit systems. Next, get the best guidebooks you can find and, if possible, a copy of the city's local magazine. If you don't have access to a newsstand that sells out-of-town publications, get the address and phone number of the magazine from the tourist office and order a copy by phone. If your community does not have a good travel bookstore, order by mail from those in the resource list on page 319. The Internet is another valuable resource for information and books.

When you have assembled your materials, read the brochures and books to learn about the character of the city and its special attractions for tourists. Use the magazine to find out what the people who live there are doing and where they are going right now.

Now make a list of the places you most want to see and circle them on the street map. Although it is hard to get an accurate sense of scale from a map of a strange city, you can easily see which attractions are close together and plot your days by grouping places in the same geographic area. Check the transit maps against the street map to see which places can be easily reached by bus or tram.

Next, make a tentative day-by-day schedule of what you hope to do and see, ranking the sights each day from most to least important. That way, if something proves fascinating, you can find extra time by dropping the least important items on the agenda. If a top choice turns out to be a disappointment, you have plenty of options to fill your time.

In a brand-new city, I always start the first day with a local sight-seeing tour. This gives you a quick sense of the locations of important sites and streets. These tours often include inconvenient areas that you may not get back to easily on your own. Sometimes when I actually get a look at a place that sounded wonderful in the guidebooks, I realize it is not so great in reality, and I strike a further visit off my list.

I also like to leave time on my schedule for guided walking tours in interesting or historic areas of the city. Walking tours have fewer people than bus tours and are far more personal and interesting; they are an excellent way to meet people. In foreign cities, walking tours with English-speaking guides are the best way to seek out fellow travelers as well as a welcome respite from struggling to speak the language. With a really knowledgeable local guide, you'll get colorful inside information that isn't found in any book. The best current walking tours aren't always listed in guidebooks, but they are usually included in city magazines. You can also ask about these at your hotel or the local tourist office after you arrive.

Schedule plenty of time just to wander when you explore a new city—this is one of the great pleasures of solo travel. As long as you stay in safe neighborhoods, don't worry about getting lost. (Ask at your hotel about parts of the city that should be avoided.) Some of the best discoveries may lie on little side streets that don't show on the map. Even in a foreign city, if you write down the name and address of your hotel and mark it clearly on the street map, you will be able to get directions or find a cab when you want to return. One of the pleasant discoveries when you travel alone is that people everywhere seem particularly willing to go out of their way to help a solo visitor.

When you go exploring, you may find you get more out of your journey by pretending that you are a travel writer who will want to bring the place alive for your readers. Take your time, look closely, window-shop, talk to people, ask questions, take mental notes, and make written ones. Make lists of the unusual shops and galleries you pass, take photos, and keep a nightly journal of your impressions. A journal is fun—it keeps you company, and it will vividly bring back the pleasures of your trip every time you open the pages back home. If you return to the city in the future, your journal will become your personal guidebook leading you back to the best places.

How much time you allot to shopping beyond souvenirs for friends and family depends on your own disposition. If you are like me and seldom find time for relaxed shopping at home, an afternoon to yourself for

City Smarts:
An Assortment
of Tips
on U.S. Cities

- San Francisco has an exceptional number of small, well-priced hotels. Especially recommended for solo travelers are the Kimpton and Joie De Vivre Hotels. These lodgings are attractive, conveniently located, and moderately priced. Kimpton's complimentary wine reception each afternoon provides a chance to mingle with other guests. Many also offer coffee or a continental breakfast in the morning. The hotels I've personally inspected include Monaco, Monticello Inn, Triton, Villa Florence, Vintage Court, Juliana, and the Tuscan Inn. Recommended Joue de Vivre properties include the Maxwell and two budget properties, the Bijou and the Commodore.

- In Chicago, the choicest hotel location is on or near North Michigan Avenue's "Miracle Mile," where fine dining and most of America's top retailers are found within a 20-block stroll, and buses can be boarded to all the city museums. Surprisingly situated in this posh neighborhood is a high-rise Motel 6, one of the city's best buys.

- Charleston, one of America's most beautiful strolling cities, is an ideal destination for solo travelers since most of the lodging, dining, and sight-seeing is in the easily walk-able Historic District. If you can afford the tab, Charleston Place, a luxury hotel in the center of things, is ideal. Their restaurants offer a Single Diner program to encourage solo guests to come to dinner, including special wine and appetizer tastings and special visits by the manager and chef on duty. They even present a silver tray with a selection of magazines, papers, postcards, and books to keep you occupied between courses. Among dozens of appealing smaller inns, my top recommendation (when the budget allows) is 2 Meeting Street.

- Wherever you go, look for multi-day passes on city transit systems; they invariably save money.

browsing stores in a new city is a treat. When I buy clothing or unique local handicrafts on a trip, they come with a bonus of happy memories. Some of my favorite souvenirs have been paintings or folk art purchased on my travels. Looking for them invariably means talking to people and learning a lot about the local scene.

....

Choosing a Place to Stay

The circles you've marked on a city street map will help you choose a convenient area for your lodging. There are a few ways to consider accommodations when you are alone; the ultimate choices are dictated by budget and personal preference—and whether you are in the United States or abroad.

U.S. Accommodations

If you can afford the splurge, it's a special pleasure to stay at a top hotel when you are traveling alone. Being surrounded by luxury is even more of a treat when you are by yourself, and the better hotels offer an important practical advantage as well: the concierge.

Now found widely in hotels in the United States as well as Europe, the job of the concierge is purely and simply to make your stay more pleasant. Besides taking care of all your transportation and ticket arrangements, a good concierge should know the city inside out—the best places to shop, the best ways to sight-see, and the places where single diners will feel comfortable. Well-connected concierges provide a lot of business to the city's restaurants, and when they phone in a reservation and say a good word, you can be sure that you won't be shunted to a cramped corner or ignored by your waiter. A good way to determine the quality of the concierge service in advance is to find out whether the head concierge wears the golden keys of Le Cle d'Or, the prestigious international concierge association.

At the other end of the scale, the small, charming budget hotels available in Europe just don't exist in most cities in the United States. With a few exceptions, our budget lodgings are at best impersonal and at worst, shabby and dreary. Luckily, now that the bed-and-breakfast craze has moved into big American cities, there is a cheerier choice when funds are limited. A bed-and-breakfast apartment or a home in a pleasant neighborhood provides an insider's advice on the city from your host, plus someone to talk to at breakfast and when you get home at night. As a bonus, you get a better sense of the real life of the city away from the business district. Dining is almost always more reasonable in the neighborhoods than in the business center of town—if you have fellow lodgers, you may even wind up with company for dinner.

Bed-and-breakfast reservations can be made through services that handle a large number of locations in each city. You'll find a sampling of these services in the box on page 235, and there are plenty of books with further suggestions. The lodgings themselves vary from lavish to modest, with either private or shared baths. Be very specific about your needs and desires when you make your reservation. Most of all, be sure the location is convenient to public transportation. If you think there may be times when you will return to your lodging late at night, find out whether cabs are readily available from midtown and the approximate fare to your destination.

Another plus for bed-and-breakfast accommodations is that, unlike hotels, they often give a generous break to single travelers. It isn't that hotels don't like singles, but the overwhelming majority of their rooms are designed for two people, and they seem to feel it is not good business to lose the extra revenue. That means one guest pays a single supplement, making the rate almost the same as for two.

When you do get a single room in a hotel, it may be the smallest and least attractive in the place. Don't be afraid to speak up and ask for a better one.

The single supplement remains the biggest gripe of solo travelers, so perhaps if enough people write to hotel managers or major hotel chains to complain, some savvy hotels will begin to change this discriminatory policy.

While they may not have done much about improving their single rates, a number of U.S. hotels have begun offering a few services that make life pleasanter for their guests who are traveling alone. These amenities are aimed at attracting business travelers, but they are equally welcome to vacationers. One innovation commonly available in large hotels is a special "executive floor" where continental breakfasts and complimentary hors d'oeuvres are served in a special lounge. You pay extra for a room on this floor, but the lounge is a very easy setting for finding company, and the complimentary breakfast and snacks are pleasant money-savers. Executive floors also tend to provide extra security, with floor concierges on duty and special elevator keys.

European Accommodations

Bed-and-breakfast homes have long been available in Europe, but, unlike in the United States, there's also a good chance of finding small and reasonable hotels that have local character and at least a modicum of charm. I favor staying in a hotel in a city where I don't speak the language, because I feel more secure in a central location when I don't know my way around. Most tourist offices as well as guidebooks offer listings of both small hotels and bed-and-breakfast lodgings.

By choosing smaller accommodations you can hold down the cost of traveling on your own, but you may have to make arrangements yourself by mail, fax, e-mail, or phone. Travel agents are businesspeople, after all, and these time-consuming reservations usually pay no commission. It's a simple matter to make your own arrangements, and the fax makes it easy to make contact. If you must communicate by mail, allow plenty of time for letters to make their way across the ocean and back.

If you are willing to make a move after you arrive, you can try another technique. Make a hotel reservation for the first night or two, and then take a morning to check out a list of small, less-expensive hotels in person, reserving a room in your favorite for the rest of your stay. If you find that you have booked a hotel that is disappointing, do the same—pay for the first night and look for a more pleasant alternative. Having the option to look around for lodgings is another reason to avoid traveling during busy peak seasons when desirable hotels are likely to be filled.

When you are hotel-shopping, don't hesitate to ask to see rooms—or

U.S. City
Bed-and-Breakfast
Registries

- **New York**

  City Lights B&B Ltd., P.O. Box 20355, Cherokee Station, New York, NY 10021;
  (212) 737–7049.

  Urban Ventures, 38 West 32nd Street, Suite 1412, New York, NY 10001;
  (212) 594–5650.

  At Home in New York, P.O. Box 407, New York, NY 10185
  (212) 956–3125.

- **Boston**

  Host Homes of Boston, P.O. Box 117, Waban Branch, Boston, MA 02168;
  (617) 244–1308 or (800) 600–1308.

  Greater Boston Hospitality, P.O. Box 1142, Brookline, MA 02146; (617)
  277–5430.

- **Chicago**

  Bed & Breakfast, Chicago, P.O. Box 14088, Chicago, IL 60614–0088; (312)
  951–0085 or (800) 375–7084.

- **Washington, D.C.**

  Bed & Breakfast League/Sweet Dreams and Toast, P.O. Box 9490, Washington,
  D.C. 20016; (202) 363–7767.

- **Philadelphia**

  A Bed and Breakfast Connection/Bed and Breakfast of Philadelphia, P.O. Box
  21, Devon, PA 19333; (610) 687–3565 or (800) 448–3619.

- **San Francisco**

  American Family Inn/Bed & Breakfast San Francisco, P.O. Box 420009, San
  Francisco, CA 94142; (415) 477–1913 or (800) 452–8249.

For a list of reservation services in other cities, contact The National Network
(TNN), Box 4616, Springfield, MA 01101.

to ask if a less expensive room is available. Contrary to what many people think, room prices are often negotiable if the hotel is not filled.

Making Your Own Travel Arrangements

Saving on Airfare

If you are making your own travel arrangements, one way to save on transportation costs is to investigate some of the consolidators who offer bargain airfares. You'll see ads from these companies in almost any big-city newspaper, listing fares to major cities that are far below the going official rate. How do they do it? They buy blocks of seats that the airlines do not expect to be able to sell themselves, mostly on international routes. A good example: Air India flies to Bombay from New York with a stop in London. There are often empty seats on the New York–London leg that will be occupied in London. Consolidators can offer the trip to London at a big discount.

Some of these companies may specialize in specific regions such as Hawaii or the Orient. Rates and dates vary from one firm to another, so comparison shopping is essential.

There can be drawbacks to dealing with a consolidator. It is more difficult to get a refund, and you may not always get frequent-flyer mile credit. You may not be transferred to another carrier in case of cancellation or delay of a flight, and you may have to juggle your dates to coincide with the flights that are available.

Consolidators are not recommended for inexperienced or nervous travelers who might panic if complications arise. For those who feel confident about coping in case of emergencies, however, the consolidators offer flights on regular scheduled airlines at a very substantial savings.

Dealing with a reputable consolidator is important. Two that come well recommended are:

TFI TOURS
34 West 32d Street, New York, NY 10001; (800) 745–8000 or (212) 736–1140.

Savvy Travel Tips for Solo Travelers

- Always ask for the corporate rate at a hotel, even if you don't work for a big company. It usually saves you 20 percent. Few hotels ask for I.D. when you arrive, and if you do, a business card is usually all you need to show.
- Don't call the 800 number to reserve at big hotel chains; they don't always know about local specials.
- Don't accept the first rate offered at a hotel; always ask if something cheaper is available. If they aren't full, most hotels are amenable to a little bargaining. Be sure they incorporate lower weekend rates into your bill.
- In the United States, big savings are available from hotel discount services, sometimes as much as 50 percent off the published rate. Two major services are Express Reservations (800–356–1123) for New York and Los Angeles, and Quikbook (800–789–9887) for Atlanta, Boston, Chicago, Los Angeles, New York, San Francisco, and Washington, D.C. Hotel Reservations Network (800–96–HOTELS) handles hotels in London and Paris, as well U.S. cities.
- No rooms available at the hotel? Call back after 6:00 P.M.; that's when rooms saved for no-shows become available.
- Can't get through to the airlines during a fare sale? Try calling at 7:00 A.M. or after 11:00 P.M., when you're less likely to get a busy signal.
- During bad weather months, avoid delays by flying early in the day and choosing nonstop flights. When you must change planes, look for winter hubs like Dallas, Atlanta, or Las Vegas rather than northern cities such as Chicago, Denver, or Detroit. Don't book the last flight of the day; if it is canceled, you are out of luck.
- To avoid getting stuck in the middle seat on a plane, always ask for seat assignments when you reserve your ticket. Check in at least twenty minutes before departure in order to hold your seat. Early arrival is doubly important to claim your seat, since boarding passes have been eliminated, causing longer lines for check-in.
- Always pay for tickets and tours with a credit card; it is your insurance in case the airline or the tour company goes out of business.

GLOBAL DISCOUNT TRAVEL SERVICES

4052 SOUTH INDUSTRIAL ROAD, LAS VEGAS, NV 89103; (800) 497–6678;
WWW.LOWESTFARE.COM.

If you are looking for discounts on domestic travel within the U.S., the outfit with the dubious name of **Cheap Tickets, Inc.** does deliver them; I've used them myself. Call (800) 377–1000 (or check www.cheaptickets.com).

Remember also that many tour operators offer independent tours that do not require traveling with others. They simply give you the benefit of a group rate for airfare and hotels and sometimes a free sight-seeing tour. The hotels tend to be commercial, but you may want to compare these group rates with those you are quoted on your own.

Those with access to the Internet will find several sites for finding lowest fares. Two of the best are www.travelocity.com and www.expedia.com.

The airline also post specials on their Web sites; many bargains are available for those who can travel on short notice.

Traveling by Train in Europe

European trains are a pleasant surprise for first-time American travelers. They are fast and comfortable; they run frequently and are almost always on time. Trains like the TGV, running on new high-tech tracks, travel 130 to 170 miles per hour—so smoothly that you can hardly believe how fast you are moving. They allow you to relax and see the sights and to arrive at a central location where both taxis and public transportation are usually available. There are no guarantees, but trains sometimes can be a way to meet people, too.

The Eurailpass is one of Europe's best buys. For a specified period, fifteen days to three months, it allows unlimited first-class travel on speedy trains that go almost everywhere in seventeen countries. Since distances are small and trains run often, you can cover a lot of ground in a short time. The pass must be purchased in this country before you leave; it is not available in Europe.

If you want to base yourself in cities and do day or overnight trips, the Eurail Flexipass is ideal, allowing a certain number of travel days within a twenty-one-day period. For those under the age of 26, the Eurail Youthpass offers economy second-class travel. But there is nothing second class about those second-class seats—they are perfectly comfortable and recommended for anyone who wants to save a bit of money on travel.

You can adapt a train trip to almost any kind of European itinerary. I had a wonderful journey recently, seeing Swiss mountain villages on day trips from Lausanne, then whizzing to Paris in 3½ hours on the TGV, that amazing high-speed superliner. After several days in Paris, a 1½-hour train ride took me to Blois, which became my home base for an excursion into the Loire Valley chateau country. I didn't need a car in Blois—there were daily bus excursions from the railroad station to the great chateaus of Chambord, Chenonceaux, and Amboise. Blois itself was a charming, small medieval town with its own famous chateau within walking distance of my hotel.

Stays in the countryside also provide a way to stretch your budget, since hotels and restaurants are far less expensive than those in big cities. In Blois I stayed at a stylish, modern, three-star hotel where three-course gourmet dinners were half the price of comparable meals in Paris.

Each European country has its own national railroad featuring special money-saving passes; you can learn about these from the local tourist office. If you plan to visit only one country, these may be a better choice than a Eurailpass.

A great thrill is taking the Eurostar, the train that runs through the tunnel beneath the English Channel to whisk you from the center of London to midtown Paris or Brussels. It is just as quick as flying (if you include time getting to and from airports) and much more fun, since you can watch the countryside as you whiz by; the actual time in the underground tunnel is very short. Rail Europe has excellent packages that include the "Chunnel" trip as does BritRail, the British rail service, which also issues passes for unlimited train travel in Ireland, Scotland, Wales, and a round-trip ferry crossing of the Irish sea.

Because trains in Europe run more frequently than they do in the United States, it is possible to tour short distances with almost as much flexibility as you would by car, and train stations are often centrally lo-

Tips on European Train Travel

- Most trains can be boarded without reservations, but the TGV and certain other special trains require advance seating. These are clearly marked with an R (meaning reservations required) on Eurail timetables so be sure to check.
- Remember that if all your travel is within one country, the national rail is often cheaper than Eurail.
- Porters may not turn up when you need them, but many stations have an ample supply of luggage carts. It takes exact change to get one, however, so find out in advance what coins are required and have them ready.
- Some European cities have more than one train station. Paris, for example, has six. Be sure to find out from which station your train is leaving.
- Avoid travel on Friday and Sunday afternoons when weekending Europeans jam the trains.
- Remember that the Eurail pass can be purchased only in the United States.

For more information on Eurail train travel package and reservations, see a travel agent or contact Rail Europe, 226 Westchester Avenue, White Plains, NY 10604; (800) 438–7245 (www.raileurope.com).

Contact BritRail at 1500 Broadway, New York, NY 10036; (888) BRITRAIL (www.britrail.com).

cated for sight-seeing in the old parts of the cities.

My first European travel on my own, in fact, was a one-week, low-budget train trip through Holland, a compact country that is ideal if you want to see a lot in a short time. I used a suitcase small enough to fit into station lockers, and traveled much the way I might have by car. Fifteen minutes out of Amsterdam, I got off the train, checked my bag, and went out to see the charming city of Haarlem, walking the old square and visiting the Franz Hals Museum. (Finding your way is a cinch in

Holland, since the VVV, the local information office near each train station, provides walking maps and has an English-speaking staff.)

After lunch in the square, I reboarded the train for the old university town of Leiden, another short ride away, where I did more browsing. Later, I boarded a train for The Hague, where I settled in for a couple of days. From there, day trips by train took me to Delft, Gouda, and Rotterdam, and a trolley ride brought me to the seaside resort of Scheveningen. The entire journey was inexpensive and easy, and I never felt nervous for a minute.

Famous scenic tours can be taken by train. The Bernina Express and the Golden Pass Route in Switzerland, the Bergen Express in Norway, and Loisrail in France follow routes through magnificent scenery that you can sit back and enjoy from your picture window. Most long-distance trains have either a dining car or will serve meals at your seat. You can also reserve a sleeper—your own little bedroom—and use the train as your hotel, making the most of your travel time.

You'll find that train travel is not intimidating in most foreign countries. Signs in stations are easy to read; pictures point out lockers and checkrooms. Reservations offices are marked with a big *R* and information offices with a big *I*. In larger cities there is always someone in either of those offices who speaks English. The trains, their track numbers, and departure times are clearly listed on big boards. Even in countries where you can't understand the loudspeaker announcements, you need only spot the track number, line up at the right place, and you'll know when to board when you see the crowd starting to move.

With most major trains, it's hard to make a mistake, since the side of each car bears an identification panel showing the name of the city where the train originated, the final destination, and the major stops in between. Trains sometimes switch cars en route, so always check the destination on your car. First- and second-class cars are identified with large numbers, and a smaller number clearly identifies the cars with reserved seats.

Traveling by Train in North America

Amtrak trains are an underrated resource for people traveling alone in the United States. Getting to and from centrally located train stations is much easier than the hassle of traveling to airports. Seats are wide and comfortable, and you can walk to the lounge car for refreshments or conversation if you get restless.

Trains can also substitute for driving alone when you want to tour. Well-priced All Aboard America fares are good for a thirty-day period in one of three regions (the eastern, central, or western U.S.) with three stopovers permitted. Amtrak offers its own tour packages using local hotels, as well. Trips crossing regions can be arranged for an extra fee.

Roomettes and single slumbercoaches designed for one adult allow you to save money and time by using the train as a hotel and covering many miles while you sleep. Fares include all meals while you are on board; tea, coffee, or fruit juice and a newspaper are complimentary in the morning.

Along the eastern corridor, Boston, New York, Philadelphia, Wilmington, Baltimore, Washington, Fredericksburg, and Richmond are a straight run from conveniently located midtown stations. The trains run often, making for easy city tours.

You can also let Amtrak do the driving while you enjoy the scenery on some fine fall foliage routes. The *Montrealer* runs from Washington, D.C., through New York's Adirondack Mountains to Montreal. The *Vermonter* goes through the Green Mountains. Both the Vermonter and the *Ethan Allen Express* can take you to Vermont ski areas, avoiding the worry of winter driving to the slopes.

In the western United States, bilevel superliners allow you to sit back and enjoy the scenery through big picture windows, and Sightseer Lounges with windows extending all the way into the roof are great places to meet people.

Canada's Rocky Mountaineer offers one of the most spectacular train routes in the world—the journey from Vancouver to Calgary through Jasper, Banff, and the Canadian Rockies. You can also tour comfortably on VIA, the national railway, from Montreal to Quebec City to Toronto

Top Scenic U.S. and Canada Train Routes

If you don't want to tour the whole seaboard or criss-cross the country, consider some of these choice segments:

- New York to Albany along the Hudson River
- New Haven to Boston along Long Island Sound
- Philadelphia to Harrisburg through Pennsylvania Dutch country
- Chicago to Seattle crossing over the Mississippi River, the Continental Divide, and the Columbia River Gorge
- Chicago to San Francisco via the Rocky Mountains
- Vancouver to Calgary through the Canadian Rockies

at a speedy 95 miles per hour. Canrail passes allow twelve days of travel within a thirty-day period, allowing for plenty of sight-seeing time. Like Eurail passes, these must be purchased before leaving home.

For information on AMTRAK service, call (800) USA–RAIL (www.amtrak.com); for Rocky Mountaineer, (800) 665–7245 (www.rkymtnrail.com) ; for VIA Rail Canada, (800) 561–3949 (www.viarail.ca).

Some excellent guides to train travel include:

- *Eurail and Train Travel Guide to The World,* Gena Holle, Editor, Houghton Mifflin, New York
- *U.S.A. by Rail* by John Pitt, The Globe Pequot Press, Old Saybrook, CT.
- *Traveling Europe's Trains* by Jay Brunhouse, Pelican Publishing Company, Gretna, LA.

- *Europe by Eurail* by George and La Verne Ferguson, The Globe Pequot Press, Old Saybrook, CT.
- *Britain by BritRail* by George and La Verne Ferguson, The Globe Pequot Press, Old Saybrook, CT.

Meeting Local People Abroad

Spending time in a new country is always far more meaningful if you are able to meet and really talk to the people. When you are traveling alone, the chance to visit with local residents is doubly welcome. A few organizations help make this possible.

U.S. SERVAS COMMITTEE, INC.

11 JOHN STREET, NEW YORK, NY 10038; (212) 267-0252; WWW.SERVAS.ORG.

This nonprofit, interracial, and interfaith group is affiliated with the United Nations as a nongovernmental organization. Its purpose is to promote peace through person-to-person understanding and friendship, which they do by opening doors for travelers to "homes and hearts" in more than 100 countries.

Servas maintains a roster of approved hosts abroad (and throughout the United States) who welcome foreign visitors to stay in their homes, usually for two nights; no money is exchanged. To apply for membership, each applicant fills out a detailed form, which subsequently serves as a letter of introduction to hosts. This form must be submitted with two letters of recommendation. A personal interview by a volunteer is required before a new applicant is accepted for the program. If approved, members pay an annual fee plus a refundable deposit for host directories in specific countries. Travelers then write or phone these hosts to ask for hospitality, giving each reasonable notice.

Members are asked to learn as much as possible in advance about the customs and cultures of the places they plan to visit. They are also requested not to stay only in major cities since hosts in suburbs and smaller

Meet the People

Several tourist offices keep lists of local people who are happy to meet with visitors and spend a few hours showing them the city. Usually there is a match with someone who has an occupation or interests similar to the visitor; in foreign countries, these friendly volunteers are bilingual. Local tourist offices can put you in touch with these organizations, which include:

- *Big Apple Greeters (New York City) (212) 669–8159*
- *Meet the People Program (Jamaica) (800) 233–4582*
- *People to People Program (Bahamas) (242) 326–5371*
- *Japan Goodwill Guides Program (212) 757–5640*

communities often have more time to welcome visitors. The purpose of visiting is to share yourself, your country, and your interests, and travelers are urged to be respectful of their hosts' values and customs. When the program works well, lifelong friendships can be formed, and many hosts eventually visit former guests.

FRIENDSHIP FORCE

900-57 FORSYTH STREET NW, ATLANTA, GA 30303; (404) 522–9490.

An international organization begun in 1977 and now active in nearly 60 nations, Friendship Force members travel as "ambassadors" from their home country to other lands, where they are welcomed for stays with local host members who enjoy sharing their culture. Participating countries range from Russia to Australia and Brazil to Japan. Planned tours include sight-seeing itineraries in each destination as well as homestays. Recent offerings have included a trip to Vietnam with a five-day homestay in Hanoi and six days of touring, and a seven-day homestay in

Freiburg, in the Black Forest of Germany, with an aded three-day tour to Zurich, Switzerland. You can join the Friendship Force and receive a quarterly magazine and new of trips by paying a $12 annual dues or join a local club with regular meetings and add activities at home as well as travel opportunities. A list of local clubs and contacts is available from the Atlanta office.

FRIENDS OVERSEAS

68-04 DARTMOUTH STREET, FOREST HILLS, NY 11375; (718) 544-5660 (BETWEEN 9:00 AND 11:00 A.M. OR 5:00 AND 7:00 P.M., EASTERN TIME).

American tourists can write to this organization if they would like to meet Scandinavians, couples or singles, during their visits to Denmark, Sweden, Norway, and Finland. American participants receive the names and addresses of Scandinavian members who are eager to meet compatible Americans and begin a correspondence before the visitor leaves the States. This can lead to invitations to an evening out or a day of sight-seeing, and perhaps an invitation to visit a home. Sometimes accommodations in homes may be offered. Send a self-addressed, stamped, business size envelope for full information.

FRIENDS OVERSEAS—AUSTRALIA, at the address above, is a meet-the-people program that introduces Americans to residents of Australia who are willing to give advice by mail and personal guidance in their country.

AMERICAN INTERNATIONAL HOMESTAYS, INC.

P.O. BOX 1754, NEDERLAND, CO 80466; (303) 642-3088 OR (800) 876-2048.

Since 1988 this organization has organized homestays with English-speaking families in somewhat unusual destinations abroad. About 200 American travelers ages 40 to 70 take advantage of this opportunity for in-depth and inexpensive travel each year. You can choose bed-and-breakfast arrangements or have a home-cooked dinner with your host family each night. There is a choice of staying in one place for three nights or more or following a pre-planned itinerary on two-night stays through countries of Central Europe and the Baltics, as well as Russia, China, India and Nepal, Australia, New Zealand, and Tahiti.

WOMEN WELCOME WOMEN
(SEE PAGE 211)
Offers homestays for women in many countries around the world.

American Youth Hostels: Travel on a Shoestring

Short of travel funds? Not to worry. If you don't demand luxury, you can still travel happily on a tight budget. American Youth Hostels (AYH) are not only for the young. Many a canny traveler takes advantage of their rock-bottom rates for dorm rooms (divided by sex) and shared cooking facilities. Lodging goes for $8 to $25 per night; in some locations, when available, you can even splurge on a private room usually occupied by couples and still save a bundle over other lodging choices. Ante up $25 a year to join AYH, and you can make reservations with a credit card at 150 U.S. locations and take advantage of nearly 5,000 hostels in seventy countries around the globe. (Hostels are open to nonmembers, as well, for slightly higher fees per night.)

In the U.S., AYH uses many interesting converted historic sites, such as an ironmaster's home built in 1827 in Pennsylvania, an 1810 townhouse in Baltimore, a Victorian mansion in Sacramento, an old lifesaving station on Nantucket, and an art deco hotel on Miami Beach. Some locations even have recreational facilities. The organization has won the National Preservation Honor Award from the National Trust for Historic Preservation for its contributions to preservation in saving these historic properties.

If you will be sharing a dorm with strangers, it only makes sense to leave valuables at home and to keep your money and camera with you at all times. With a bit of care, hostels can be a sociable and money-saving opportunity. For information, phone (202) 783–6161 or check www.hiayh.org.

Dining Alone

The one part of traveling solo that people seem to dread most is dining alone. Even the most worldly travelers may hate it. Some people refuse to travel by themselves just to avoid it.

In part, this is understandable since it is undeniably a lot pleasanter to share a meal. But often the reluctance is strictly a matter of point of view. When *Travel & Leisure* magazine talked to businesspeople who frequently travel alone, many of them said that after a hectic day it is actually a relief to be able to relax and not have to make conversation with strangers. Many also considered a room service dinner a wonderfully indulgent luxury.

The same can be true after a busy day of sight-seeing. It really isn't so bad relaxing over a drink by yourself and thinking back over the day— unless you think it is. Some diners are so self-conscious they bury themselves in a book, thereby missing out on the pleasure of people-watching in the restaurant—or maybe even starting up a conversation with someone at the next table.

One of the reasons that solo diners may feel ill at ease is that busy restaurants don't always seem pleased to see them. It's that same old problem—most tables are designed for two. The smaller tables inevitably seem to be stuck back near the kitchen. And, understandably, it may be true that waiters would be happier getting tips from two instead of one. If you make the effort to be friendly, however, explaining that you are a solo traveler, and enlisting advice about the menu and even about what to see and do in the city, you may find a staunch ally in your waiter.

Sometimes I shift my schedule so I can eat an early dinner before restaurants are filled and when I know they are happier to see a solo diner. Often I'll have this early meal in the neighborhood where I spent the afternoon, which gives me a chance to try places in areas I might not venture into on my own later in the evening.

When I want to eat at a really posh place by myself, I usually go for lunch. This is not only cheaper than evening dining but usually leaves me wanting very little for dinner that night. I've found that if you stop by in advance and explain to the captain that you are in town alone and ask which day they might best be able to accommodate you for lunch or dinner, you'll likely get a more cordial reception—and a reservation. Don't try this visit during the height of the lunchtime rush.

I have a female friend with another technique. She phones to reserve tables for one under the name of "Dr. Glenn." Somehow the title seems to do the trick; she isn't turned down, and she is welcomed when she arrives.

Though you don't want to miss out on some of the really great restaurants in a new city, as a rule, when you travel alone, it is a lot more comfortable going to smaller, more casual dining places. The less formal dining rooms in large hotels are always a good bet for single travelers, since management is quite used to serving them; you'll notice that these rooms tend to have a lot of small tables. You don't have to be staying in a particular hotel to take advantage of its dining facilities, so you can have a number of comfortable evenings simply by surveying the local hotel scene.

If I am looking for variety and I have no concierge to guide me, I always scout the blocks around my hotel during the day for promising little places within walking distance. This may or may not be successful, depending on the neighborhood and the city.

A surer technique is to seek out the trendy city neighborhoods that attract a lot of browsers. Usually as you stroll along you can count on finding small cafes in these areas. Watch for outdoor terraces with empty tables or little cafes with lots of small tables by the windows or along the walls. These are often used to serve single diners; you will probably spy some who have arrived before you.

Other best bets in every city are restaurants with bars serving complete meals as well as beverages. These may be among the city's most popular restaurants, as you'll see from some of the places listed beginning on page 250. Sushi bars are always fine for dining alone, as are restaurant bar areas and wine bars in many cities that also serve light meals. I've found that Chinese restaurants tend to be relaxed places where single diners need not feel self-conscious.

Good sources of ideas are the Zagat restaurant surveys, which are made up of opinions from local residents and always include suggestions for dining alone as well as listings of places where local singles gather. The Zagat guides are available for most major U.S. cities. For ordering information contact Zagat Survey, 4 Columbus Circle, New York, NY 10019; (800) 333–3421 or (212) 977–6000.

One other option: take an evening sight-seeing tour that includes dinner and you'll definitely have company. That's the way I saw San Francisco's Chinatown for the first time.

Wherever you go, you'll be better received in a restaurant if you are reasonably well dressed. I met one traveler who told me she always dresses up when she goes out to dine by herself. She also carries a notebook and asks lots of questions about the restaurant and the menu. She hopes she will be mistaken for a food critic, and so far, she says she has been treated well wherever she has tried her little game.

Another way to find dining companions in a city in the United States is to look into the meeting dates of the local chapters of any professional organization or alumni club you may belong to, or the scheduled dinners of the local Single Gourmet group. Contact the national Single Gourmet organization listed on page 195 for local addresses. And don't hesitate to look up friends of friends.

The best way to find nightlife is to read local publications. If you are 35 or under, look for alternative papers such as the *Boston Phoenix* or the magazine *Time Out* in New York. If you are hesitant about venturing alone, check into nighttime tours.

Singles bars still exist, but they are far less attractive to travelers in this age of AIDS. A brief romance in a strange city once might have seemed romantic, but today it is a bit like playing Russian roulette. A good rule for females always is to pay your own way at bars or in restaurants. If you are meeting someone you don't know well, always do so at a public place, never at your hotel.

For those who prefer specific dining destinations to browsing, here are some solo suggestions from restaurant critics who were kind enough to share their expertise on three major U.S. cities:

Boston

Mat Schaffer, former restaurant critic for *Boston Magazine,* offers these suggestions:

GALLERIA ITALIANA

(77 TREMONT STREET; 617-423-2092) is known for superb Northern Italian fare. Order a full meal (the pasta is homemade) or graze on antipasto at Miss Kitty's Salon, the crimson-curtained wine bar area at the front of the Galleria. The party atmosphere is contagious; the owners make you feel as if you're a member of the family.

DAILY CATCH

(313 HANOVER STREET IN THE NORTH END; 617-523-8567) specializes in seafood, especially squid—fried, stuffed, sautéed, even minced into marvelous meatballs served in tomato sauce over linguini. Located in the city's Italian neighborhood, the tiny dining room is conducive to meeting diners at adjoining tables.

JAE'S CAFE

(520 COLUMBUS AVENUE; 617-421-9405) has a Pacific Rim menu of Thai, Korean, and Japanese dishes. If you dine at the sushi bar downstairs, you're guaranteed to strike up a conversation with the person next to you.

CHARLIE'S SANDWICH SHOP

(429 COLUMBUS AVENUE; 617-536-7669) is a neighborhood breakfast and lunch spot where everyone shares tables. Be ready for long lines on Saturdays, and be sure to order the turkey hash.

STEPHANIE'S ON NEWBURY

(190 NEWBURY STREET; 617-236-0990) dishes out terrific American comfort food, sandwiches, and salads to a fashionable clientele in a *très chic* setting. Alfresco dining on the sidewalk out front features some of the city's best people-watching.

HAMERSLEY'S BISTRO

(553 TREMONT STREET; 617-423-2700) is nationally recognized as one of Boston's finest restaurants. The roast chicken is spectacular. Chef Gordon Hamersley is the lanky guy in the open kitchen with the red hair and ever-present baseball cap. The intimate seating makes it virtually impossible not to spark up a conversation.

BREW MOON

(115 STUART STREET; 617-523-6467) is one of the city's most popular brew pubs. The food is cutting-edge eclectic and is designed to complement brewmaster Tony Vieira's excellent beers. The bar is popular with singles after work and on weekends.

LALA ROKH

(97 MOUNT VERNON STREET; 617-720-5511) is a Persian restaurant in the basement of a Beacon Hill townhouse. Allow the well-informed wait staff to guide you through the pleasures of an exotically delicious cuisine with influences from the Near East to the Far East.

RIALTO

(IN THE CHARLES HOTEL, HARVARD SQUARE, CAMBRIDGE; 617–661–5050) serves the foods of southern Spain, France, and Italy. Make a reservation—Jody Adams is rightfully considered one of Boston's most accomplished chefs. The lounge is a good place to meet the local intelligentsia.

MR. & MRS. BARTLEY'S BURGER COTTAGE

(1246 MASSACHUSETTS AVENUE, CAMBRIDGE; 617–354–6659) is a Harvard Square landmark that has been serving huge hamburgers to Harvard students forever. Every other customer dines solo—many with his or her head in a book.

COMMENTS *E.B.: When I am in Boston alone, I always head for the bar/counter at* Legal Seafoods, *27 Columbus Avenue, 617–426–4444, behind the Park Plaza Hotel. There are waiting lines, but a single diner sometimes gets a seat while couples wait. The seafood is super; the chowder is heaven.*

A couple of trendy favorites that have dining bars are Mistral *(221 Columbus Avenue, 867–9300), a great looking South End spot known for fine food, and* Restaurant Zinc *(35 Stanhope Street, 262–2323), a French restaurant where even the bar is elegant. If you are looking for a sushi bar, try* Ginza *(16 Hudson Street, 338–2261).*

Biba *(272 Boylston Street, 617–426–5684) made* Esquire *magazine's list of twenty best places in America for a solo meal. The bar offers a terrific tasting menu.*

Another possibility is Durgin Park, *a longtime landmark in the North Building of Quincy Market (617–227–2038), where diners are seated at long communal tables and served big portions of roast beef and other hearty American fare by waitresses renowned for their grumpiness. It's definitely touristy, but do it once anyway.*

Chicago

Penny Pollack, Dining Editor of *Chicago Magazine*, recommends:

BERGHOFF

(17 WEST ADAMS; 312–427–3170) is a genuine Chicago institution serving traditional German cuisine and house-made brews since 1898!

BIG BOWL CAFE

(159½ West Erie; 312-787-8927) is a casual, fun Asian cafe created in the noodle-house tradition. Simple, fresh noodle-based dishes under $10 are the mainstay here. An interactive stir-fry bar adds to the fun.

ED DEBEVIC'S SHORT ORDERS

(640 North Wells at Ontario; 312-664-1707) provides 1950s nostalgia, burgers served to the blare of rock and roll, and a gum-cracking, smooth-talking wait staff.

FRONTERA GRILL

(445 North Clark; 312-661-1434) serves the most sophisticated Mexican food in town. Single diners may sit at the bar, and often avoid a line for tables so long you could grow old waiting.

BLUE CRAB LOUNGE

(21 East Hubbard; 312-527-2722) is under the same roof as Shaw's Crab House. It offers raw-bar items plus a few more ambitious entrees served mostly at high stools along the bar. If you prefer table seating, Shaw's is a good choice, too.

CAFE SPIAGGIA

(980 North Michigan; 312-280-2764) treats you to all the flavors of Northern Italy in a casual-chic setting overlooking Michigan Avenue—and for considerably less money than in its elegant next-door sibling, Spiaggia.

SEASONS CAFE

(at the Four Seasons Hotel; 120 East Delaware; 312-280-8800) provides a cozy nook off the main dining room where you can enjoy expertly prepared soups, grilled fish, pastas, and salads.

BISTRO 110

(110 East Pearson; 312-266-3110) serves typical bistro standards accompanied by crusty baguettes at this lively spot just off Michigan Avenue.

MITY NICE GRILL

(at Water Tower Place; 835 North Michigan Avenue; 312-335-4745) has the decor and feel of the forties and the comfort food of the nineties. The perfect stop after shopping on Michigan Avenue.

MRS. PARKS TAVERN

(at the Doubletree Guest Suites at 198 East Delaware; 312-280-8882) is a sophisticated spot in a sophisticated neighborhood. The kitchen benefits from the talent and style upstairs at the pricier Park Avenue Cafe.

BRASSERIE JO

(59 West Hubbard; 312-595-0800) is a sizzling, bustling River North hot spot for robust Alsatian food and custom-brewed beer.

CHEESECAKE FACTORY

(in the John Hancock Center at 875 North Michigan Avenue; 312-337-1101) sports eclectic, over-the-top decor and provides great people-watching, an enormous California-style menu, and delectable cheesecakes.

MASHED POTATO CLUB

(316 W. Erie, 312-255-8579) has a gimmick—gazillions of toppings (from chocolate chips to caviar) for baked or mashed potatoes. The place is outrageous—you half expect a drag show to start any minute—and fun. Watch the prices, those toppings can add up quickly.

OKNO

(1332 North Milwaukee Avenue, 773-395-1313) is rocking by 9 P.M., full of trendoids who would look at home in the hottest hip NYC restaurant. Sit at the bar and graze on appetizers such as lamb chimichangas or Mongolian barbecue duck roll. Every night a different DJ every night adds to a raucous scene.

312 CHICAGO

(136 North La Salle Street, 312-696-2420) attached to the new Allegro Hotel in the ever-evolving Chicago Loop, this clubby room makes singles feel welcome. Whether seated at the counter fronting the kitchen or comfortably ensconced in a tapestried armchair, light-handed American interpretations of French and Italian techniques make for a pleasing bill of fare.

COMMENTS *E.B.: Chicago pizza is not to be missed. Local critics say it isn't as good as it used to be, but as an out-of-towner, I'm still impressed with* Giordano's *(at 747 West Rush Street; 312–251–0747 or at 1840 North Clark Street; 312–944–6100), the place that made "stuffed pizza" famous. Also worth noting is* Gordon, *(500 North Clark Street; 312–467–9780), one of the city's better restaurants, it recently has featured "Gordon's Table," where solo diners gather. Such features don't always last, so call to be sure before you go.*

San Francisco

Patricia Unterman, respected restaurant reviewer for the *San Francisco Chronicle*, suggests these singles-friendly places:

IL FORNAIO

(1265 Battery Street; 415-986-0100) a bustling Italian trattoria with a comfortable counter.

LITTLE JOE'S

(523 Broadway; 415-443-4343) is a busy, old-fashioned Italian restaurant known for its pasta and veal; it's inexpensive and has a counter.

HAYES STREET GRILL

(320 Hayes Street; 415-863-5545) specializes in fish and has a number of smaller tables for singles. Zagat ranks it among the city's best for seafood.

STARS

(150 Redwood Alley between Polk and Van Ness; 415-861-7827) offers both counter seating and an informal cafe in a large au courant restaurant in the Civic Center; owner Jeremiah Tower is a culinary star.

VICOLO PIZZERIA

(201 Ivey Street; 415-863-2382) is an upscale pizzeria with counter seats and small tables.

VIVANDE PORT A VIA

(2125 Fillmore Street; 415-346-4430) is a wonderful Italian deli and cafe with a counter and small tables. Note that it is open only until 7:00 P.M.

HAWTHORNE LANE

(22 Hawthorne Street; 415-777-9779) is in the blooming SOMA area. It's pricey but well recommended.

Ms. Unterman adds that many San Francisco restaurants now feature a bar or counter where you can stop in for a fine meal alone, including Kuleto's (221 Powell Street, 415-397-7720). Designer Pat Kuleto, whose imaginative settings are found in many of the city's favorite dining places, has made eating bars one of his trademarks. They can be found at Boulevard in SOMA (1 Mission Street, 415-543-6084), Farallon near Union Square (415-956-6969), and Jardiniere near the Opera House (300 Grove Street, 415-861-5555).

Another favorite with a dining bar facing the kitchen is Rose Pistola in North Beach (532 Columbus Avenue, 415-399-0499).

Four Favorite Cities

EVERYBODY HAS HIS OR HER OWN FAVORITE CITIES. I'VE chosen Amsterdam, Montreal, Paris, and New York, not only for their beauty or excitement but because I have found them to be especially easy cities to be in by myself. My descriptions are not meant to be used as a substitute for a comprehensive guidebook—they are simply personal impressions to share what I've found most enjoyable when traveling on my own.

Amsterdam

There's a fairy-tale quality to the tilty, gabled townhouses on the tree-lined canal streets of Amsterdam. Though apartments, boutiques, and cafes may hide behind the historic facades, the beautiful, old city has not changed since the seventeenth century. No matter how many times you walk along the canals, they are always enchanting, even in busy midday when traffic and whizzing bicycles dispel the old-world illusion. The loveliest times for walking are on a silent Sunday morning or on a summer evening when the old facades are floodlit.

The contrasting aspects of this city equally well known for its Rembrandts and its red-light district are endlessly fascinating. Amsterdam is small, so you can cover most of it on foot, savoring such details as the charming, no-two-alike gables atop the houses, the growing number of kicky boutiques, the many art galleries, the tempting bakeries, and the masses of flowers in the colorful, floating flower market. Outdoor markets for everything from postage stamps to parakeets to "junk-tiques" are another intriguing part of the cityscape that you need no company to enjoy.

Amsterdam's polyglot population is another part of its appeal. The freewheeling atmosphere makes everyone, young and old, feel at home. The street music characterizes the happy spirit of the city. On one recent stroll in Amsterdam I counted six kinds of music from various music makers: a classical violinist outside the concert hall, a folksinger-guitarist near the van Gogh museum, a rock group in front of the train station, a carillon ringing from a church steeple, an organ concert wafting from an open church door, and the tinkly tunes of a barrel organ in Dam Square. All are typically Amsterdam.

Several things make Amsterdam particularly easy for solo travelers. First, everyone speaks English. Second, if you stay within the confines of the old city, you can easily walk to see the Rembrandts in the Rijksmuseum and the priceless collections in the Vincent van Gogh Museum, as well as to concerts and restaurants. If you tire, cheerfully clanging trolley cars are waiting on every major street. To save money buy the trolley tickets that are good for a whole day or get a strip of tickets good for a number of rides. Tickets are also available for individual rides if you think you won't make good use of the more economical multiple-ride tickets. For a wonderful way to see the city, sign up for a bicycle tour and join the Dutch on their bikes. Check with the tourist office for current offerings.

Because the center of the city is small, almost any hotel is conveniently located, but two with particularly sociable bars are the American Hotel, an art deco landmark at 97 Leidsekade (31–20–624–5322), and the Pulitzer, an amalgam of seventeenth-century townhouses at 315 Prinsengracht (31–20–627–6753). The Ambassade at 341 Herengracht, (31–20–324–5321) made up of six patrician canal houses, is one of the more interesting luxury hotels. Among less-expensive canal-house hotels with special charm are the Canal House at 148 Keizersgracht, (31–20–622–5182); the Hotel Agora at 462 Singel, and Seven Bridges at 31 Reguliersgracht (31–20–623–1329).

What's best of all about Amsterdam when you are by yourself is that it is a city where people like to "hang out"—in sidewalk cafes in summer and in coffee shops and local taverns, known as "brown bars," in winter. There's always a place where you can comfortably have a cup of coffee, a drink, or a meal without feeling out of place because you are alone. And if you need to, it is easy to watch your budget. At dozens of restaurants, you'll see the knife-and-fork symbol indicating a tourist menu, which means a price-fixed three-course meal. You'll no doubt make your own dining discoveries as you wander, but the following are some recommended spots.

The busy square called Leidseplein is the center of Amsterdam's nightlife, and together with the side streets perpendicular to its edges it offers a wide range of cafes from casual to chic. These cafes deserve special recommendation:

CAFE-RESTAURANT AMERICAIN
(IN THE AMERICAN HOTEL AT 97 LEIDSEKADE) is a high-ceilinged art deco rendezvous for everything from reading a newspaper over a cup of coffee to indulging in a full dinner menu. Theatergoers, actors, musicians, and tourists all can be found here or on the big terrace cafe outside. One of the city's most popular gathering spots, it's perfect when you are alone.

OESTERBAR
(10 LEIDSEPLEIN) offers a top seafood restaurant upstairs with an informal, tiled dining room on the street level with tables and a counter.

You might also try these nearby restaurants:

HAESJE CLAES
(275 SPUISTRAAT) is small, narrow, wood-paneled, atmospheric, and inexpensive.

DE KNIJP
(134 VAN BAERLESTRAAT) offers a range of choices from quiches to six-course feasts in a pleasant spot with a garden.

CAFE HANS & GRIETJE
(27 SPIEGELGRACHT) is a quaint place with an upstairs restaurant and a downstairs bar/cafe.

PULITZER COFFEE SHOP
(IN THE PULITZER HOTEL AT THE CORNER OF KEIZERSGRACHT AND REESTRAAT) has rattan furnishings, contemporary art, and a menu that runs the gamut from snacks to substantial meals.

KEUKEN VAN 1870
(4 SPUISTRAAT) has the plainest Dutch cooking at the lowest prices. Patrons share tables, so it is a good place to meet Amsterdammers.

CASA DI DAVID
(426 SINGLE) is a family-run Italian restaurant overlooking the canal. It offers reasonably priced homemade pastas and pizza.

PANCAKE BAKERY
(191 PRINSENGRACHT) is a restored canalside warehouse with more than fifty kinds of Dutch pancakes—great for lunch or a light dinner and very light on the pocketbook.

L'OPERA
(27–31 REMBRANDTSPLEIN) is a split-level art deco restaurant-cafe and bar with a big, popular terrace.

KANTJIL EN DE TIJGER
(291 SPUISTRAAT) is the place to sample a multi-dish Indonesian rijsttafel.

SALAD GARDEN
(75 WETERINGSCHANS), located near the Rijksmuseum, has much more than salads—light meals are served downstairs; formal dining is above. A perfect place for afternoon tea.

HOLLANDS GLORIE
(220–222 KERKSTRAAT), longtime local favorite, serves up popular-priced food in a wonderful Old Dutch setting of copper and tiles.

For further information on Amsterdam, contact the Netherlands Board of Tourism (NBT) at 355 Lexington Avenue, New York, NY 10017 or 225 North Michigan Avenue, Chicago, IL 60601 or call (888) 464–6552 (www.goholland.com). Recommended guides include *Eyewitness Guide to Amsterdam,* Dorling Kindersley, London and New York, and *Cadogan Amsterdam,* Cadogan Books, London.

Montreal

Here's a touch of French *joie de vivre* right over the border—and you don't even have to know the language. Montreal is an easily manageable city of 1.8 million people with the life, charm, and sophistication of a city many times its size. Promenaders on the streets and laughter in the sidewalk cafes last well into the night!

The setting is unusual and scenic: an island in the middle of the St. Lawrence River, with a little mountain, Mont Royal, providing acres of greenery right in the middle of town. The street and shop signs, much of the food and the ambience are strictly French and foreign, yet almost everyone in Montreal is bilingual, so you'll not have to open your phrase book unless you want to.

The marvel of Montreal is its Metro, a subway system that is not only clean, safe, and speedy but a tourist attraction in itself. Buy a day pass for a discount, and ask for a free pocket-sized map card of the city and the Metro system. Miles of the Metro's wide, well-lit, attractive corridors connect the city's main shopping complexes and offer hundreds of shops in the corridors themselves. The system provides something to do no matter what the weather. The entertainers who make your strolling and waiting time tuneful are top-rate musicians who have auditioned to compete for their spots.

The efficient train system also makes it easy to visit far-flung attractions such as the Olympic Stadium or the former site of Expo 67, now a complex of gardens, museums, and the elegant Casino de Montreal, housed in the former French Pavilion. The guided tour of the Olympic Park includes visits to the city's fine Botanical Garden, one of the largest in the world, known for its Japanese and Chinese gardens. Other attractions are the unique Insectarium, the Biosphere (where the St. Laurence–Great Lakes ecosystems come alive), and the Biodome, which has four ecosystems under one roof.

Quaint Old Montreal on the banks of the St. Lawrence is the city's tourist mecca. Browsing is pleasant, though many of the shops are decidedly commercial. For a fascinating history tour of the area, take one of the walks given daily from late June through September with one of Guidatour's English-speaking guides. For information, call (800) 363–4021.

The city's history is displayed in the new Pointe-a-Calliere Museum of Archaeology and History of Montreal, located on the site on Place Royale where the city was founded. The upstairs cafe has a wonderful view of the port.

Self-guided walking tours printed in the free official Tourist Guide take you through some of the city's other neighborhoods—the elegant

Sherbrooke Street area that boasts the city's top hotels and boutiques and the handsome McGill University campus; Saint-Denis, the lively "Latin Quarter" of student life filled with boutiques and cafes; Avenue Laurier, a burgeoning area of upscale shops and restaurants, and Boulevard Saint-Laurent with its mix of nationalities, trendy bistros, discos, and cigar bars. Everywhere you go, you'll find sidewalk cafes where you can have a rest and a view of the passing scene.

On Sherbrooke, the Montreal Museum of Fine Arts is housed in two buildings; the spectacular newer pavilion was designed by noted Israeli architect Moshe Safdie with a fourth-floor atrium that offers a grand view of the city. The collections range from Rembrandt to Rodin.

Shopping is one of this city's greatest pleasures, and one you need no company to enjoy. The fashions are French, and the prices are Canadian, a great combination for travelers with American dollars. Boutiques and department stores on Sainte-Catherine Street vie with the most elegant of those to be found at city shopping centers anywhere. Ogilvy's, for one, is an old-world treasure filled with five floors of lovely boutiques.

Two centers are modernistic dazzlers and good places for informal meals as well. Les Cours Mont-Royal, a former hotel on Peel Street, has been converted to a fourteen-level elegant mall of interior courtyards, skylights, fountains, and glittering chandeliers. The mall is shared by more than fifty fine shops, movie theaters, condominiums, and offices. Its black-and-white food court, called Noir et Blanc, has among its tenants one of the city's best restaurants, Guy et Dodo Morali.

Place Montreal Trust, between McGill College Avenue and Mansfield, boasts a number of cafes and 120 boutiques on its five multicolored levels, including such familiar names as Fendi, Rodier, Bally, and Crabtree and Evelyn, as well as dozens of shops featuring exclusive designer creations. This is also the home of Montreal's Planet Hollywood.

If you have dreamed of buying a fur coat for yourself or to give as a gift, Montreal is definitely the place. The selection and the prices are superior, and the American dollar goes far. The fur district is centered around Mayor Street.

Where to stay? The top-of-the-line hotels are on Sherbrooke West, the Ritz-Carlton at 1228 (800–426–3135), and the Westin-Mont Royal at 1050 (514–284–1110). They are top-notch and conveniently located near the cafes on convivial Crescent Street. The more moderately priced Courtyard by Marriot is about 6 blocks away at 410 Sherbrooke West (800–449–6654). Chateau Versailles (1659 Sherbrooke West; 800–361–7199), a small hotel comprising four Victorian houses, is also a good value.

The safe and efficient Metro makes this an ideal city for bed-and-breakfast lodgings. For reservations, contact Montreal Bed and Breakfast, P.O. Box 575, Montreal H3X 3T8; (514) 738–9410 or (800) 738–4338.

When it comes to restaurants, you can hardly go wrong in Montreal. The gastronomic capital of Canada, it is a city all but dedicated to wining and dining. This is a sophisticated city, and no one raises an eyebrow when you enter a restaurant alone. Take your pick of the places in the following areas:

Crescent Street between Sherbrooke and Sainte-Catherine is a favorite area of Montreal's over-30 smart set. A host of good, informal choices await, many with outside terraces. Les Halles at 1450 Crescent is one of the city's gourmet landmarks; it's probably a better bet at lunchtime if you are alone. Nearby streets such as Bishop and Stanley have their own share of charming cafes. A few recommendations are:

THURSDAYS
(1449 CRESCENT) French, with a lively young crowd.

LE CHRYSANTHEME
(1208 CRESCENT) Interesting Chinese.

LE MAS DES OLIVIERS
(1216 BISHOP) French.

L'AUTRE SAISON
(2137 CRESCENT) A good lunching spot with super salads.

The lower part of Saint-Denis Street near the University of Quebec draws younger patrons to its wall-to-wall lineup of cafes of all nationalities. The farther up the hill you go, the more sophisticated the restaurants and the older the crowd. During the late-June Jazz Festival, the lower street sings with impromptu concerts. Suggestions in this neighborhood are:

L'EXPRESS
(3927 SAINT DENIS) French bistro.

TOQUE

(3842 SAINT DENIS) "Vertical cuisine," a unique experience.

LALOUX

(1250 AVENUE DES PINS EAST) French bistro.

LA SILA

(2040 SAINT DENIS;) Italian.

Prince Arthur Street and Duluth Street, not far from the Saint-Denis area, are filled with Greek and other ethnic restaurants with big outdoor patios. They're all inexpensive and strictly BYOB —bring your own bottle of wine. Prince Arthur is also a pedestrian mall where guests enjoy street entertainment along with the modest dinner tabs. Just pick a place with an empty seat out front.

You'll find more tourists than locals in Old Montreal, but you'll also find street musicians and a host of outside cafes. This neighborhood is not my favorite part of the city, but I did enjoy a meal at Claude Postel (443 St. Vincent). It offers excellent French food. Another good choice is Bonaparte (443 St. Francois-Xavier), where lunch is a good value.

Another good bet is found in The Alcan Building (Maison Alcan) at 1188 Sherbrooke Street West. In the inner court of this interesting building is Brulerie Saint-Denis, a perfect place for lunch, light suppers, or desserts.

The Ritz Garden is nearby at 1228 Sherbrooke Street West. Don't miss the beautiful outdoor setting and delicious food. The gracious Ritz staff will make you comfortable, but if you are shy about dinner, come for lunch, a fabulous breakfast, or high tea. Also not far away are the restaurants in the Westin-Mont Royal Hotel at 1050 Sherbrooke Street West. Opus, located right off the lobby, offers extraordinary French cuisine, and Zen is a Chinese extravaganza with moderate prices.

For further Montreal information, send for the free Tourist Guide and other excellent materials put out by the Montreal Tourisme. You can find them at www.tourism-montreal.org or get information in the U.S. by phone at Tourisme Quebec (800–363–7777).

Paris

Can the most romantic city in the world really be a good place to be alone? I know none better. Paris is dazzling, incredibly beautiful, and interesting at every turn. There are never enough days to begin to cover all the neighborhoods to be explored, all the fascinating shops for browsing, and all the incredible museums to be visited. No matter how many times you go, there is always something new to see. The splendid additions to the Louvre, the soaring d'Orsay Museum filled with Impressionist works, and the charming Picasso Museum are visual treats. The old Place de Vosges neighborhood grows more beautiful each year. And since there is always some controversial modern building going up, it's fun to have a look and form an opinion about places like the Pompidou Center, the new Les Halles, the pyramid entrance at the Louvre, and the Bastille Opera.

Of course, a visit to Paris may be more enjoyable if you speak a modicum of French. Some lessons before you leave home are helpful, and a phrase book is a necessity. On my last visit I noticed that a remarkable number of Parisians now are willing to speak some English, and I found residents extremely kind and helpful. The three-star restaurants may not be overly warm to American-speaking guests, but in the less-rarified stratas of the city, in my opinion, Paris no longer deserves its longtime reputation for coldness.

Unfortunately, you can't always count on the cab drivers to speak English. When I travel around Paris, I always carry the indispensable street guide, the little red *Cartes Taride,* which locates every single address in each of the city's *arrondissements* or districts. It also includes a detailed map of each arrondissement as well as maps of the Metro subway system and the bus routes. All you need to do is add an *X* to mark your spot, and you'll always be able to find your way. You can find the *Cartes Taride* in larger U.S. bookstores, or you can buy one when you arrive in Paris.

The Metro is simple to figure out. Stations are marked with a large *M*, and many have elegant turn of the century art nouveau entrances. You can buy *un carnet* ("uhn kar-*nay*"), a book of ten tickets good for train or bus at a discount. If you will be in town for five to seven days, a better bet is the Carte Orange, which gives you a week of unlimited travel; come prepared—you'll need two passport-size photos of yourself. Whichever you use, remember to take your ticket when the machine returns it. You sometimes need it to exit.

To find the right train, find your destination on a Metro map and trace the line by following the color coding and the number of the line. At the end of the line you will see the number of the last stop—it will guide you to the right train. The name of the last stop is also indicated on the platform. Inside the train is a chart of all the stops, so you can follow your route. You'll find a neighborhood map at almost every Metro exit.

You might prefer to take your time and ride the bus, since every route in this city makes for a scenic tour. A bus map is available at the big tourist office on the Champs-Elysées. Each bus is clearly marked with a route number and its final destination. Traveling across town by bus may require more than one ticket; ask the driver. Just a few of the outstanding sight-seeing routes are:

- LINE 24, WHICH CROSSES THE SEINE FOUR TIMES AND PASSES MOST OF THE CITY'S FAMOUS SITES.
- LINE 29 FROM THE OPERA TO THE BASTILLE.
- LINE 38 FROM LES HALLES ACROSS ILE DE LA CITÉ AND UP BOULEVARD SAINT-MICHEL TO THE LUXEMBOURG GARDENS.
- LINE 63, A LEFT BANK ROUTE THROUGH THE SAINT-GERMAIN-DES-PRES AREA.
- LINE 84 FROM THE MADELEINE UP RUE ROYALE, AROUND THE PLACE DE LA CONCORDE THROUGH THE HEART OF THE LEFT BANK TO THE LUXEMBOURG GARDENS AND AROUND THE PLACE DE PANTHEON.
- LINE 96 FROM MONTPARNASSE THROUGH SAINT-GERMAIN-DES-PRES TO SAINT PAUL.

Check a current map before you board to be sure that routes have not changed and remember that bus service is limited on Sundays and evenings.

Not even the most magnificent ride will satisfy for long in a city made to order for walking. One of the best ways to get to know Paris on a first visit is with Paris Walking Tours, run by a personable young English couple. Ninety-minute tours, which vary from week to week, may take in Notre-Dame, Sainte-Chapelle, the Luxembourg Gardens, Hemingway's Paris, the old village of Montmartre, medieval Paris, the Invalides, Paris of the Impressionists, the Ile St.-Louis and the Seine, the Marais and the Opera House. The company also does bus trips to Malmaison and

Versailles. Reservations for walks are not necessary; groups meet at a designated Metro stop. For information, phone (33–1) 48–09–21–40.

It's also nice for those of us who haven't mastered French that the Louvre offers regular tours in English. Check at the information desk for the time schedule.

Besides tours, the many English-language bookshops afford an excellent way to find other English-speaking people in Paris. **Brentano's** (37, avenue de l'Opera) is the largest of these and a good place to pick up information through the little paper called *American in Paris,* which lists activities of interest to Americans. You might find such events as a "quintessential July Fourth party." Restaurants advertising in this paper are those where Americans living in the city are likely to be found.

My favorites of the English-language bookstores are **W.H. Smith's** combination restaurant, tearoom, and bookshop at 248, rue de Rivoli (also a fine place for a meal or a snack), and **Shakespeare and Company,** 37, rue de la Boucherie, an atmospheric gem of a used bookstore on the Left Bank. When I last visited the latter, you could borrow (they'll ask you to leave a deposit) a copy of *Pariswalks,* one of the best guides to self-guided walking tours, and have free tea upstairs on Sunday afternoons at 4:00 P.M. If you are staying in the city long enough, you might want to sign up for language lessons at the Alliance-Francaise, 101, boulevard Raspail, another place to meet your countrymen.

Of course you haven't come all the way to Paris only to meet other Americans, but when you have no companion in a city where few people speak your language well, it is a relief to take a break occasionally and talk freely to someone from home.

While you're in Paris, read all you can about the city to discover some of the special small pleasures that you might overlook, such as the concerts held at Sainte-Chappelle, illuminated by daylight through the church's glorious stained-glass windows. Check the "Bests" section in the guidebook *Paris Access* for other treasures favored by a number of noted Paris visitors. The "Star Sights" noted in the *Eyewitness Guide to Paris* offer a good roundup of special sights not to be missed.

Any guidebook can tell you about the grand hotels of Paris, but there are many small, reasonable hotels with some amount of charm (albeit small rooms) where you can be comfortable by yourself and not spend a fortune. Among those that have been recommended to me are: the Hotel de la Bretonnerie, 22, rue Ste-Croix de la Bretonnerie (48 87 7763), in the lovely Marais district; Hotel Des Deux Iles, 59, rue St. Louis-en-L'Ile (43 26 1335), on the Ile St. Louis; Hotel Burgundy (8 rue Duphot, 01–42-60–34–12, two converted 1830s townhouses on the posh Right Bank, Hotel L'Abbaye St. Germain (10 rue Cassette, 01–45–44–38–11), a one-time convent turned into a boutique hotel on the Left Bank near the Luxembourg Gardens, Hotel Littre, (9 rue Littre, 01–45–44–38–68) another Left Bank choice, and the Louvre Forum (25 rue du Vouloi, 01-42-36-54-19), a simple, clean, and centrally located budget hotel on the Right Bank.

Unless you are determined to try the famous culinary palaces of Paris, dining alone in this city is a snap. There are cafes and bistros in every neighborhood, many with big outdoor terraces, and dozens of tiny eateries where solo diners are commonplace. Attractive tearooms are perfect places for lunch, as are wine bars. And though the street has become a bit tacky, the Champs-Elysées offers a lineup of reasonably priced cafes offering the traditional steakfrites (beef steak and French fries); lone diners are not at all unusual in this neighborhood.

An expensive but wonderful way to enjoy French cuisine with company—and to take home the ability to cook it yourself—is to sign up for the Gourmet Sessions at the famous cooking school, Le Cordon Bleu (8, rue Leon Delhomme). Courses are available from a half day to a month. A one-day class of particular interest for visitors is a visit with chefs (and an English interpreter) to a city market, followed by a light buffet and a cooking demonstration in the afternoon. Demonstration lessons are also open to the public. For a schedule and information in the United States, phone (800) 457–CHEF. Le Cordon Bleu also supplies students with a list of hotels where they receive special rates.

Check the *Michelin Guide to Paris* if you want the latest count on star chefs in Paris; if you can afford the bill, you can probably eat better in this city than anywhere in the world. This small selection concentrates on atmospheric neighborhoods where you can roam and almost take your pick of comfortable spots to dine. Here are a few specific recommendations; broken down by neighborhoods:

The Marais
BOFINGER

(5, RUE DE LA BASTILLE) is a lively and pretty landmark brasserie dating back to 1864.

CHEZ JO GOLDENBERG

(7, RUE DE ROSIER) is on the main artery of the old Jewish ghetto, a local landmark.

Ile de la Cité
BRASERIE DE L'ILE ST. LOUIS

(55, QUAI DE BOURBON) popular newly chic old-timer dating to the 1880s.

Saint-Germain
AU PACTOLE

(44 BOULEVARD ST. GERMAIN) fine chef; fixed price menus can be good value.

LE PETIT ZINC

(25, RUE DE BUCI) is known for good food and always busy. The block of rue Gregoire-de-Tours between rue de Buci and boulevard Saint-Germain has about fifteen similar cafes.

The famous brasseries where Sartre, Hemingway, and other literary lions once assembled are now said by many to be overpriced and filled with nothing but tourists, but they are landmarks I wanted to see on my first visit to Paris and perhaps you will, too. You will find two on boulevard Saint-Germain: Café de Flore at 172, and Brassierie Lipp at 151. La Coupole is at 102, boulevard du Montparnasse. Aux Deux Magots is a 6 Place St.-Germain-des-Pres.

Other Recommendations
You might also try:

RESTAURANT DE PALAIS D'ORSAY

(62, RUE DE LILLE) is in the marvelous d'Orsay Museum and is open for lunch and dinner.

CAFE DE LA PAIX
(12, BOULEVARD DES CAPUCINES, PLACE DE OPERA) is a restored national landmark. Come for meals or tea between 3:00 P.M. and 6:00 P.M.

FAUCHON
(26, PLACE DE LA MADELEINE, 8TH ARRONDISSEMENT). This is the best cafeteria in Paris. You'll eat standing up, but it's still a "don't miss" for lunch.

AUDROUËT
(6 RUE ARSENE-HOUSSAYE) A new home for an old favorite once adjoining a fine cheese shop. Every dish includes cheese.

CAFÉ DROUANT
(18 RUE GAILLON) is the sibling of a famous restaurant and offers good value, given the quality of the food. The shellfish motif on the ceiling is famous.

RUE DE LA HUCHETTE, a Left Bank street near the Shakespeare and Company bookshop, is lined with inexpensive, small Greek restaurants—good to know about if your budget is running low.

If you are really low on cash and homesick, there are dozens of McDonalds and Burger Kings, plus scores of sound-alikes all over Paris. What is the culinary world coming to?

Guides to Paris
Eyewitness Guide to Paris, Dorling Kindersley, London and New York. Wonderful photographs and guided walking itineraries.

The Best of Paris and Provence, by Andre Gayot (Gault Millau, Incorporated AGP). Good for restaurants, hotels, and shopping tips.

Paris Access, by Richard Saul Wurman (AccessPress, Ltd., 59 Wooster Street, New York, NY 10012). Detailed neighborhood walking tours that include sights, shops, and dining places where you need them.

Michelin Guides, Paris. The old standbys, with green for sight-seeing, and red, with those much-desired star ratings, for dining. The guides stay popular because they tell you what you need to know quickly, and the narrow size is easy to carry in your pocket or purse.

New York

This is my city. Almost all of us who live here have a love-hate relationship with the place. We grumble about the traffic, the subways, the rents, the prices, and the crowds. What keeps us here, however, are the same elements that make New York a fabulous place to visit: It is one of the most diverse and exciting cities in the world, overflowing with cultural riches, theater magic, marvelous food, and wares from around the globe. The old saying is true: If you can't find it in New York, it probably doesn't exist.

The pace and pulse of the city are tangible, maybe daunting at the start but eventually drawing you in to pick up your step and share the excitement. If you can't have a wonderful time here, you just aren't trying.

The New York subway is intimidating to strangers and sometimes even to natives. To feel secure getting around the city, familiarize yourself with the bus system. Buses are slow but sure, and they provide a great way to see the sights as well as the natives. Also, they cost just $1.50 per ride. You won't mind the traffic nearly so much if you aren't watching a taxi meter tick. You'll need exact change before you board, and no bills are accepted, so bring lots of change with you. Better yet, go down into any subway station and buy a Metrocard, which is also accepted on all buses. You can buy the Metrocard in any denomination over $5; each ride is automatically deducted when you board and slide the card through a slot. The card is gradually replacing the old New York subway tokens.

Contrary to what many out-of-towners expect, getting your New York bearings is easy because most of Manhattan is laid out on a straight grid, with avenues running north to south and streets running east to west. The central business district is only about 16 blocks wide, and you'll spend most of your time within eight to ten of them. Bus transfers are free if you need to change from a "crosstown" (east-west) bus to one heading uptown or downtown (or vice versa). This is automatic with a Metrocard, but without one you have to ask for a transfer when you board the first bus, not when you are getting off.

Bus routes are clearly marked on maps at most bus stops. A bus map is also printed on the back of the subway maps available free at token booths at the main city stations, or you can write to the New York

Only-in-New York Pleasures

Some favorite New Yorkers' pleasures that can be shared by visitors include:

- Biking the car-free roadways on the weekend or jogging around the reservoir any day in Central Park (both activities recommended for daylight hours only).
- Sitting on the steps of the Metropolitan Museum of Art on Sunday afternoon and watching the street performers and the passing parade.
- Visiting the farmer's Green Market in Union Square on Wednesday, Friday, or Saturday.
- Weekend brunching and gallery-hopping in SoHo along Broadway, West Broadway, and the cross streets between.
- Wandering Eighth Street, West Fourth Street, Bleecker, and other Greenwich Village streets along with young and young-at-heart New Yorkers.
- Walking the promenade along the East River from the World Financial Center through Battery Park City, with the Statue of Liberty in view all the way.
- Evenings at the city museums. The Museum of Modern Art is open until 8:30 P.M. (voluntary donation after 5 P.M.) on Thursday and Friday; the Metropolitan Museum of Art to 8:45 P.M. on Friday and Saturday; the Whitney Museum until 8:00 P.M. on Thursday (free admission after 6:00 P.M.); the Guggenheim to 8:00 P.M. on Friday (voluntary donation) and Saturday, and the American Museum of Natural History to 8:45 P.M. on Friday and Saturday.

Convention and Visitors Bureau (see page 275).

No one should miss a heart-stopping, skyscraper-high view of the city at night. Nothing else shows you so vividly why New York is unique. The Empire State Building observatory is open until midnight, and the top floor of the World Trade Center is open until 9:30 P.M. You might want to have a drink in the lounge of the Rainbow Room on the sixty-fifth floor of the RCA building, at City Lights on the 107th floor of the World Trade Center, or atop the Beekman Tower Hotel at First Avenue and 49th Street. A magical time to see the city from above is at dusk, when you can watch millions of city lights go on.

New Yorkers are champion walkers and they like exploring their city as much as visitors do, so when it comes to seeing specific neighborhoods on foot, you'll find a great choice of walking tours around almost every part of the city each weekend from late spring through fall. Some of these groups also offer bus excursions that make it easy to visit suburban attractions. Here are some of the leading organizations that offer guided walks and tours:

MUNICIPAL ART SOCIETY, 457 MADISON AVENUE AT 50TH STREET, NEW YORK, NY 10022; (212) 935-3960.

92ND STREET Y, 1395 LEXINGTON AVENUE, NEW YORK, NY 10128; (212) 996-1105.

BIG ONION TOURS; (212) 439-1090.

Two of the city's landmarks offer free tours, the magnificent public library at Fifth Avenue and 42nd Street each Saturday at 11:00 A.M and 2:00 P.M. and the beautifully restored Grand Central Station, 42nd Street and Lexington Avenue, each Wednesday at 12:30 P.M.

Central Park is one of the city's glories, a beautiful site and the best place to see a microcosm of city life from baby strollers to rock concerts. In summer it is the scene of free concerts by the Metropolitan Opera and the New York Philharmonic, free Shakespeare in the Park, and a whole series of popular and rock music known as Summerstage. The park is perfectly safe in daylight and is filled with hundreds of people. If you are nervous, however, join one of the guided Urban Park Ranger tours; schedules are available at The Dairy building in the park near 64th Street.

On a first trip to New York, Little Italy and Chinatown can be confusing and might well be better seen on a guided walking tour. But here are

some suggested neighborhoods to roam safely on your own to get a sense
of the city and its diversity (buy a book of self-guided walking tours to
find out who lived where as you wander):

- THE POSH UPPER EAST SIDE RESIDENTIAL STREETS, ROUGHLY BETWEEN 70TH AND 90TH
  STREETS FROM FIFTH TO PARK AVENUES.
- THE CHARMING WEST SIDE NEIGHBORHOODS FROM CENTRAL PARK WEST TO WEST END
  AVENUE BETWEEN 68TH AND 86TH STREETS.
- THE CHIC MADISON AVENUE SHOPS FROM THE 60S TO THE 90S.
- THE OVERPRICED BUT ENTICING BOUTIQUES ON COLUMBUS AVENUE FROM 68TH TO 81ST
  STREETS.
- THE WINDING STREETS AND HISTORIC TOWNHOUSES OF GREENWICH VILLAGE, THE OLD HEART
  OF LITERARY NEW YORK.

Shopping is a favorite New York pastime. Besides the special merchan-
dise carried by the hundreds of small shops, out-of-towners often find the
variety of wares in the big department stores such as Macy's, Saks Fifth
Avenue, and Bloomingdale's a revelation. Most of the branches in major
cities can't compare with the home stores. And the advent of superstores
like Bed, Bath and Beyond means stocks so enormous you can hardly get
through the whole store.

If you are brave and you know your labels, you can venture down to
bargain hunt on the crowded Lower East Side. Note that stores are closed
on Saturday in this old Jewish neighborhood, and Sunday is the busiest
shopping day. It is a good idea to go armed with one of the special shopping guides to the area sold in most bookstores.

Another pleasure not to be missed by book lovers is the city's trove of
wonderful specialized bookstores. Among the many stops providing
hours of happy browsing are the beautiful Rizzoli store at 31 West 57th
Street, specialty shops such as The Biography Bookshop at 400 Bleecker
Street; The Drama Book Shop for theater books at 723 Seventh Avenue
at 48th Street; Kitchen Arts & Letters at 1435 Lexington Avenue between 93d and 94th Streets; The Military Bookman at 29 East 93rd
Street, Hacker Art Books, 45 West 57th Street; and Murder Ink., two
stores full of mystery novels at 1465 Second Avenue and 96th Street and
2486 Broadway at 92nd Street. Check the Yellow Pages for addresses of

the big Barnes and Noble superstores now found all over town, most with a coffee bar for browsers and favorite meeting spots for single New Yorkers. Remaindered books and bargains can be found at the original Barnes and Noble at 105 Fifth Avenue, and used-book treasures are available at the Strand at 828 Broadway at 12th Street, the Argosy at 116 East 59th Street, and the Gotham Book Mart at 41 West 47th Street. The Yellow Pages will guide you to dozens of other specialists for everything from comic books to collectors' volumes.

No trip to New York is complete without a visit to the theaters and concert halls. To avoid spending a king's ransom, take advantage of the TKTS booth (Times Square Ticket Center) at 47th Street and Broadway. Half-priced tickets for Broadway and off-Broadway shows are sold on the day of the performance starting at 3:00 P.M., and at 10:00 A.M. for matinees on Wednesday, Saturday, or Sunday. If you happen to be sight-seeing downtown, there is a branch of TKTS, usually with much shorter lines, on the mezzanine at 2 World Trade Center. The hours are Monday to Friday 11:00 A.M. to 5:30 P.M. and Saturday 11:00 A.M. to 3:30 P.M.

Contrary to another popular belief, everything in New York does not cost pots of money. Television shows are one favorite free pastime, but you must get your request in early—at least one month in advance and often as much as six months ahead for the hot shows. Some networks will mail out ticket requests received by phone; others ask you to send in a postcard. At times, standby tickets may be available the morning of the show. Singles have a good shot. You can also pick up same-day tickets on occasion at the New York Visitors Bureau at 810 Seventh Avenue at 53rd Street. For up-to-date information on your favorite show, it's best to phone. Network numbers are: ABC, (212) 456–3054; CBS, (212) 975–2476; NBC, (212) 664–4000. Everyone is welcome to watch the *Today* show through the window daily 7:00 to 9:00 A.M at Rockefeller Plaza and 49th Street.

It won't cost you a cent to take in a master class or attend high-quality, free concerts by faculty and students at the noted Juilliard School; phone in advance for schedules and ticket information at (212) 799–5000. Thursday morning rehearsals of the New York Philharmonic at Avery Fisher Hall are open to the public for a modest fee.

There are numerous free concerts as well in building atriums (such as the glorious Winter Garden at the World Financial Center), museums, and outdoor plazas around the city. Check *New York* or *Time Out* magazines or the Convention and Visitors Bureau at (212) 484–1222; for a free guidebook, phone (800) NYC–VISIT (www.nycvisit.com).

Any guidebook will list the city's leading hotels. If you can't afford the top listings, but you prefer a small hotel to bed-and-breakfast homes, here are a few inexpensive and moderate recommendations. All are area code 212.

PICKWICK ARMS
(230 EAST 51ST STREET; 355-0300) offers no frills but a good, safe, East Side location.

HOTEL METRO
(45 EAST 35TH STREET; 947-2500) is breezy and cheerful and offers complimentary breakfast.

EDISON
(228 WEST 47TH STREET; 840-5000) is a refurbished hotel in the heart of the theater district; it saves searching for cabs after the show.

WYNDHAM
(42 WEST 58TH STREET; 753-3500) provides big, pretty rooms, dated plumbing, and the best values in town. This is a favorite with show-biz people; reserve far ahead to get in.

Assuming that new owners don't change things all of the Gotham Group hotels are highly recommended for solo travelers. They include breakfast, a sociable ambience, and sometimes even evening dessert. These stylishly renovated older properties include the Franklin (164 East 87th Street; 369–8000), the Wales (1295 Madison Avenue; 876–6000), the Shoreham (33 West 55th Street; 247–6700), and the Mansfield (12 West 44th Street; 944–6050). The Wales and the Franklin are located on the Upper East Side, a bit far from midtown but convenient for museum visits.

Consider leaving the midtown business center and seeing New York like a native by taking advantage of the city's bed-and-breakfast registries (see page 235). They'll show you what real life is like in the Big Apple, where in warm weather people sunbathe in the parks on Sunday and sit around in sidewalk cafes. Having checked out a number of these lodgings for a recent article, I was surprised at the lovely apartments available as B&Bs. It says a lot about the price of housing in New York that so many people are welcoming paying guests.

Where to dine alone in New York? There are plenty of options. If you want ambience, you'll find cafes even in some of the tiniest hotels. You'll no doubt make your own discoveries as you walk around, but some suggested havens for dining alone, by neighborhood, include:

Midtown

THE OYSTER BAR

(LOWER LEVEL IN GRAND CENTRAL STATION, 42ND STREET AND LEXINGTON AVENUE) provides counter service and a number of small tables; it's tops for seafood.

ASIA DE CUBA

(237 MADISON AVENUE BETWEEN 37TH AND 38TH STREETS) is a trendy favorite for its fusion menu and a singles favorite for the big communal table.

CARNEGIE DELICATESSEN

(854 SEVENTH AVENUE BETWEEN 54TH AND 55TH STREETS) is a New York landmark with wisecracking waiters, long, cramped tables, and legendary corned beef and pastrami sandwiches.

CHEZ NAPOLEON

(365 WEST 50TH STREET) is a homey, family-run French bistro, convenient for theatergoers.

CHINA GRILL

(60 WEST 53RD STREET AT THE CORNER OF SIXTH AVENUE) is a trendy favorite with a French-Chinese menu and long dining bar.

COMING OR GOING

(38 EAST 58TH STREET) is a tiny American spot, with charm and good home-style food; A good choice.

OSTERIA DEL CIRCO

(120 WEST 55TH STREET) has playful circus decor, tasty (if a bit pricey) Italian food, and a most convivial dining bar. Men love the female bartenders.

LA VINERIA

(19 WEST 55TH STREET) is a small, friendly Italian cafe with excellent food and reasonable prices.

EDISON CAFE

(AT THE HOTEL EDISON AT 228 WEST 47TH STREET) offers potato pancakes, blintzes, matzo ball soup, and the chance that show-biz biggies will stop in between shows.

LA BONNE SOUPE

(48 WEST 55TH STREET) is good for a light dinner.

PALIO

(151 WEST 51ST STREET) is an elegant Italian restaurant that serves meals at the knockout downstairs bar.

PEN & PENCIL

(205 EAST 45TH STREET), a business lunch favorite, offers cluster seating that encourages inter-table chatting among separately seated guests. Solo diners also receive a complimentary glass of the house pear grappa.

Upper West Side

Browse Columbus Avenue and its side streets between 65th and 81st Streets for limitless possibilities—just pick a cafe that doesn't have a line spilling out the door! If you aren't going to Lincoln Center, come after 8:00 P.M. when the crowds are smaller. A few recommendations:

MUSEUM CAFE

(COLUMBUS AT 77TH) offers a pleasant ambience.

CAFE FIORELLO

(1900 BROADWAY BETWEEN 63RD AND 64TH STREETS) have a seat at the antipasto bar and feast before an evening at Lincoln Center, just across the street.

RIKYU

(COLUMBUS BETWEEN 69TH AND 70TH STREETS) is Japanese with a choice of small tables or a sushi bar.

LINCOLN SQUARE COFFEE SHOP, RESTAURANT AND BAKERY

(COLUMBUS AVENUE BETWEEN 65TH AND 66TH STREETS) has a varied menu and a super salad bar.

Upper East Side

Browse Second Avenue between 74th and 86th Streets, and 86th Street east or west of Second Avenue and you'll have experienced a mini world tour of cuisines. Try one of these:

PAMIR

(1437 SECOND AVENUE BETWEEN 74TH AND 75TH STREETS) is a pretty little spot with Afghanistan specialties, a delicious and delicate blend of Indian and Middle Eastern fare.

MOCCA

(1588 SECOND AVENUE BETWEEN 82ND AND 83RD STREETS) is a European-style Hungarian cafe; it has good goulash and good prices.

WU LIANG YE

(215 EAST 86TH STREET BETWEEN 2ND AND 3RD AVENUES) is one of the best of the neighborhood's many Chinese choices.

LE PAIN QUOTIDIEN

(1131 MADISON AVENUE BETWEEN 83RD AND 84TH) serves breakfast, lunch, and early dinnier (to 7:00 P.M.) at a congenial 26-foot-long communal table.

BELLA CUCINA

(1293 LEXINGTON AVENUE AT 87TH STREET) is a pleasant, reasonably priced Italian eatery.

VIAND

(300 EAST 86TH STREET AND ALSO AT 1011 MADISON AVENUE AND AT 673 MADISON AVENUE) is an upscale coffee shop with wide-ranging diner-style menus and surprisingly good food. The upper Madison Avenue address is ideal if you are visiting the Metropolitan or Whitney museums.

Greenwich Village/SoHo

Pick any block and you'll likely find tiny, welcoming restaurants. Here are some possibilities:

CUCINA STAGIONALE

(275 BLEECKER STREET) produces Italian food that pleases both palate and pocketbook.

JOHN'S PIZZERIA

(278 BLEECKER STREET) is generally agreed to be New York's best, as attested by the long lines. Come at an off-hour.

WHITE HORSE TAVERN

(HUDSON AND 11TH STREETS) is a 106-year-old neighborhood classic.

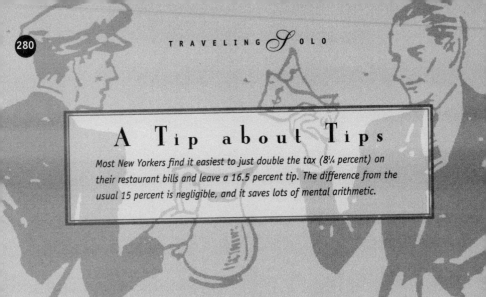

A Tip about Tips

Most New Yorkers find it easiest to just double the tax (8¼ percent) on their restaurant bills and leave a 16.5 percent tip. The difference from the usual 15 percent is negligible, and it saves lots of mental arithmetic.

ZOE
(90 PRINCE STREET) has a popular counter where diners can watch the chef in action.

CHEZ BRIGETTE
(77 GREENWICH AVENUE) is a hole-in-the-wall spot with counters—and incredible French food. Great for onion soup at lunch.

Don't leave the Village without sampling its coffee houses.
Two suggestions are:

PATISSERIE LANCIANI
(271 WEST FOURTH STREET) located between Perry and 11th Streets, has a light menu in addition to coffees.

CAFFE VIVALDI
(32 JONES STREET) offers incredible desserts.

The East Village

Here's where young New York eats on a budget. A few favorites are:

"LITTLE INDIA," covering all of 6th Street between First and Second Avenues, and spilling over onto First Avenue, is lined with tiny Indian restaurants, most BYOB. There are at least a dozen to try. **Mitali East** at 334 East Sixth Street, gets good reviews—or just pick the decor that pleases you; some people joke that they all use the same kitchen, anyway.

CHRISTINE'S

(208 FIRST AVENUE BETWEEN 12TH AND 13TH STREETS) has zero decor but is noted for inexpensive and hearty Polish home cooking.

TERESA'S

(103 FIRST AVENUE AT 6TH STREET) is another downtown Polish choice.

UNION SQUARE CAFE

(21 EAST 16TH STREET) is farther uptown and in another world. A stylish cafe that is one of the city's favorites, it has an innovative menu and a long bar where singles dine comfortably.

GOTHAM BAR & GRILL

(12 EAST 12TH STREET, 620–4020) Another of the city's top restaurants, welcomes with special trays that attach to the bar to make single diners comfortable. Their prix fixe lunch ($19.99 or $20.00, depending on the year) is a great deal.

Guides to New York

Recommended guides to the city are:

Eyewitness Guide to New York, (Dorling Kindersley, London and New York)

Nooks and Crannies: A Walking Tour Guide to New York City by David Yeadon (Charles Scribner's Sons, New York)

AIA Guide to New York City by Elliot Willensky and Norval White (Harcourt Brace, New York). A knowledgeable architectural guide for walking tours.

Frommer's Irreverent Guide to Manhattan (Macmillan, New York). An honest appraisal of what's good and bad around the city.

ACCESS NEW YORK CITY

(HarperCollins, New York). Handy street-by-street format.

Bring the *Kids*

USY SINGLE PARENTS WHO TAKE DOUBLE RESPONSIBILITY FOR their kids most of the year really deserve a vacation. They most often want to share that vacation with the children. They look forward to rare relaxed and unscheduled time to have fun together, family time to really talk and share. Having kids for company actually solves certain travel problems, such as solitary meals.

Yet, while shared family vacations can be wonderfully rewarding, single parents also need a break. In fact, each generation benefits from time off for relaxing and socializing with people in their own age group. For parents, that doesn't necessarily mean looking for romance—just a bit of adult companionship and conversation. So, the most successful single-parent outings with the kids offer both the opportunity for togetherness and time to be apart.

For that reason, some traditional family vacations aren't really great for single parents. One parent trying to keep up with two or three kids at Walt Disney World might be exhausted instead of exhilarated. Car trips can be miserable with no one to share the driving or the disciplining of the children. And resorts with children's programs can be populated mostly by couples who are relishing time together while *their* kids are busy, and they are therefore not much company for a parent alone. Luckily, there are options that offer both togetherness and a chance for separate activities.

Some Practical Pointers

Start by planning something *you* really want to do, regardless of the kids. Ranches are wonderful places for family vacations, but if you hate the idea of getting on a horse, life on a ranch isn't going to be any more appealing just because the children are along.

As with any family outing, arrangements generally work out better if the youngsters are involved in the planning and are excited about the trip. If there are choices to be made, even preschoolers can look at color brochures and have some say in what looks great to them. Let the children help write for brochures and information, using their own names so that the mail comes back addressed to them. If you decide on a city vacation, have them participate in making lists of what you hope to do each day. Readers can make a trip to the library to get books about the area you will be visiting.

A productive pretrip activity is to have children put together a scrapbook with space for preplanning and a day-to-day diary with room to paste in souvenirs as you travel. It helps build anticipation beforehand and keeps them busy along the way.

Older kids can also help put together those tried-and-true travel games, such as making a list of states that can be checked off when their license plates are spied. Another family favorite is printing the alphabet down the side of a sheet of notebook paper for each child, with space to fill in objects spotted for each letter. Don't forget to bring favorite books, toys, and other games to keep everyone happily occupied.

When you pack, choose comfortable, fast-drying clothing in dark colors so you needn't nag about keeping clothes clean on vacation. Be sure to include rainwear in case of bad weather.

Two issues that make for crabby tempers on family vacations are fatigue and hunger. Do your best to avoid both. Be prepared with snacks during travel times and in hotel rooms. Unfamiliar beds and schedules and the excitement of new places can wreak havoc with bedtimes, so plan time out for rest each day. It will do you good, too.

Keep traveling time to a minimum. Pack a small bag for each child with pajamas, toothbrush, toothpaste, and a favorite blanket and toy, so they can settle into a new place fast. If you need cribs and high chairs, call ahead to double-check that they are available and in place.

You'll find many more practical suggestions and ideas for traveling with children in the *Great Family Vacations* series by Candyce Stapen (The Globe Pequot Press, Old Saybrook, CT).

Singular Parent Choices

Some of the vacation choices recommended for single adults are equally comfortable for single-parent families. Active adventure vacations are wonderful for youngsters who are old enough to enjoy them. Almost all are appropriate for teens, and some can accommodate much younger children. Ask the operator about the ages recommended. Some groups that explicitly welcome children are listed below along with learning options that have separate programs for youngsters.

Ranch vacations are made to order for single parents, and all the guidance on page 22 is appropriate for families. Cruising from a family point of view is covered later in this chapter. See page 108 for information on windjammer cruises. Teenagers love the adventure of these big sailing ships, but restless younger children are not well suited to these trips. For them, stick to the ocean liners. If you want to go to a resort, check for tennis, sailing, or golf schools that are resort-based and have children's programs. Those arrangements will give you a focus, and you can make friends while the children enjoy their own brand of fun.

Here are a variety of vacation suggestions for single parents:

CLUB MED

40 EAST 57TH STREET, NEW YORK, NY 10019;
(800) CLUB-MED. (SEE PAGE 198.) (M–E)

Club Med doesn't just tolerate children—they welcome them, and they welcome single parents, too. Five Club Med villages have been designated for families, and at two of these, Eleuthera in the Bahamas and Ixtapa in Mexico, there are "Single Parenthood" programs featuring a private cocktail party for single parents at the start of each week and a sign-up board to make it easier to find a partner for sailing, tennis, or golf.

Kids' programs entertain and teach children aged 1 to 11 with non-stop activities, meals, and amusements, supervised and coordinated by a special staff, all at no additional cost. Programs run from 8:00 A.M. to 9:00 P.M. daily, and there are optional kid-pleasing early lunches and dinners to give parents the chance to enjoy conversation with other adults at meals.

Other villages for families include Sandpiper in Florida, Punta Cana in the Dominican Republic, Caravelle and St. Lucia in the Caribbean, and many other locations worldwide. Each has Petit, Mini, and Kids Clubs divided by age and geared to ages 2 to 11. Kids can stop by for one favorite activity, for an hour, or for the entire day. Sandpiper has a Baby Club with sitters for babies and toddlers 4 months to one year, and supervised sleeping for tots from 7:30 P.M. to 11:00 P.M. Potties and baby monitors are supplied free of charge. Little ones get their own wading pools, and at some clubs there is a private dining room with high chairs and furniture scaled to youngsters. Baby Clubs are equipped with cribs, playpens, and toys. Strollers, potties, and baby monitors can be borrowed at no extra charge. They even sell diapers in the boutiques. How family-minded can you get?

Activities vary from village to village. Among the fun possibilities are lessons in waterskiing, sailing, golf, and tennis, plus arts and crafts, archery, boat rides, picnics, puppet shows, and swimming. Lots of children love the Club Med circus workshops where they learn juggling, magic, trampolining, and how to walk a tightrope (with a net right below, of course). Organized evening programs keep the kids happy during adult dinner hours.

At certain times of the year, one child age 1 to 5 comes free with each adult. The time periods and the specific clubs offering this package may vary, so it's best to check for current information.

Teenagers have their own programs at Huatulco in Mexico and at Copper Mountain in Colorado during ski season.

GOLF DIGEST INSTRUCTION SCHOOLS

5520 PARK AVENUE, BOX 395, TRUMBULL, CT 06611;
(800) 243-6121 OR (203) 373-7130. (SEE PAGE 20.) (EE)

This large golf program offers a special parent/child program. Open to youngsters ages 12 and up; the instruction is geared to both age groups. A sharing and learning experience that builds closeness as well as golfing prowess, the program is limited to sixteen parent/child teams. In the past these three-day parent-child schools have been held at Sea Island, Georgia; check for the current locations.

SIERRA CLUB FAMILY OUTINGS

c/o Sierra Club, 730 Polk Street, San Francisco, CA 94109;
(415) 776-2211. (See page 90.) (I)

Introducing families to the joys of camping and the outdoors is one of the missions of the Sierra Club. Half a dozen outings each summer are designated especially for families, and the catalog notes that single parents as well as uncles, aunts, and grandparents are welcome. The difficulty of the trips varies. Some trips are lodge-based; others are at campsites. All offer opportunities for nature study, day hikes, fishing, swimming, and solitude. The group meets for breakfast and supper; lunch for outings is packed at breakfast. Most activities are informal and unstructured, and the group usually makes its own fun in the evening.

Among recent offerings were "Toddler Tramps" in state and national parks; these are appropriate for very young children. Other adventures included trips to Hawaii and wilderness adventures designated for children six years and older. The Sierra Club catalog also notes other types of trips that are suitable for families.

FAMILY GOES TO CAMP
SHERI GRIFFITH EXPEDITIONS

P.O. Box 1324, Moab, UT 84532;
(800) 332-2439 or (435) 259-8229. (See page 112.) (M)

The most exciting river runs are recommended for ages 10 and up, but this special five-day, four-night family trip of about 94 miles through the canyons of the Green River is full of big, rolling waves that are fun but not difficult and is open to children from age 5. A three-day program on the Colorado River features calm waters and camping in the tepees; it is open to children from age 3. Camping is on sandy beaches. Hiking excursions are part of the trips. Meals take pint-sized tastes into account by including hamburgers as well as steak. After dark come campfires, roasted marshmallows, and plenty of talk and song.

Guides also take the children on separate outings. Parents can join in
or take this time for themselves—for quiet relaxation beside the river, a
leisurely walk, or a demanding hike. According to the operators, many of
the adults are single parents.

FAMILY RAFTING
O.A.R.S. RAFTING ADVENTURES
Box 67, Angels Camp, CA 95222;
(209) 736–4677. (See page 113.) (I)

For families who want to be introduced to the fun and excitement of river-
rafting, special discounts are offered on half a dozen selected family dates
for trips on the many rivers this company navigates. The regular trips offered
by this group also welcome children of specified minimum ages, starting at 4
years for some of the shorter, easier trips and starting at 16 years for the more
rugged rivers.

FAMILY RAFTING
DVORAK'S RAFTING EXPEDITIONS
17921–B U.S. 285, Nathrop, CO 81236;
(800) 824–3795 or (719) 539–6851. (See page 114.) (I–M)

On specified family weeks, this outfitter invites one child under the
age of 13 to come along free with an adult. These trips on the
Green and Dolores rivers are planned with kids in mind. Reserve early—
they fill up fast.

Other short trips suitable as an introduction to river-running offer discounts for families of three and up.

CONSERVATION SUMMIT YOUTH PROGRAMS
NATIONAL WILDLIFE FEDERATION
8925 Leesburg Pike, Vienna, VA 22184;
(703) 790–4363 or (800) 245–5484. (See page 121.) (I)

Most of the programs for adults offer separate supervised activities
for children of all ages. "The Big Backyard," running from 8:00
A.M. to noon for three- and four-year-olds, is a nature discovery program
including micro-hikes, touch-and-feel expeditions, and fun-with-nature
crafts. "Junior Naturalists," for ages five to twelve, divide into age groups

for nature hikes, stream studies, wildlife investigations, bird walks, folktale hours, outdoor games, and arts and crafts. Their day runs from 8:30 A.M. to 3:00 P.M. A separate Teen Adventure program is adventure-oriented, with the chance to learn hiking, orienteering, and rope skills.

CORNELL'S ADULT UNIVERSITY

626 THURSTON AVENUE, ITHACA, NY 14850-2490;
(607) 255-6260. (SEE PAGE 47.) (I–M)

Although the title says adult, kids are far from forgotten here. More than 100 youngsters from all over the United States enroll in the Youth Program, having fun while their parents are learning on their own level. Families always have breakfast and dinner together, but child supervision is available from 8:30 A.M. to 11:15 P.M. for those who want it.

Programming is provided for five age groups. Infants and tots under 3 have no formal schedule, but qualified baby-sitters are available. Li'l Bears (ages 3 to 5) learn and play in a Cornell preschool facility. Art, music, crafts, expeditions across campus, and time to rest are all part of their fun. (Children enrolled must be potty trained.) Tykes, (five- and six-year-olds who have been to school) have their own similar sessions.

Sprouts (ages 7 and 8) have a learning program as well as hikes, games, sports, crafts, and cookouts. Junior Cornellians (ages 9 to 12) meet in the morning for a choice of classes and have recreational activities, outings to state parks, visits to campus facilities, and presentations and demonstrations by members of the faculty during supervised afternoon and evening programs. They can choose from a variety of classes including cooking, animal behavior, outdoor adventures such as ropes and wilderness hiking, horseback riding, windsurfing, and sailing.

Teens (ages 13 to 16) have an even wider selection, and they have their own reserved dormitory floor and dining place.

CHAUTAUQUA INSTITUTION

CHAUTAUQUA, NY 14722;
(716) 357-6200. (SEE PAGE 51.) (I–M)

While parents enjoy the multitude of classes and cultural events during the summer at Chautauqua, youngsters can enroll in the diverse children's programs offered. Programs are for one week to a full season.

Children's School, held from 9:00 A.M. to noon daily, is an early childhood center for preschoolers from age 3. It includes language enrichment, pre-reading, early math concepts, and exposure to the arts as well as creative free play. The Boys' and Girls' Club for ages 7 to 15 is organized as a day camp where children get a full schedule of summer recreation such as swimming, sailing, canoeing, arts and crafts, drama, music, archery, basketball, soccer, volleyball, and baseball. The group is divided into sections according to age.

For teenagers, the Youth Activities Center is open daily from noon to 11:00 P.M. It has its own beach (with diving board), a snack bar, amusement machines, Ping-Pong equipment, table games, and color television. Dances, cookouts, guest speakers, and movies are offered at night.

YOSEMITE FIELD SEMINARS

P.O. Box 230, El Portal, CA 95318;
(209) 379-2321. (See page 125.)

Activities for families include three-day "Adventure-A-Day" programs featuring day hikes in different areas of the park, ranging from 2 to 4 miles. Family backpacking expeditions, also lasting three days, are an easy introduction to camping in the beautiful wilderness of Tuolumne Meadows. Programs are recommended for children ages 6 to 12.

BACKROADS BICYCLING VACATIONS

1516 Fifth Street, Berkeley, CA 94710;
(800) GO-ACTIVE. (See page 97.) (I–M)

Several of this group's tours, both camping and with inn lodging, are designated as family outings. Recent destinations have included Washington State's Puget Sound, the Canadian Rockies, Maine, Vermont, Nova Scotia, and excursions in France and Switzerland. Family weekend trips in California are also planned.

ALASKA WILDLAND ADVENTURES

P.O. Box 389, Girdwood, AK 99487;
(800) 334-8730. (See page 96.) (EE)

Family safaris each summer are designed for parents and children ages 6 to 11.

RASCALS IN PARADISE
650 FIFTH STREET, SUITE 505, SAN FRANCISCO, CA 94107;
(415) 978-9800 OR (800) U-RASCAL; WWW.RASCALSINPARADISE.COM. (EE)

Hawaii and Honduras, Alaska and Africa, Florida and Fiji are among the far-flung family offerings of this California-based group. Age minimums vary with the difficulty of the trip and are as low as 3 years for many destinations. To make the experience easier for families, on many trips the group establishes one home base and goes exploring on day trips. Babysitters are available as needed. Kids have a separate menu, and mealtimes bring familiar foods even in remote climes. Groups are usually composed of four to six families; if four or more families sign up, an escort goes along.

The operators also specialize in booking family-oriented resort and ranch vacations. They can tell you which have special rates for single parents, and they are familiar with the differences in offerings at resorts in Jamaica (such as F.D.R. and Boscobel Beach) that specialize in family vacations.

....

Family Cruise Vacations

Children love cruise ships. They love climbing the steps or riding the elevators from one deck to another; they like the pools and the gyms and all the activities and entertainment on board; they adore scampering down the gangplank to see a brand-new port. The constant parade of food is a treat, especially since it usually includes familiar favorites like hamburgers and ice cream as well as sophisticated fare. Teens enjoy it too—provided they find company aboard. Some ships provide special video/disco centers where they can meet others their age.

Cruising certainly is not an inexpensive family vacation, but it can be a memorable one, and many of the problems of cruising alone are solved when you have your family along.

Questions for Cruise Lines

Here are a few pertinent questions to ask when you compare family cruises:

- Are cabins large enough to comfortably accommodate families? Are there any connecting cabins? Is there room for a crib if you need one?
- What are children's rates? Are there periods when these are discounted?
- Are there breaks for single parents?
- When can you count on supervised activities for children?
- How large is the children's staff? What training do they have?
- What is the average size of the group they supervise?
- Is there a children's center on board? What does it offer?
- Is there a separate center for teens?
- Are children's meals offered during the early sitting if parents are signed up for the later serving?
- Are booster chairs available in the dining room?
- Are any evening activities planned for young passengers?
- Are baby-sitters available in the evening?
- Is there any provision for baby-sitting for young children while the ship is in port?
- Are there any special shore excursions for youngsters? Any special children's rates on regular excursions?

Almost any itinerary seems exciting, but The Disney Cruise Line (Box 22804, Lake Buena, FL 32830; 800–511–1333) specializes in families and offers the largest dedicated space for kids at sea, with age-specific programming from morning to night. Parents are given beepers when they drop off the kids so they can be reached if necessary. Older teens have their own teen club and game arcade. Of course, Disney characters are around to please the kids, and the lavish entertainment is planned for families. Three- and four-day cruises are offered from Cape Canaveral to the Bahamas, and they can be combined with visits to the Disney theme parks.

Most cruise lines today recognize that families are good business and provide special activities, from baby-sitters to crafts programs to pizza parties. Many have children's playrooms. Norwegian, Royal Caribbean, Celebrity, and Princess are among the lines with special age-appropriate activities for cruisers age 3 to 17.

Many cruise lines allow children under 3 to share their parents' staterooms, and most have special children's rates or reduced fares for the third and fourth passengers in a cabin. Costa specifically mentions special rates for single parents. Reduced rates and children's programs vary with the seasons, and some lines offer them only during school breaks. Choose carefully so that you can look forward to smooth sailing on a family vacation. Cruise specialists listed on page 181 can help. World Wide Cruises publishes a pamphlet, *Guide to Family Cruising,* that details facilities on all the major lines. An excellent guide for more information is *Cruise Vacations with Kids* by Candyce Stapen, 1999 (Prima Books, Rocklin, CA).

Ski Weeks

Skiing is a wonderful family sport. Even the youngest children take to the slopes with glee, and thanks to nurseries and lessons for children, parents can find free time to take off at their own ability level. The bigger ski resorts typically have centers that accommodate children from infants to ages 6 or 8. You can leave the children for an hour or two or for the day.

As the kids get older, skiing allows for plenty of independence. After one or two family runs, everyone usually goes off to his or her own challenges, reuniting for lunch and at day's end. If the weather is uncooperative, parents can stay by the fire or read a book in the lodge while gung-ho youngsters brave the elements. In our family, skiing was the one family vacation that remained popular even after my children were in college and traveling on their own.

If you can afford it, the ideal situation for families is a lodge within walking distance of the slopes or one that has shuttle service to the mountain. This means eager beavers can be first on the slopes while parents get needed rest, and everyone can quit and go home when they are ready.

Another good bet is Club Med at Copper Mountain in Colorado, where special lessons are available for children ages 3 to 12. Younger ones get a basic initiation, those 6 to 12 have two hours of lessons in the morning and afternoon. Besides skiing, the Mini Club is open from 9:00 A.M. to 9:00 P.M. with staff-supervised activities and meals for the kids.

Every ski area offers money-saving ski week packages with or without lessons, and many have additional savings for children who stay in parents' rooms. Families also may choose less expensive, less crowded smaller ski areas while children are still young and need less challenge. The best plan is to pick several areas that interest you and write for current programs.

Single Grandparents

Single grandparents and their grandchildren can make great traveling companions. Each generation widens the other's perspective, and a trip affords them a wonderful chance to get to know each other better and bond for life.

GRANDTRAVEL, C/O THE TICKET COUNTER
6900 WISCONSIN AVENUE, SUITE 706, CHEVY CHASE, MD 28015;
(800) 247-7651 OR (301) 986-0790

Grandtravel was the first to make it easier to arrange this type of trip, usually scheduled during school breaks. These escorted tours take care of all travel arrangements, and they provide time for each generation to be alone with their peers as well as ample time together. The kids might go roller skating while the grandparents go out for a gourmet dinner. The grandparents typically are in their 60s or early 70s, the grandchildren ages 7 to 14. Among the U.S. destinations are the western national parks, Washington, D.C., Colorado, southern California, the desert Southwest, and Alaska. Foreign itineraries have included New

Zealand, China, England, and Scotland, barging in Holland, and safaris in Kenya.

The Sierra Club (see page 287) also has a special week in its family programs set aside for grandparents, and several cruise lines are offering discounts for passengers older than 55 during certain periods.

City Safaris

Parents who prefer an outing solely for their own family would do well to think about visiting a city. Kids really wax enthusiastic about picking a city and planning what to see and do. All you have to do to keep everybody happy is to allot a fair share of time for activities that appeal to youngsters as well as grown-ups.

For the happiest outings, plan an itinerary alternating your choices with those of the children. Intersperse museum visits with trips to the zoo, the beach, or an aquarium, for example. If you insist on shopping with children along, reward them with a performance at a children's theater or a children's movie. Look for boat rides, major league baseball games, and other sure-to-please treats everyone can share. While you are researching reasonable family-priced dining, look out also for the best local ice-cream emporiums. Above all, provide plenty of breaks such as excursions to city parks where kids can run and play or use up excess energy on a rented bike. Parks offer a bonus for parents, for while the smaller members of the family are letting off steam, adults can gain a special perspective watching everyday local life they might otherwise have missed.

The growth of all-suite hotels with two rooms for the price of one is a real boon for families. These are equivalent in price to standard hotels and offer space, privacy, refrigerators, and separate TVs; some even have cooking facilities. While you may not want to spend your vacation cooking, having snacks, drinks, and breakfast ingredients on hand is a real money-saver. Some of the all-suite chains also include a free breakfast.

Most bed-and-breakfast facilities, however, are not good choices for families with young children. Healthy, noisy little ones often feel much too restricted in someone else's home. And somehow, even a budget motel seems more exciting, more of a special outing.

Almost any major city presents opportunities for family adventures, but those with easy and inexpensive public transportation systems offer a special advantage.

Chicago

Chicago is my top pick for family fun. It is filled with kid-pleasing attractions, is easy to navigate, and is easy on the budget. You can stay in a high-rise Motel 6 in the heart of the city! Most of the city's museums have a free admission day, and the Lincoln Park Zoo is free whenever you visit. Too much sight-seeing? Take a break at Oak Street beach, right in town.

Navy Pier and its 150-foot Ferris wheel is almost reason enough for a visit. The revitalized 1916 pier, a city landmark, is a spectacular playground on the lake with more than fifty acres of parks, an old-fashioned carousel, ice skating in winter, and a big, bright children's museum.

Cruises leaving from Navy Pier and along the Chicago River, which runs through the city to the lake, are a wonderful way to appreciate the great architecture in this town where the skyscraper was born. The Chicago Architecture Foundation runs the most informative river trips, but kids may prefer the Wacky Pirate Cruise, an hour of singing and surprises that still manages to highlight the city's notable buildings.

Another popular perspective on the skyline is from the 103rd-floor sky deck of the Sears Tower, the tallest skyscraper in the world.

The Art Institute, home to many of the world's most famous works of art, has a wonderful interactive introduction to art for kids in the Kraft General Foods Education Center, where paintings are hung at kids'-eye level. Family Days are planned to highlight various parts of the collection.

Also fun for families is a walk past the veritable museum of outdoor sculpture around Chicago's downtown commercial center, known as The Loop. A free brochure, "Round & About the Loop," available at the city's three visitor centers, points the way to a hunt for treasures—works by the likes of Calder, Chagall, Picasso, and Miro.

Allow plenty of time for the Museum of Science and Industry, Chicago's most visited attraction, a vast building covering more than fifteen acres with more than 2,000 exhibits, including the chance to descend into a realistic reproduction of a coal mine, tour an actual U-505 submarine, and be strapped in for a simulated space-shuttle flight.

Grant Park on the lakefront includes three major museums. The Field Museum of Natural History features a four-story brachiosaurus, the world's largest mounted dinosaur, and the Adler Planetarium has a special Sky Show for kids. Everyone enjoys visiting the beluga whales, sea otters, and penguins at the Oceanarium in the Shedd Aquarium.

Farther north on the lake is Lincoln Park and its thirty-five-acre zoo, home to more than 2,000 mammals. There is a separate children's zoo where many baby animals can be seen and small animals like rabbits can be petted, plus the Farm in the Zoo, a working farm with the chance to see milking every day. All of this is free.

At dinnertime, sample Chicago's famous deep-dish pizza, drop in at Michael Jordan's place, or visit the one and only Rock 'N Roll McDonald's.

Boston

Another of my favorite cities to visit with children is Boston, home of the New England Aquarium, with its exciting dolphin shows, a fabulous Children's Museum, and the country's only Computer Museum, a surefire hit with most youngsters. In Boston, kids can have a lively history lesson walking the red line of the Freedom Trail, tossing their own chest of tea overboard on the Boston Tea Party ship, and boarding "Old Ironsides," the USS *Constitution*. A visit to Paul Revere's home and the Old North Church in the North End can be followed by dinner at one of the area's many Italian restaurants, with unbeatable cannoli for dessert.

The National Park Service offers Freedom Trail guided tours from its information center at 15 State Street, or you can sign up for a citywide family tour, Boston by Little Feet (617–367–2345), designed for ages 6 to 12 (accompanied by adults).

The famous swan boats are out in the Public Garden in warm weather, offering rides near the spot made famous by Robert McCloskey's classic children's picture book *Make Way for Ducklings*. Read the book before you go.

Kids also love visiting the food booths at Quincy Market, where lavish choices for every taste include pizza and brownies as well as a whole world of ethnic fare, all to be enjoyed at outdoor tables to the tune of free entertainment by street musicians. This is also a great city for sports lovers; especially popular are the baseball games at Fenway Park, one of the country's last classic arenas.

Don't overlook the Esplanade beside the Charles River, a great place for watching roller skaters, joggers, rowing crews, and sailboats in action. A walk up Beacon Hill is a wonderful way to see what cities were like in America a long time ago. Trolley tours and double-decker buses allow on and off privileges around the city all day, a good investment at least one day of your visit.

Philadelphia

Children love Philadelphia—and vice versa. Besides the perennial attraction of the Liberty Bell and Independence Hall, this city makes youngsters welcome with many attractions. The "Please Touch" Museum was the first museum in the nation designed especially for children under age 7. Another surefire favorite is the imaginative Treehouse at the Philadelphia Zoo, where kids can find out how it feels to climb through a 35-foot-high honeycomb or hatch out of a giant egg in the Everglades swamp. The nation's oldest zoo also offers a separate Children's Zoo, where kids can board Noah's Ark to pet the furry passengers, see how cows are milked, ride a pony, or watch a sea lion show.

History, Philadelphia-style, becomes a hands-on experience at Franklin Court, a fabulous little museum devoted to Benjamin Franklin. A telephone hotline there allows you to call anyone from George Washington to John F. Kennedy to hear what they had to say about the remarkable Mr. F. At Dial-A-Witticism, you can call up a Franklin quip on almost any subject.

Not far away on the river, Philadelphia's waterfront is blooming, with a maritime museum, historic ships for boarding, and a boat that shuttles back and forth to the New Jersey Aquarium just across the Delaware River.

The big Franklin Institute ranks as one of the nation's great science museums. It is full of participatory exhibits: Climb aboard a steam locomotive or take a walk through the chambers of a giant walk-through heart. The newest addition, the Meyer Center, is a whirring, blinking world of participatory exhibits that show what we can expect in the future from medicine to transportation to fashion. Even the youngest visitors can enjoy touring a space station and imagining themselves as astronauts. The museum offers a leaflet suggesting other exhibits that can be enjoyed by children under age six. Adults are as fascinated as the kids.

Philadelphia also offers the nation's largest city park, filled with diversions.

There is good eating both at the family restaurants near South Philly's colorful Italian Market and at Reading Terminal Market, where generations of Philadelphians have shopped for fresh produce and meat—and where knowing locals come for lunch at stands offering everything from freshly carved turkey sandwiches to Greek gyros or hot enchiladas. And don't miss a sampling of Philly's gourmet junk food, the cheese steak, at Jim's at Fourth and South Streets.

Washington, D.C.

This city is guaranteed fun for both generations, though it is best to wait until children are old enough to be interested in the workings of government. The Tour Mobile allows you to get on and off all day, seeing the many monuments and sights without wearing out shoe leather. If you can, visit when Congress is in session. Get in touch with your Congressman or Senator in advance to request passes that admit you to the public galleries without being part of a tour. Stop into your representative's office, and you may get to meet your congressperson and/or learn from his or her staff just what goes on in an office in the Capitol. You can get a schedule of committee meetings and sit in on one to see your government in action.

The FBI tour is a special treat for most young visitors, and the Mall allows for stretching young legs. Every kid loves climbing on the prehistoric animals outside the Museum of Natural History and gazing at the spacecraft in the National Air and Space Museum. The National

Museum of American History is another popular spot where you can salute the original "Star-Spangled Banner" or watch the earth rotate an inch or two under the Great Pendulum. Every kind of Americana is found here, from the original set of *Sesame Street* to the inaugural gowns of our First Ladies.

Many hotels are within walking distance of the main sights, but don't hesitate to save by staying outside the city, as long as your accommodations are near a stop on the Metro; it's the cleanest, quietest subway you'll ever ride.

San Francisco

It almost seems that this city was designed with children in mind. Few amusement park rides can equal the fun of the trolley cars clambering up and down the hills of San Francisco, and harbor seals frisking around Fisherman's Wharf are the best free entertainment around. And how can you match the thrill of walking or biking across the Golden Gate Bridge?

San Francisco also has one of the nation's first and best museums for children, the huge Exploratorium, where you can explore science with dozens of imaginative participatory exhibits, from learning to "paint" on a computer screen to entering the Tactile Dome, a pitch black crawl through a variety of touch experiences.

Families can easily spend a day in Golden Gate Park. You can ride on a circa 1912 carousel, go boating on lakes, or watching miniature sailboats in action. You can visit the California Academy of Sciences, where the gem and mineral hall is a favorite, or enjoy the funny antics at the Steinhart Aquarium, home to more than 14,000 denizens of the deep.

Older kids think it is really cool to take the boat trip for a tour of infamous Alcatraz Island; reserve well in advance for this is one of the city's most popular excursions. Best of all, the places that kids love best in the city have almost equal appeal for moms and dads.

The special excitement of any of these great cities will make for meaningful, shared memories for everyone in the family—which is what family vacations are all about.

At Fisherman's Wharf have a look at the figureheads, ship models, and photos in the ship-shaped Maritime Museum in the San Francisco Maritime National Historic Park and the lineup of historic ships at Hyde Street Pier. Experience some of the excitement of sailing 100 years ago by prowling the passageways of the three-masted 1886 square-rigger *Balclutha,* the last of the historic Cape Horn fleet. You can also tour the engine room of the impressive 1890 steam-powered ferryboat *Eureka.*

Take time out for a chowder and sourdough snack while you watch some of the city's free entertainment—the fishing fleet and the seals. Then take a stroll to see some of the street performers in action around the wharf and its shopping centers, especially at the Cannery. Balloon sculptors seem to win the biggest audience of fascinated kids. If you're feeling flush, your children may lure you into the amusements at Pier 39. The attractions include a Cinemax theater and Underwater World, an aquarium that "floats" visitors on a moving walkway through an ocean environment. You can also tour the 312-foot submarine U.S.S. *Pampanito* at Pier 45, or board a boat at Piers 39 or 41 for a harbor cruise, a picnic on Angel Island, or a visit to Sausalito or Tiburon.

"Chequing"
the
American
Traveler

Traveling Safe and Smart

W hether you are joining a group or traveling on you own, with or without children in tow, when you set out without another adult along, it is doubly important to be a smart traveler. Traveling alone carries some built-in stresses: no one to help watch the bags or read a map, no one can share the aggravations. But there are many practical steps you can take to keep yourself feeling confident and in control.

Practical Packing

R edcaps never seem to be around when you need them most, so remember when you pack your suitcase that every item inside is something you may have to carry. Use the smallest suitcase you can get along with and pack a folding tote bag to hold any extras you might acquire on your trip. If you need a lot of clothing, two smaller bags or a small case on wheels and a garment bag that goes over your arm or shoulder are easier to manage than a giant suitcase.

A soft-sided bag with a frame is the best combination I've found for both light weight and protection. Cordura is an excellent sturdy choice as a luggage material. Strong wheels make a bag easy to transport. The most stable bags are those with retractable handle across the wide side of the top and two big wheels that carry the weight when you tilt the bag. Suitcases on four wheels pulled by a strap are easy to tip over. If your luggage lacks wheels, a wheeled carrying cart can be a lifesaver.

Other helps are padded shoulder straps or bags that can convert into a backpack, freeing your hands for finding tickets or change. Don't keep valuables in a backpack, where you cannot see them when the pack is on your back.

Be merciless when it comes to paring your travel wardrobe. Unless you are going to a resort where dressing up is the rule, all a woman really needs for a week of normal travel is three dark skirts or slacks, three daytime tops and three tops for evening, a sweater, a jacket, and a raincoat, preferably one that easily folds up. Pack a folding umbrella, as well—the smaller the better.

A similar basic wardrobe suits men, who may add a tie or two for evening for some destinations. One pair of comfortable walking shoes (already broken in!) and one pair of dress shoes complete the picture for both sexes, unless you need to add a warmer coat for colder climates. If you need a coat, wear it or carry it, don't try to pack it.

Expect unexpected weather. Be prepared for a cold, rainy spell in July or a January thaw. For extra warmth, bring silk long underwear, the kind that skiers wear; it is lightweight and can be rolled up into almost nothing when you pack. Avoid bulky items as much as possible. If you are going to a cold climate, think like those skiers and wear layers—underwear, cotton turtleneck, flat-knit sweater, wind-resistant jacket.

So many hotels have indoor pools these days that you may want to take along a bathing suit no matter what the season. Packing a couple of plastic bags to hold wet or soiled clothing is another good idea.

The best travel advice is that old adage: Bring half as many clothes and twice as much money as you think you'll need.

The most important item in your travel wardrobe is a pair of comfortable walking shoes with nonskid soles—a pair that has been broken in at home *before* your trip. Two important small items are a sewing kit for quick repairs and a travel alarm to be sure you don't oversleep.

Bring plenty of film with you. It's almost always cheaper at home, and you don't want to run out where there are no refills available. Don't trust airport x-ray machines with your precious vacation pictures. Buy a film-shield bag or hand your film (and camera if it is loaded) to the guard for manual inspection.

Before you set off on your trip, be sure your luggage is locked securely and clearly tagged, and remember to put your name, home address, and next destination address inside your suitcase as well. Tags sometimes get detached, and if your bag is lost, inside identification will help locate you.

It's also not a bad idea to jot down the brand, size, color, and any other

Packing
Tips

- Make a packing list. It will keep you from forgetting important items and will come in handy if your luggage goes astray and you need to account for the contents.

- Organize your wardrobe around one basic dark color (brown, black, or navy) to cut down on accessories.

- Transfer shampoo and lotions into mini-bottles of lightweight plastic. Don't fill them to the top: pressure may cause the contents to expand. Put spillables into a plastic bag, just in case.

- Pack heaviest items first; put shoes along the side of the bottom of the bag.

- Pack tightly; don't waste precious space. Fill in spaces with underwear, socks, and hose. Roll pajamas, sweaters, and other casual wear to fit into small spaces.

- Pack suits, dresses, shirts, and blouses in plastic dry-cleaner bags to cut down wrinkling, or put layers of tissue paper between garments.

- Drape slacks, dresses, and any longer garments across the suitcase with the ends hanging over the sides. Put shirts and blouses in the center and fold the long ends over. The center clothing acts as a cushion to prevent wrinkles.

- Pack some old clothes and discard them after you wear them, lightening your load as you go or leaving room for new purchases.

- Don't force your suitcase to close; it may mean broken hinges or zippers when you can least cope with them. If the suitcase won't close, remove a few items.

- Lock your luggage to avoid accidental opening and to discourage thieves. Wrap a tape around the bag to discourage them further.

- A bright piece of ribbon or yarn will help you spot your bag among the look-alikes on the luggage carousel.

- Remove old claim tags so baggage handlers won't be confused about your destination.

aids for identifying your luggage in case it is delayed or lost by an airline. They will ask you to write a description, and sometimes memories play tricks under stress. A close-up snapshot is a reminder that is easy to take along.

Another important tip: Make copies of your tickets, confirmations of hotel reservations, passport, and other important documents, and keep them separate from the originals. The copies will be a big help should you need replacements. Electronic ticketing takes away the worry of lost tickets, but I like to keep a copy of the airline's letter of confirmation, just for my own peace of mind.

Above all, never pack valuables, jewelry, travel documents, or medicines in luggage that you intend to check. Always put them in your hand luggage. Always pack one change of clothes in your carry-on luggage, just in case. If you arrive in a warm climate in winter clothes and your bag is delayed, you'll bless that one lightweight outfit!

Incidentally, if your bag is delayed more than a few hours, airlines often will advance you cash to buy a few necessities, so always ask; they may not volunteer!

Easy Departures and Arrivals

Be sure to allow extra time for the airport. Check-in and baggage inspection lines are longer and slower now that airlines are taking extra security precautions and since boarding passes are no longer issued in advance. Extra time means you won't feel panicked about missing your plane. Better to leave calm and collected than in a frantic rush.

Remember to take photo identification with you; you won't be allowed to board without it. And be sure to get seat assignments in advance. Those without assigned seast stand a greater risk of being "bumped" when planes are over-booked.

If you are traveling into an unfamiliar city from the airport alone, you'll find yourself a lot more confident if you know what to expect.

Find out from your travel agent, tour operator, or hotel, airport, or airline personnel how long it takes to get into the city and the options for getting there. Is there a convenient bus or limo to your hotel? Does the hotel have courtesy van service? Are cabs plentiful? What is the difference in cost between public transportation and usual cab fare? The Airport Transit Guide, available through the Magellan Catalog listed on page 310, can give you much of this information on many cities.

If you take a cab, you will save hassles by knowing in advance the normal rate to town. *Before* you get into the cab, ask the driver what the fare will be. If it is out of line with the expected rate, wait for another cab.

As mentioned earlier, I've learned that, abroad and even sometimes in the United States, it is a good idea to write down the name and address of your destination clearly before you get into a cab and to mark the spot on a street map. You can't assume that foreign drivers know English or that all cab drivers know their cities well.

The more you know and are prepared in advance, the more you will have that all-important feeling of control in an unfamiliar place.

Money Matters

Nobody likes to think of bad things happening on vacation, but the surest way to prevent them is to be prepared. Overladen solo travelers juggling bags and bundles can be a tempting target. Money holders to hide your cash and guard against pickpockets give great peace of mind when you travel.

Protection comes in many forms. Some money holders are slotted to fit on a belt and tuck into your skirt or slacks; others have straps that either hang around your neck or across your shoulder like a holster or fit around the calf of your leg under trousers. For women, there are half-slips with zip-pockets in the bottom of the hem. Money belts have zip compartments hidden on the inside. There's even a waterproof plastic money holder on a neck cord that solves the problem of where to put your cash if you go swimming alone.

Many travelers use hikers' day packs or a "fanny pack" that fits around the waist. These are convenient, but they identify you as a tourist so may not be the wisest choice. If you do use a fanny pack, look for a strong, wide belt; thieves have been known to come up behind and cut the straps. Always keep the pack in front, in your sight.

I often carry a lightweight but sturdy cloth tote bag with straps long enough to go over my shoulder but short enough that I can tuck the bag under my arm when I walk. It allows me to bring along a pad and pencil and an extra sweater or umbrella; I keep my wallet and camera in the very bottom of the bag, out of sight.

I picked up a great little tip from the Travel Companions newsletter for countries like Brazil where thefts from tourists are a big problem. A reader noted that a Brazilian friend had taught her to carry her camera and valuables in a supermarket plastic bag, which made her look like a native rather than a tourist.

No matter which of these safety measures you find most convenient, the point is to keep your cash, tickets, passports, and valuables safe—and preferably out of sight.

Travelers checks are still a standby to avoid losing cash, but the prevalence of ATM bank cash machines in the United States and Europe that accept Cirrus, Plus, and other common banking networks means you don't have to carry as much money with you as in the past. Not only can you get money easily twenty-four hours a day, but you get a preferred exchange rate abroad; the bank gets a wholesale rate that is not available to individuals. Most bank machines offer instructions in English. The fee charged for the transaction is also likely to be less than the hefty exchange charges abroad. It still makes sense, however, to keep transactions to a minimum, since there is a charge each time you withdraw money.

Always use credit cards for large purchases; you get the preferred exchange rate, and you have someone to come to your aid if there are problems with the purchase.

If you use traveler's checks, you probably know to keep the receipts separate from the checks, in case you have to make a claim. It is also a good idea to separate your credit cards and cash into two wallets kept in two different places; if one disappears, you have another resource.

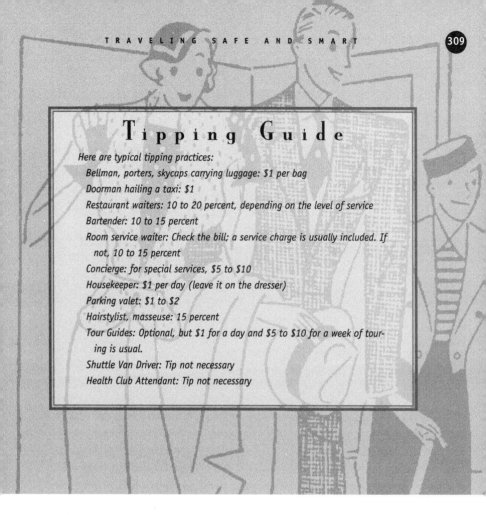

Tipping Guide

Here are typical tipping practices:

Bellman, porters, skycaps carrying luggage: $1 per bag

Doorman hailing a taxi: $1

Restaurant waiters: 10 to 20 percent, depending on the level of service

Bartender: 10 to 15 percent

Room service waiter: Check the bill; a service charge is usually included. If not, 10 to 15 percent

Concierge: for special services, $5 to $10

Housekeeper: $1 per day (leave it on the dresser)

Parking valet: $1 to $2

Hairstylist, masseuse: 15 percent

Tour Guides: Optional, but $1 for a day and $5 to $10 for a week of touring is usual.

Shuttle Van Driver: Tip not necessary

Health Club Attendant: Tip not necessary

Another money suggestion before you set out: Be sure you have small bills for tips and enough change on hand to use the telephone or mass transit systems. If you are traveling to a foreign country, "trip packs" of foreign currency for this purpose can be bought in major U.S. airports. If you exchange money in the airport on arrival, remember to ask for small bills and change; the tendency is to hand out larger bills. If you use a cash machine, ask the hotel to give you smaller change as soon as you arrive.

The practice of tipping puzzles many travelers. If you are going to a foreign country, read up on local customs before you leave home. In many countries, the tip is included in the price of the meal. In the United States, the usual percentage may vary in different parts of the country.

Handy Companions

Some terrific gadgets have been devised to help you feel and look cool and collected on the road. One valuable traveling companion is a compact clothes steamer to remove wrinkles in a hurry when you unpack; they really work. Just remember to have the right adapter plugs if you are traveling in a foreign country.

Other handy travel gadgets include inflatable hangers for drip-dry clothes; tiny sponges that expand in water when you find yourself without a washcloth; portable clotheslines and individual packets of laundry soap; portable alarm clocks; and tiny calculators that help you figure foreign currency rate in a flash. I love my Banana Republic unisex Gore-Tex hat that packs flat but can be popped into shape to ward off both sun and rain. Again, remember that folding umbrella. It's expecting too much to think a thundershower will wait until you're within convenient reach of shelter or an umbrella store. Christine Columbus (see below) has a model that folds absolutely flat.

Shop your own department store notions department, or browse through stores like Brookstone and Sharper Image for these and many other intelligent travel items. If you don't have access to a good selection, here are three mail-order companies that specialize in travel gear; write for their catalogs:

MAGELLAN'S

110 WEST SOLA STREET, SANTA BARBARA, CA 93101; (800) 962-4943; WWW.MAGELLANS.COM. This company provides a fifty-five-page comprehensive roster of useful accessories.

TRAVELSMITH

60 LEVERONI COURT, NOVATO, CA, 94949; (800) 950-1600; WWW.TRAVELSMITH.COM. Official outfitters for many top adventure travel operators, this enterprise's catalog features outdoor gear, luggage, gadgets, and many clothes in wrinkle-proof fabrics.

CHRISTINE COLUMBUS

(800) 280-4775; WWW.CHRISTINECOLUMBUS.COM This on-line catalog is geared to women travelers.

LE TRAVEL STORE

745 FOURTH AVENUE, SAN DIEGO, CA 92101, (800) 713–4260 OR (619) 544–0005;
WWW.LETRAVELSTORE.COM, is stocked with everything a traveler might need,
guidebooks to gadgets to gear. They do not print a catalog, but do take
mail orders, and much of their stock can be browsed online.

Staying Healthy

When you are tired or not feeling well, minor problems loom twice
as large. To maintain a feeling of calm and control, it's wise to do
what you can to minimize the fatigue of traveling and to take sensible
precautions to keep yourself healthy.

Air travel is particularly tiring because seating space is tight.
Experienced travelers make the best of the situation by asking for seat assignments as soon as they make plane reservations. To be sure that you
enjoy the most leg room available on board, ask for a window or aisle
seat. Always avoid the squeezed-in middle seats if you can. Aisle versus
window is a matter of preference—the aisle makes it easier to leave your
seat, the window provides a headrest for napping. Inflatable pillows con-
toured to support the neck are a smart investment to rest better on
planes, trains, or buses and to leave your transportation without a stiff
neck as a souvenir of your trip. Use the little pillow given out on the
plane as a back support.

On most planes, the lower-numbered seats near the front of the cabin
get the quickest meal service and the best chance of getting your meal of
choice; sometimes the most popular dish is no longer available by the
time the meal cart gets to the back.

However, this matters less now that so little food is served on planes. If
you are taking a plane trip of less than four hours, remember to bring along
a snack or sandwich unless you want to survive on a tiny bag of peanuts.

Rows 10 to 20 are often the best choice for a quick exit; on many
planes they are closest to the door. If you are serious about getting the
best seat for seeing the movie or stretching your legs, you can invest in
the *Airline Seating Guide,* a reference that comes in U.S. and overseas edi-

tions. For information, contact Forsyth Travel Library, Box 2975, Shawnee Mission, Kansas 66201–1375; 800–FORSYTH.

As for jet lag, no one has solved the problem. Only time really helps your body clock to adjust when you cross several time zones. Some strategies may help to reduce fatigue, however. Begin a few days before departure to gradually shift your meal and sleep times to fit the new time zone. Adopt the new time immediately when you arrive at your destination, and spend time out of doors—daylight somehow seems to help adjust the body's rhythms. Avoid overeating or excessive drinking on the plane—as well as at your destination. Whether you are better off traveling by day or night depends a great deal on how well you sleep on a plane. Some travelers find that taking a mild sleeping pill helps them rest better and feel fresher at journey's end. In general, arriving at night is easier on the system because you have time to rest.

Don't leave your sunglasses and suntan lotion behind just because you are heading for a city; sight-seeing often puts you out of doors for long periods.

Bring along bandages and medication from home. Be sure to include remedies for the most common travel maladies such as headaches and diarrhea. You'll be thankful you did if the need arises when pharmacies are closed. Just in case you might need them in the middle of the night, remember to look for extra blankets or pillows as soon as you check into your hotel room. The middle of the night may be too late.

If you are traveling to countries where hygiene is a problem, you no doubt have been warned to drink only bottled water. Remember to avoid drinks with ice as well. Eat only cooked fruits and vegetables or those that can be peeled, and eat only meat that is well done. Many people even play safe by using bottled water for brushing their teeth.

Time for rest should be a must in your travel schedule. Travelers generally are better off seeing one less sight and getting more out of what they do see. Being tired is a special problem when you are alone. It magnifies the difficulties and gets you down, making you less willing to reach out to meet other people. Allow plenty of time for sleep and plenty of rest breaks in your day. If you are traveling to a high-altitude destination, remember to allow extra rest time until you adjust.

Safety Tips on the Road

- Use the peephole in your hotel room door to identify visitors. If you don't recognize the person, call the front desk to verify identification.

- Don't accept delivery of items or services you did not request; ask that the items be left at the front desk.

- When you ride in elevators alone, stand next to the floor button panel. If you sense any problem, press the button for the next floor and get off as soon as possible. Don't press the emergency stop button; it could leave you trapped inside the elevator waiting for assistance.

- When you leave your room, leave a light on and close the curtains if you plan to return after dark.

- Ask hotel personnel to point out unsafe areas on your street map so that you can take care to avoid them.

- Don't keep all of your cash and credit cards in one place; otherwise, you may be left without funds if a pickpocket strikes. Keep your main stash of cash and your passport (when traveling abroad) in a money belt or a safe travel pouch that can be worn out of sight.

- Have keys ready when you get to your guestroom door so you won't have to fumble for them in a corridor. Ditto for cash to pay for cabs or bus fare.

- Don't let a stranger touch your belongings. A common travel scam starts with spilling coffee or ice cream on a tourist and offering to clean it up. While the traveler is distracted, the thief or his partner is cleaning out his wallet. Another distracting ploy: a big "welcome to my country" hug at the airport; the accomplice comes up behind and startles the victim with a punch in the back so the hugger can get the loot.

Be good to the feet that are doing extra duty getting you around. When you return to your room after tours of sight-seeing, elevate your legs to give them a rest. Even if you are a confirmed shower-taker at home, you'll find that a soak in the tub does wonders for a travel-weary body.

Playing It Safe

When you are traveling alone, safety in hotel rooms is a concern. Ask for a room near the elevator; don't accept a room at the end of a long corridor. In a large hotel, someone from the front desk should always escort you to your room when you check in. The employee should unlock the room door, check to be sure no one is in the bathroom, and pull back curtains over any sliding glass doors. Sliding doors should have a secure lock, preferably in the floor track. If not, ask for some type of rod to put into the track. The hall door should have a chain as well as a bolt lock and a peephole so that you can see who is outside the door.

Never hang the MAKE UP MY ROOM sign on the door; it announces to the world that the room is unoccupied. To discourage intruders, do the opposite—when you are not expecting the maid, hang out the DO NOT DISTURB sign as you leave the room and leave the radio or television playing softly.

It's also wise to check the location of the fire exit nearest to your room. A helpful booklet published by the federal government, *A Safe Trip Abroad,* suggests that a room between the second and seventh floors is the best bet, high enough to prevent easy entry from outside but low enough for fire equipment to reach.

Chances are that nothing will happen to spoil your trip, but you'll sleep easier away from home if you take intelligent precautions.

Driving Safety

Just you in the car? Chances are you'll be just fine, but don't take chances. Here are some tips to keep you rolling along safely:

- Keep the doors locked and the windows up. Use the air conditioner if necessary. Be extra-sure the windows are up when you stop for a light.

- Keep the gas tank full. When the gas level gauge reaches the halfway mark on your dashboard indicator, fill up. Don't wait for the gauge to read "empty."

- Park only on well-lit streets or parking lots. Check for loiterers when you get out, even in your own neighborhood.

- Have keys out and ready so you can get into the car quickly.

- Never stop if a stranger signals that something is wrong with your car—not even if two or three cars go by with the same message. They may be working as a team. Keep going to a service station to check it out.

- If you think you are being followed, head for the nearest police or fire station or a well-lit grocery store or gas station. Hit the horn hard in short, insistent beeps. If you can't find a place to stop, keep moving and keep beeping. You'll attract attention—maybe even the police, which is just what you want.

- If you have car trouble in the daytime, lift the hood and tie a cloth to the antenna or outside door handle to signal for help. In the nighttime, turn on headlights and emergency flashers and get back in the car and lock the door. If a stranger stops, lower the window slightly and ask him to call for help.

- If you are arriving at an airport late at night, stay at an airport hotel and get your car in the morning rather than trying to make your way to an unfamiliar destination on dark roadways.

Worry Insurance

One final matter to think about before you travel is insurance. Most tour companies and several independent companies now offer trip cancellation insurance. The average cost is low compared to the price of a trip and can prove a worthwhile investment whenever you plan far ahead for a very expensive journey. Cruises, for example, offer sizable discounts for early booking, but if it's necessary for you to cancel your plans at the last minute, you can lose your entire payment without insurance. Insurance also includes coverage for any costs that may occur due to travel delays en route.

Your U.S. health insurance probably will not cover you outside the United States, but travel insurance is available. Access America, Inc. (800–284–8300), Mutual of Omaha (800–228–9792), and GlobalCare (800–821–2488) are among several organizations providing this service. Travel agents and tour operators can supply names of other groups that will provide coverage. If you are traveling to remote places, be sure that emergency evacuation coverage is included.

Holders of gold Visa, MasterCard, and American Express cards also may be entitled to many travel benefits, from life insurance to car rental discounts to a help-line abroad with an English-speaking operator who can advise on medical or legal problems. It pays to check what your card offers, as it may be worth upgrading if you travel often.

Be Ready for the Blues

Vacations serve a great many important functions. They are our best chance to rest from routine and revive the spirit, to hone old skills and acquire new ones, to learn about other life-styles and appreciate other cultures. However, many of us have the fantasy that vacations will be happy and exciting from beginning to end. That is not reality, whether you travel alone or with a companion.

Leaving familiar surroundings creates stress—pleasant stress, yes, but a strain nonetheless as you learn your way around a new place. You may not sleep as soundly, for instance, in an unfamiliar bed. Add the fatigue of un-accustomed exercise, and it's easy to understand why solo vacation emo-tions tend to be uneven, sometimes shooting from exuberant high to lonesome low. There will inevitably be moments when you may wish there were someone close to share a beautiful sunset or a wonderful experience.

The best way to cope when those feelings arise is to let your feelings out in writing—write to a friend back home or spill it out to your jour-nal, the solo traveler's best companion. It's okay to write about your blues, but make a point of writing about the better side of the trip as well. It really helps to put good and bad in perspective.

One other suggestion: In addition to guidebooks, take along the most engrossing books you can find about your destination, either nonfiction or novels set in the locale you are visiting. You'll be learning and building excitement for the next day's outing even while you are distracting your-self from loneliness.

You will discover that traveling on your own will yield a bonus when you get home. With the knowledge and confidence gained as a successful trav-eler, you will be a more aware person—and you'll never feel quite as fearful or dependent on others again.

Probably none of us would choose to spend all of our vacations alone, but that does not mean that we cannot reap the special pleasures and re-wards that come with solo travel. With the right preparation and an opti-mistic outlook, single can be a singular way to go!

Travel

Information

Sources

Other Books for Solo Travelers

Travel Alone and Love It:
A Flight Attendant's Guide to Solo Travel

SHARON B. WINGLER, CHICAGO SPECTRUM PRESS, EVANSTON, IL, 1996.

Practical advice on health, safety, packing, and traveling along with first-hand enthusiasm about the pleasures of solo travel.

A Journey of One's Own:
Uncommon Advice for the Independent
Woman Traveler

THALIA ZEPATOS, EIGHTH MOUNTAIN PRESS, PORTLAND, OR, 1996.

More practical advice, this time with emphasis on extended budget travel to offbeat destinations. Good suggestions on safety and socializing and first-hand accounts from women travelers.

Travelers' Tales: Gutsy Women, Travel Tips, and Wisdom for the Road

MARYBETH BOND, TRAVELERS' TALES, INC. 1995

Mail-Order and Retail Travel Book Sources

THE COMPLETE TRAVELER

199 MADISON AVENUE, NEW YORK, NY 10016; (212) 685-9007.

THE TRAVELERS BOOK STORE

22 WEST 52ND STREET, NEW YORK, NY 10022; (800) 755-8728 OR (212) 664-0995.

BOOK PASSAGE

51 TAMAL VISTA BOULEVARD, CORTE MADERA, CA 94925; (800) 321-9785.

FORSYTH TRAVEL LIBRARY

P.O. BOX 1975, SHAWNEE MISSION, KS 66201; (800) 307-7984.

....

The Internet

If you have access to the Internet, you have a world of additional travel information at your fingertips. Books on all kinds of specialized topics can be ordered from Amazon.com., an online bookstore with more than a million titles.

Shawguides.com offers free the updated text of the most comprehensive guides published to cooking schools, art and craft workshops, and photography workshops and schools. Many of the operators listed in this book have current information on their programs under their own names on the Internet.

This is only the beginning of the vast resources to be tapped. Almost every state, city, and country now has a page on the Internet, which also carries Zagat restaurant listings and some guidebooks. You can browse through pictures of bed-and-breakfast inns, get transportation information, and even make reservations via computer. And you can ask for tips from travelers who have recently visited your destination. Wherever possible Web sites have been added throughout this book.

European Travel

The European Travel Commission publishes a booklet, *Planning Your Trip to Europe,* that includes highlights of their twenty-six member countries and names and addresses of their U.S. tourism offices. To request a copy, write to European Planner, P.O. Box 1754, New York, NY 10185.

....

U.S. State Offices of Tourism

These offices can also supply contacts for tourist information in specific cities in the state. Internet users can phone to get the current Web site.

Alabama Bureau of Tourism and Travel, P.O. Box 4927, 401 Adams Avenue, Montgomery, AL 36104; (800) ALABAMA or (334) 242–4169.

Alaska Division of Tourism, Box E, Juneau, AK 99811; (907) 465–2010.

Arizona Division of Tourism, 1702 North Third Street, Suite 4015, Phoenix, AZ 85004; (800) 842–8257 or (602) 230–7733.

Arkansas Department of Parks and Tourism, 1 Capitol Mall, Little Rock, AR 72201; (800) 643–8383.

California Division of Tourism, P.O. Box 1499, Dept. 200, Sacramento, CA 95812; (800) 862–2543, ext. 200.

Colorado Tourism Board, 1625 Broadway, Suite 1700, Denver, CO 80202; (800) 265–6723.

Connecticut Tourism Division, 865 Brook Street, Rocky Hill, CT 06067; (800) CT–BOUND or (860) 258–4355.

Delaware Tourism Office, 99 Kings Highway, Box 1401, Dover, DE 19903; (800) 441–8846; in state, (800) 282–8667.

District of Columbia Visitors Association, 1212 New York Avenue, NW, Washington, D.C. 20005; (202) 789–7000.

Flausa, P.O. Box 1100, Tallahassee, FL 32302; (904) 487–1462 or (888) 735–2872.

Georgia Tourist Division, Box 1776, Atlanta, GA 30301; (800) VISIT–GA or (404) 656–3590.

Hawaii Visitors Information, 2270 Kalakaua Avenue, Suite 801, Honolulu, HI 96815; (808) 923–1811.

Idaho Travel Council, 700 West State Street, Boise, ID 83720; (800) 635–7820.

Illinois Bureau of Tourism, 100 West Randolph Street, Suite 400, Chicago, IL 60601; (800) 223–0121 or (312) 814–4732.

Indiana Tourism Development, Indiana Division of Tourism One North Capitol, Suite 700, Indianapolis, IN 46204; (800) 289–6646.

Iowa Tourism Office, 200 East Grand Avenue, Des Moines, IA 50309; (800) 345–4692 or (515) 242–4705.

Kansas Travel and Tourism Division, 400 West Eighth Street, Suite 500, Topeka, KS 66603; (913) 296–2009.

Kentucky Department of Travel Development, Capital Plaza Tower, 22nd Floor, Frankfort, KY 40601; (800) 225–8747.

Louisiana Office of Tourism, Box 94291, Baton Rouge, LA 70804; (800) 33–GUMBO or (504) 342–8119.

Maine Publicity Bureau, P.O. Box 2300, Hallowell, ME 04347; (800) 533–9595 or (207) 623–0363.

Maryland Office of Tourism Development, 217 East Redwood Street, Ninth Floor, Baltimore, MD 21202; (410) 767–3400 or (800) 543–1036.

Massachusetts Office of Travel and Tourism, 100 Cambridge Street, Boston, MA 02202; (800) 447–MASS or (617) 727–3201.

Michigan Travel Bureau, Box 30226, Lansing, MI 48933; (888) 784–7328 or (517) 373–0670.

Minnesota Office of Tourism, 375 Jackson Street, 250 Skyway Level, St. Paul, MN 55101; (800) 657–3700 or (612) 296–5029.

Mississippi Department of Tourism, Box 1705, Ocean Shrimp, MS 39566; (800) 927–6378.

Missouri Division of Tourism, Box 1055, Jefferson City, MO 65102; (800) 877–1234 or (314) 751–1433.

Montana Travel, 1424 Ninth Avenue, Helena, MT 59620; (800) 541–1447 or (406) 444–2654.

Nebraska Division of Travel and Tourism, 301 Centennial Mall South, Box 94666, Lincoln, NB 68509; (800) 228–4307; in state, (800) 742–7595.

Nevada Commission on Tourism, Capitol Complex, 600 East Williams Street, Suite 207, Carson City, NV 89710; (800) NEVADA or (702) 687–4322 or (800) 237–0774.

New Hampshire Office of Vacation Travel, Box 1856, Concord, NH 03301; (800) 258–3608 or (603) 271–2343.

New Jersey Division of Travel and Tourism, C.N. 826, Trenton, NJ 98625; 800–JERSEY7 or (609) 292–2470.

New Mexico Tourism, 491 Old Santa Fe Trail, Santa Fe, NM 87503; (800) 545–2040; in state, (505) 827–0291.

New York Department of Economic Development, Tourism Division, 1 Commerce Plaza, Albany, NY 12245; (800) CALL–NYS or (518) 474–4116.

North Carolina Division of Travel and Tourism, 430 North Salisbury Street, Raleigh, NC 27603, (800) VISIT–NC or (919) 733–4171.

North Dakota Tourism Promotion, Liberty Memorial Building, 600 East Boulevard Avenue, Bismarck, ND 58505; (800) 437–2077.

Ohio Division of Tourism and Travel, Box 101, Columbus, OH 43266; (800) 282–5393 or (614) 466–8844.

Oklahoma Tourism and Recreation Department, 215 NE 28th Street, Oklahoma City, OK 73105; (800) 652–6552.

Oregon Tourism Division, 775 Summer Street. NE, Salem, OR 97310; (800) 547–7842.

Pennsylvania Bureau of Travel Development, Chamber of Commerce Forum Building, Harrisburg, PA 17120; (800) VISIT–PA or (717) 787–5453.

Rhode Island Tourism Division, 1 West Exchange Street, Providence, RI 02903; (800) 556–2484 or (401) 277–2601.

South Carolina Division of Parks and Tourism, P.O. Box 71, Columbia, SC 29202; (800) 346–3634 or (803) 734–0122.

South Dakota Department of Tourism, 711 East Wells Avenue, Pierre, SD 57501; (800) 732–5682.

Tennessee Tourism Development, Box 23170, Nashville, TN 37202; (615) 741–2158.

Texas Tourism Division, Box 1272, Austin, TX 78711; (800) 888–8839 or (512)462–9191.

Utah Travel Council, Council Hall, Capitol Hill, 300 North State Street, Salt Lake City, UT 84114; (800) 200–1160 or (801) 538–1030.

Vermont Travel Division, 134 State Street, Montpelier, VT 05602; (800) VERMONT or (802) 828–3236.

Virginia Division of Tourism, 901 East Byrd Street, Richmond, VA 23219; (800) VISIT–VA or (804) 786–4484; D.C. office, (202) 659–5523.

Washington State Department of Trade and Economic Development, 101 General Administration Building, P.O. Box 4250, Olympia, WA 98504; (800) 544–1800 or (206) 586–2088.

West Virginia Tourism Division, 2101 Washington Street East, Charleston, WV 25305; (800)CALL–WVA.

Wisconsin Division of Tourism Development, 123 West Washington Avenue, Box 7606, Madison, WI 53707; (800) 372–2737 or (608) 266–2161.

Wyoming Travel Commission, I–25 and College Drive, Cheyenne, WY 82002; (800) 225–5996; in state, (307) 777–7777.

Index